The Colombian
Political Novel 1951–1987

Hispanic Studies: Culture and Ideas

Volume 71

Edited by
Claudio Canaparo

PETER LANG

Oxford · Bern · Berlin · Bruxelles · Frankfurt am Main · New York · Wien

Alvaro Quiroga-Cifuentes

The Colombian
Political Novel 1951–1987

A Critical Contribution

PETER LANG

Oxford · Bern · Berlin · Bruxelles · Frankfurt am Main · New York · Wien

Bibliographic information published by Die Deutsche Nationalbibliothek.
Die Deutsche Nationalbibliothek lists this publication in the Deutsche National-
bibliografie; detailed bibliographic data is available on the Internet
at http://dnb.d-nb.de.

A catalogue record for this book is available from the British Library.

Library of Congress Control Number: 2015950320

Cover illustration: Tropical Spectrum, 2015. Acrylic on paper. © aoqcifuentes.

ISSN 1661-4720
ISBN 978-3-0343-1978-2 (print)
ISBN 978-3-0353-0758-0 (eBook)

© Peter Lang AG, International Academic Publishers, Bern 2015
Hochfeldstrasse 32, CH-3012 Bern, Switzerland
info@peterlang.com, www.peterlang.com, www.peterlang.net

This publication has been peer reviewed.

Printed in Germany

Contents

Acknowledgements

This book has been put together after a PhD completed at University College London. I am indebted to every single author I read and consulted for it is their works that gave me the real support to illuminate the volume in all its length.

My thanks are due to Professor Stephen Hart from the Department of Spanish and Latin American Studies at University College London for his supervision of the thesis during the years of research and writing and to Professor Christopher Abel from the Department of History at University College London for his guidance in the first year of research.

To Hilary Furey for her support and encouragement during these long years; without her love I would not have been able to carry it out.

This book was actually begun in the early 1990s, after the end of the project 'Actores y Regiones' carried out at IEPRI (Instituto de Estudios Políticos y Relaciones Internacionales / Universidad Nacional de Colombia) and Colciencias, in which I participated. I thank Gonzalo Sánchez for his encouragement and support then, which afterwards kept alive my interest in studying this literature. A profoundly missed friend during these years has been Darío Betancourt, whose relevant conversations on this literature in the past not only offered ideas but also encouraged me to pursue my study (in memoriam).

My thanks also to Rosa Emilia Gómez who kindly provided some information about her uncle, Ignacio Gómez Dávila.

I am grateful to Terry Eagleton for his kind permission to use extracts of his works from which I greatly benefited as they enlightened and helped me to understand the concepts that form the backbone of this work.

My thanks are in order to Alessandra Anzani, for her editorial advice, and to Jasmin Allousch for typesetting assistance. Any mistakes are only my responsibility.

For critical purposes this work uses brief quotations whose sources, either printed or electronic, are all cited in the footnotes found along the chapters, as well as in the general bibliographical section.

Every reasonable effort has been made to contact copyright holders and to obtain their permission for the use of copyright material. The publisher apologises for any errors or omissions and would be grateful for notification of any corrections that should be incorporated in future reprints or editions of this book.

Introduction

The study that follows examines the political and ideological environment, pressures and cultural contexts that shaped a number of Colombian novels published between 1951 and 1987. It asks to what extent and how the novels express the notions of politics and ideology, and its essential purpose is to move this set of novels away from the reductive focus prevalent in the criticism, into a defined and in a better contextualised scrutiny. While defining the nature of the novels' political practices and ideological commitment, together with the multiple intricacies these issues entail, I seek to demonstrate how power relationships are articulated in specific cultural practices in what the novels predicate.

These connections are explored in nine representative novels, namely *El 9 de abril* (1951) by Pedro Gómez Corena, *El día del odio* (1952) by José Antonio Osorio Lizarazo, *El Cristo de espaldas* (1952) by Eduardo Caballero Calderón, *Viernes 9* (1953) by Ignacio Gómez Dávila, *Siervo sin tierra* (1954) by Eduardo Caballero Calderón, *La mala hora* (1962) by Gabriel García Márquez, *Años de fuga* (1979) by Plinio Apuleyo Mendoza, *Una y muchas guerras* (1985) by Alonso Aristizábal and *Bulevar de los héroes* (1987) by Eduardo García Aguilar.

These works, with the exception of *Años de fuga* (1979) by Plinio Apuleyo Mendoza and *Bulevar de los héroes* (1987) by Eduardo García Aguilar, are often labelled as Novel of the Violence ('novela de La Violencia'), a term employed to associate them with the disturbances which occurred in mid-twentieth-century Colombia called The Violence (La Violencia).[1] However, I believe that these novels are more intricate than the term itself

---

1   See Lucila Inés Mena, 'Bibliografía anotada sobre el ciclo de La Violencia en la literatura colombiana', in *Latin American Research Review* (*Research Reports and Notes*), 13, 3 (1978), 95–107. Available at <http://links.jstor.org/sici?sici=00238791%281 978%2913%3A3%3C95%3ABASECD%3E2.0.CO%3B2-J> [Accessed 22 October

suggests. The novels articulate a complex vision of the political practices, ideological commitments and the pressures demanded of writers at the time the novels were written and published.

The revision of the criticism on these novels shows that the emphasis on politics and ideology was alluded to as early as 1954 by Hernando Téllez in his article 'Literatura y testimonio'; by Antonio Curcio Altamar in his pioneering and lengthy work, *Evolución de la novela en Colombia*; and also by Gabriel García Márquez in his article 'Dos o tres cosas sobre "la novela de la violencia"' in 1959, as one of the 'two or three' facts which defined the character of such novels.[2] Téllez, opening a debate on what was happening in the literary landscape during the 1950s, suggested that novels such as *El Cristo de espaldas* by Eduardo Caballero Calderón and *El día del odio* by J.A. Osorio Lizarazo were novels whose style allowed them to transcend the reality they mirrored. Remarking on how a literary rebellion was occurring, he asserted that 'el snobismo intelectual y los hábitos y costumbres de la clase social privilegiada [...] provinciana en su actitud y en su concepto del mundo' traditionally reflected in national literature were changing. The fact that a writer such as Eduardo Caballero Calderón, 'heredero legítimo de las oligarquías', had written *El Cristo de espaldas* and *Siervo sin tierra*, two novels inscribing social and political turbulence accusing his own class, Téllez maintained, was a symptom of a radical change. Reflecting their social and political character, these novels were part of a new movement depicting the people ('el pueblo') as the protagonist and not as a decorative element as it was in the past, Téllez asserted. In 1957 Antonio Curcio Altamar, in *Evolución de la novela en Colombia*, pointed to a few pivotal changes which had occurred in the novel of that time.

2007]. See also Manuel Antonio Arango, *Gabriel García Márquez y la novela de la violencia en Colombia* (México: Fondo de Cultura Económica, 1985).

2   See Hernando Téllez, 'Literatura y testimonio', in *El Tiempo, Lecturas Dominicales*, 27 June 1954, p. 1; Antonio Curcio Altamar, *Evolución de la novela en Colombia* (Bogotá: Instituto Colombiano de Cultura, 1975), (first publ. Instituto Caro y Cuervo, 1957), and Gabriel García Márquez, 'Dos o tres cosas sobre "la novela de la violencia"', in *Eco*, 34/1, 205, Bogotá (November 1978), 103–108 (first publ. in *La Calle*, 9 October 1959).

Curcio Altamar announced the appearance of certain new tendencies in the novel-writing process and alluded to a number of novels included in this study. However his views skated over the surface as far as these works were concerned, for his work was an overview of the development of the novel from 1670 to 1953. Curcio Altamar showed awareness as to the impact on fiction that national politics had, the new direction the novel was taking, and the ideology perceived in some novels. He argued, for example, that the nuanced political tone evidenced in the novel was an unfortunate development. He warned that the novel was already mirroring the conditions entailed by the bipartisanism in that it was simply reproducing scenarios resembling the national reality and its conflicts.[3] By creating conditions entailed by bipartisanism the novels were demonstrating a 'commitment' which simply reflected society and were not literary in a profound sense. Curcio Altamar's observations about the influence of bipartisanism on the novels and the tendency to political commitment have been a cornerstone of subsequent criticism on the Colombian novel of this period.

García Márquez's influential article hinted at what the real significance of these novels was.[4] He identified two factors dominating the literary environment at that time: firstly, the pressure exerted by the political ambience upon writers to write political books, since writers at the time felt disqualified when their works seemed not to be 'políticamente comprometidos de manera evidente'; and secondly, the consequent impact and effects produced by a confrontational bipartisanism. García Márquez argued that writers seemed to have buckled under the pressure to make their plots fit with what the public was expecting:

> Las personas de temperamento político, y tanto más cuanto más a la izquierda se sientan situadas, consideran como un deber doctrinario presionar a los amigos escritores en el sentido de que escriban libros políticos. Algunos, tal vez no más sectarios pero sí menos comprensivos se sienten obligados a descalificar, más en privado que

---

3   See Curcio Altamar, *Evolución de la novela*, p. 213.
4   'Dos o tres cosas' (1978).

en público, a los escritores amigos cuyos trabajos no parecen estar políticamente comprometidos de manera evidente.[5]

This statement suggests how ideology filtered the cultural spectrum and exerted its 'doctrinal duty' on writers, pressurising them to write according to a pre-established political agenda. Indeed the reasons expounded for this situation related to both the political circumstances which the upper class and their power relations had created for the country and to its society.

The overwhelming approach to the Colombian novel of this period, describing it as 'novela de La Violencia' after García Márquez's article in 1959, has led to two unfortunate consequences: firstly, it has ignored the fact that these novels are much more complex than the term suggests. Secondly, it has relegated the novels of this period to the level of documentary works or what García Márquez termed as 'novelas equivocadas'.[6] It is for this reason that a new approach is necessary given the variety of literary outputs during this period, not only in terms of story lines and style but also in terms of ideology.

This study is different in that it interprets these works as bearers of a broader agenda, including topics such as political practices for power reproduction, ideological commitments and the pressures exerted on writers at the time the works were written. This procedure draws upon Jane Tompkins's notion of the novel as the 'product of historical contingencies'. Jane Tompkins, in *Sensational Designs*, argues that literary works are the 'product of historical contingencies' considering the 'complex circumstances' on which they are built and for being bearers of a set of 'national, social, economic, institutional [...] interests'.[7] Tompkins understands fictional works 'as providing men and women with a means of ordering the world they inhabited' to, in that way, grasp the 'cultural realities that made

5   'Dos o tres cosas' (1978).

6   'Dos o tres cosas' (1978). For a discussion of the documentary character of many of these novels see Gerardo Suárez Rondón, *La novela sobre la Violencia en Colombia* (Doctoral thesis, Bogotá: Pontificia Universidad Católica Javeriana, 1966).

7   See Jane Tompkins, *Sensational Designs: The Cultural Work of American Fiction 1790–1960* (Oxford: Oxford University Press, 1985), p. xii.

the novels meaningful' at the time of their emergence.[8] I believe that the fictional works examined in this book were written more to respond to the convoluted particularities of the time and environment within which they were produced, than simply to resonate the unpleasant images of atrocity.

By adopting this approach I view the novels beyond the blanket term 'novela de La Violencia' that has masked the individual resonance of a number of novels of the period 1951–1987, thereby preventing them from being examined within the broad circumstances that linked them to their complex, historical environment. Thus, once the novels are considered from the perspective provided by Tompkins's idea of 'historical contingencies' they can be seen as works that attempted to define their social order and are distinguished by a preoccupation with contemporary social, economic, political and cultural issues, particularly those engendered by inequality in a politicised and transitional society. In this way, I distance my analysis from any pre-existing position and analyse these works as the 'product of historical contingencies'. Obviously, beyond any label, these works are clearly bonded with an emphatic response to their troubled, historical conditions.

My objective is to establish how, within the works selected, there is a code of political significance mediated by an ideological discourse lodged in the fictional plots, considering its preoccupations with contemporary social and economic issues, and observing specifically the matters generated by inequality and stagnation. Other aspects need to be considered: many of these novels refer to the events or the aftermath of 9 April 1948 in modern Colombian society, and in related but different ways they express the variables of a changing genre within an endogenously changing society which preserves the past as a constant touchstone of cultural memory. My discussion focuses in particular on the portrayal of political power, bipartisanism and alternative ideologies together with the tensions of class struggle entrenched in the works.

The interdisciplinary application of theoretical perspectives, which will consider conceptual aspects of Colombian politics, is important,

---

8   Tompkins, *Sensational Designs*, p. xii.

particularly if the novels' long period of production – over three decades – as well as its articulation of the core themes of social justice, institutional venality, social debasement, etc, as connected to the political machine, is taken into account.

A new and distinctive topic included in this book is the exploration of how Colombian politics was linked to 'letrados' (men of letters) who were also politicians, and vice versa, throughout the first half of the twentieth century and beyond, which is the most noticeable gap in the studies of the criticism on these novels. The notion of 'letrados', in itself an example of cultural contingency, is a key issue that requires to be integrated into the study of these novels, specifically because of its close link to politics. The topic is a vital part of the political and ideological questions, such as the intellectual and his role in the historical contingencies, studied in these works.[9] I also follow an interdisciplinary method built on a combination of theoretical views to support the structural positions suggested in the notion of historical contingencies.

I use Jane Tompkins's definition of the novel as the 'product of historical contingencies', because of its breadth.[10] Tompkins's notion allows us to perceive multiple articulations lodged in a novel while focusing on the complexity that a work, plot-wise, might entail, i.e. social, economic, institutional aspects. In her claim, 'novels [...] should be studied [...] because they offer powerful examples of the way a culture thinks about itself, articulating and proposing solutions for the problems that shape a particular historical moment'.[11] In this way this study observes the ideological circumstantial interconnections in the novels: 'the continuities rather than ruptures [...] the strands that connected a novel to another similar text, rather than for

---

9   The notions of 'letras' (letters) and 'letrados' (men of letters) are based on Angel Rama, *La ciudad letrada* (Hanover: Ediciones del Norte, 1984). There are occasional references to this idea in Juan Pablo Dabove, 'Los pasquines como alegoría de la disolución de la ciudadanía en "La mala hora" de Gabriel García Márquez', in *Revista de Crítica Literaria Latinoamericana*, 26, 52 (2000), 269–287. Available at <http://www.jstor.org/stable/4531133> [Accessed 26 November 2008]

10 See Jane Tompkins, *Sensational Designs*, p. xii.

11 Tompkins, *Sensational Designs*, p. xi.

the way in which the text might have been unique'.[12] These interconnected aspects become apparent as the different factors within one and the same process, which is, in the case of these novels, their political expression.[13]

The notions of politics and ideology are linked but they are not identical. For this matters I follow Terry Eagleton's definitions in that politics is 'the way people organise social life together, and the power-relations this involves', whereas ideology refers to

> The largely concealed structure of values which informs and underlies our factual statements [...] the ways in which what we say and believe connects with the power structure and power relations of the society we live in [...] more particularly those modes of feeling, valuing, perceiving and believing which have some kind of relation to the maintenance and reproduction of social power.[14]

The distinction is that politics 'refers to the power processes by which social orders are sustained or challenged', and the ideology 'denotes the ways in which these power processes get caught up in the realm of signification'.[15] While politics is more a matter related to 'technical management and manipulation', or a functional machine more associated with 'form', ideology is distinctive in that it is 'content', i.e. 'preaching and indoctrination'.[16] Thus, 'ideology is a matter of "discourse"', and this discourse is one where, indeed, power is involved.[17] An ideological unity therefore is shaped in the political solidarity and comradely feeling that brings the success of 'oppositional movements as it is part of the armoury of dominant groups'.[18] A way of explaining this is in Marx and Engels's comment in *The German Ideology* that the ruling ideas of each epoch are the ideas of the ruling

12   Tompkins, *Sensational Designs*, p. xv.
13   Tompkins, *Sensational Designs*, p. xii.
14   Eagleton, *Literary Theory*, pp. 13–14.
15   Terry Eagleton, *Ideology: An Introduction* (London: Verso, 1991), p. 11.
16   Eagleton, *Ideology*, p. 38.
17   Eagleton, *Ideology*, p. 223; *Literary Theory*, p. 19.
18   Eagleton, *Ideology*, p. 45.

class.[19] That is to say that such ideas are the ones conveyed by the ruling class regardless where they derive from. But the ideas in question may be true or false, thus ideologies exist in relation to other ideologies. This condition implies also recognition of the 'other' and such an 'otherness' may become a potentially disruptive force within the ruling order. As a consequence a dominant ideology has continually to negotiate with the ideologies of its subordinates creating an open-endedness which prevents it from achieving pure self-identity. A case in point during the second half of the twentieth century was the 'socialist ideology', which shared beliefs and inspired a group or class in the pursuit of political interests judged to be desirable.[20] This thought became synonymous with 'class consciousness', i.e. ideas 'shaped by an underlying motivation, and functional in achieving certain goals' that is common goals and motivations as 'they were not in the case of a class regarded as unjustly oppressive'.[21]

This approach offers a notion of how ideas grow in a society and the role they play in the formation of cultural values and beliefs and also the way certain social groups 'exercise and maintain power over others'.[22] In this sense ideology comprehends the idea of literature understood as a vehicle to convey ideas. Yet literature does more than embody certain social values. It also becomes an instrument for wider dissemination. Ideology has been interpreted in different ways in literary theory. Whereas, for example, Lucien Goldmann sees ideology as displaying a high degree of internal unity, Pierre Macherey considers it 'so amorphous' that 'it can hardly be spoken of as having a significant structure at all'.[23] The speaking silence is a structure that articulates social practices reproduced in the literary text,

---

19   See *The German Ideology*, in *Karl Marx: Selected Writings*, ed. by David McLellan (Oxford: Oxford University Press, 1978), pp. 159–191.

20   Eagleton, *Literary Theory*, p. 30.

21   Eagleton, *Literary Theory*, p. 32.

22   *Literary Theory*, p. 35.

23   See Lucien Goldmann, *Pour une sociologie du roman* (Paris: Gallimard, 1964); see also Pierre Macherey and Etienne Balibar, 'On Literature As An Ideological Form', in *Untying the Text: A Post-Structuralist Reader*, ed. by Robert Young (London: Routledge and Kegan, 1981), pp. 79–99.

providing an 'imaginary solution' or a 'mise en scène' of 'contradictions which are [...] political, religious, etc'.[24] This is a productive view from which to analyse the novels studied in this book since the ideology of the literary work is often more elusive than at first envisaged.

On this basis I argue that the novels produced during the period 1951–1987 in Colombia offer a minutely sensitive barometer which is able to detect the eddies and flows of a 'structure of feeling', to use Raymond Williams's suggestive term.[25] The term 'structure of feeling' expresses the idea of the sense of community and the way that intimate knowledge is communicated within society itself. It communicates the sense of 'a way of life [people] know intimately [...] the culture of a period'.[26] It may be described, in other words, as the zeitgeist of the time or the way life in the fictional work has been captured either in a character or in the society it mirrors. These notions are pointers to the ways in which the 'political machine' operates in the novels studied in this book particularly when addressing cultural issues that accompanied the political process.[27]

The role of politicians, their connection to matters of power and its direct link with the role of 'letrados' in Colombia is important in this study. The political role of the 'letrado' has been questioned by Juan Pablo Dabove in relation to *La mala hora* by García Márquez, which is interpreted as a means to disclose a glimpse of the Colombian reality through a metaphor represented in the novel by the pasquinades, as we shall see later.[28]

The category of the 'letrado', whose significance and impact in Latin America was developed by Angel Rama, refers to those individuals dedicated to the cultivation of language in all its possible dimensions. 'Letrados'

---

24 Balibar and Macherey, 'On Literature', pp. 79–99.
25 See Raymond Williams, *The Long Revolution* (London: Hogarth Press, 1992), pp. 48–49.
26 Raymond Williams, *The Long Revolution*, pp. 48–49.
27 Eagleton, *Ideology*, p. 38.
28 Juan Pablo Dabove, 'Los pasquines como alegoría de la disolución de la ciudadanía en "La mala hora" de Gabriel García Márquez', in *Revista de Crítica Literaria Latinoamericana*, 26, 52 (2000), 269–287 (pp. 270–271). Available at <http://www.jstor.org/stable/4531133> [Accessed 26 November 2008]

or men of letters, according to Rama, are men who have exercised 'the power of letters' in 'poetic' or prose language, to gain a solid position as much in society as in power.[29] The 'letrados' is a major category that has not been practically studied in the criticism on the novels 'product of historical contingencies', the 'letrados' being a crucial contingency in itself in the novels explored here. The Colombian 'letrado' portrayed in these novels is particularly complex. It illustrates a multifaceted intellectual whose ideological significance is associated with his role in the socio-political process. I have combined Rama's theory with Antonio Gramsci's notion of the organic intellectual to analyse the way in which this category grew within a process of politicisation by the mid-1950s in Colombia and how it is mirrored in the novels in question.[30]

The Criticism on these Novels

I have referred above to the political significance recognised by Téllez, Curcio Altamar and García Márquez in these novels. It is important though to return to García Márquez since his recognition of the political signifi-cance of these novels was accompanied by other clues that shed light on their ideological aspect. Accordingly, writers were encouraged not to be 'indifferent' since literature was supposed to be 'a powerful weapon that should not be neutral in the political contention'.[31] This raises one key question: what kind of 'powerful weapon' was he referring to? Was that 'powerful weapon' above all else ideological? Clearly some type of influ-ence was expected as a result of that pressure.

29   See Angel Rama, *La ciudad letrada* (Hanover: Ediciones del Norte, 1984), p. 29.
30   *Antonio Gramsci: Selections from Prison Notebooks*, ed. by Q. Hoare and G. Nowell Smith (London: Lawrence and Wishart, 1971).
31   'Dos o tres cosas' (1978).

It is on the issue of quality that García Márquez found this new type of literature to be deficient. He suggested there were 'strange interests' involving 'parcialidad política' and 'intervención clerical en los diversos frentes de la cultura'.[32] These factors led to ideologically driven, bad literature. García Márquez's views in this regard are especially interesting for they leave some doubts as to whether he actually read these novels: 'Quienes han leído todas las novelas de violencia que se escribieron en Colombia, parecen de acuerdo en que todas son malas'.[33] His statement is clearly non-committal in that respect, in that he refers to 'those who have read [...] [they] seem to agree', which suggests on the one hand political caginess. A similar caginess is found in Raymond Leslie Williams's work when he argues that novelists commonly said that there were 'no critics, while critics [...] sustained that Colombia [had] no novelists'.[34] On the other hand, García Márquez's emphasis suggested a negation of the existence of the novel as a genre in Colombia at all, when he underlines that writers had to take the time to learn how to write a novel, that there was not a novel tradition to follow, and that writers had to start from the beginning.[35]

The existence of the novel as a genre in Colombia was recognised by some critics. Hernando Téllez and Curcio Altamar, for example, pointed to the validity of the novels being written at that time. For his part, Rafael Gutiérrez Girardot argued that the 1950s novels expressed the actual tension existing in the depths of the society they depicted.[36] Gutiérrez Girardot pointed out, for instance, that an author of that time was able to 'lift the veil' that covered a structurally depressed society. He credited J.A. Osorio Lizarazo with the ability to portray human experience in a vivid way and

---

32 See 'La literatura colombiana: un fraude a la nación', *Eco*, 33/5, 203 (September 1962), 120–128.

33 'Dos o tres cosas' (1978).

34 Raymond Leslie Williams, *The Colombian Novel 1844–1987* (Austin: University of Texas Press, 1991), p. 23.

35 'Dos o tres cosas' (1978).

36 Rafael Gutiérrez Girardot, 'La literatura colombiana en el siglo XX', in *Manual de historia de Colombia*, vol. 3 (Bogotá: Procultura/Instituto Colombiano de Cultura, 1984), pp. 447–536.

hinted that Caballero Calderón was an author whose novels were narrative examples of his central meditation about Colombia and Latin America.[37] These authors' novels, as suggested by Gutiérrez Girardot, were intimately connected to the evolution and the stagnant conditions in which Colombian society was languishing. Gutiérrez Girardot's is a valuable contribution that must not be underestimated. Brief appreciations of another critic, Valencia Solanilla, with reference to the evolving process of the novels are likewise valuable. Valencia Solanilla perceived a quest for an identity individual and also collective to rebuild the past through fiction. He argued that the reconstruction of the past created by the novels required a 'polysemic reading' able to fuse documental reconstruction and 'narrative fiction'.[38] This point is also important as it denoted the existence of a hidden agenda largely overlooked by the previous criticism on the novels.

This study builds on these readings while drawing inspiration from Laura Restrepo's challenging idea which depicts the novels as an expression of social problems of everyday life, relating to ethical issues, guerrilla, 9 April 1948, the peasantry, among others. Asserting that an attempt had been made to mythicise the abstract meaning of 'La Violencia', Restrepo suggests that in all stages of the Colombian novel there was a prevailing world-view based on social class, an ideological reflection conveyed by the novels: works that 'reflejan [una] óptica de clase'.[39]

On the other hand, this book does not subscribe to Raymond Leslie Williams's study of the Colombian 'fictionalization prevalent during the 1950s and the 1960s' which he finds faulty for being 'documentary

---

37   Gutiérrez Girardot, 'La literatura colombiana', pp. 516, 527.

38   César Valencia Solanilla, 'La novela colombiana contemporánea en la modernidad literaria', in *Manual de literatura colombiana*, vol. 2 (Bogotá: Procultura/Planeta, 1988), pp. 463–510 (pp. 468–469).

39   See Laura Restrepo, 'Niveles de realidad en la literatura de la "violencia" Colombiana', in *Once ensayos sobre la violencia* (Bogotá: CEREC/Centro Gaitán, 1985), pp. 117–169 (p. 169). Laura Restrepo's observation about the inappropriate treatment of this political phenomenon in order to mythicise it as an attempt to hide the real connotations of politics coincides with the point made by social scientists such as E. Hobsbawm and G. Sánchez and D. Pécaut, as will be seen in Chapter One.

in impulse and frequently laden with crude violence'.[40] Even if violence might be found in these novels, this does not per se mean that they were 'not the kind of literature the upper class preferred to read and disseminate', in the sense that their partisan bias made them 'liberal' in the writing and therefore censured by the 'conservative establishment'.[41] The dismissive suggestion about political bias made by R.L. Williams not only belittles these novels; it also ignores the veiled structures hinted at by Gutiérrez Girardot or the possibility of a polysemic reading, as suggested by Valencia Solanilla. Williams's own recognition of some works – such as Manuel Zapata Olivella's *La calle 10* (1960), García Márquez's *La mala hora* (1962), Mejía Vallejo's *El día señalado* (1963), and Alvarez Gardeazábal's *Cóndores no entierran todos los días* (1972) – as 'more valuable' for communicating problems influenced by 'socio-political phenomena' and experience through narrative strategies, to allow the reader an active participation with contemporary events, poses the perversity of its counterpoint. That is, if there are 'more valuable' works it is because these ones are less valuable, at which point the many other novels of the period in question become reduced to a crude documentary in the best of the cases, or in the worst scenario are worthless.[42] This contradiction reinforces my argument in that it is the articulation of historical contingencies that explains the real nature of the novels, precisely for what they have in common with R.L. Williams's own selection: political contingencies.

This book does not concur either with studies which consider 'La Violencia' as the only leitmotif of the Colombian novel, such as those by Manuel Antonio Arango or Seymour Menton. Arango, for one thing, views the novels as works of violence per se, and 'La Violencia' in itself as a leitmotif that can only be measured from García Márquez's criteria.[43]

---

40 R.L. Williams, *The Colombian Novel*, p. 49.
41 See R.L. Williams, *The Colombian Novel*, pp. 49–51. It is worth noting that the publication of this work was not exempt from criticism for its views on the modern novel in Colombia. In this respect see *El Espectador, Magazín Dominical*, 426 (23 June 1991), 6–13.
42 R.L. Williams, *The Colombian Novel*, pp. 49–51.
43 See Arango, *García Márquez y la novela*, pp. 12–13.

Although Arango suggested that García Márquez's works could not be understood without taking into account the 'oppression exerted by political groups' that characterised the literary production of the time, he attributed the writing of them to a fatalistic determinism. Furthermore, for Arango, many of the early novels were only written in order to serve the purpose of inspiring writers to write more novels of violence. Pointing in a similar direction, Seymour Menton in *La novela colombiana: planetas y satélites* devised a metaphoric comparison in which the term 'planets' represents major national works, and 'satellites', the minor.[44] Menton argued that, despite their intrinsic values, the latter offer weaknesses that prevented them from achieving the category of 'planets', i.e. major works.[45] These views, first published in 1978 have not changed since then and have led Menton to suggest that only novels which treat 'La Violencia' are possible in Colombia, since there are not different possible criteria to study them.[46] The difficulties posed by the complexity of the novels shows that it has always been easier for critics to appeal to the matter of violence rather than analyse the far more important issues lodged at their core.

Indeed, these novels have not always been confined to the deterministic straightjacket dictated by Menton, Arango and R.L. Williams. Patricia Trujillo Montón, for example, underlines that these novels were not always seen as 'novelas de La Violencia'. She points out that the works represented a social realism proper to the time to which they belonged, and that the date 9 April 1948 was a valid criterion to refer to these works.[47] Paul Juten in the 1980s warned that the inaccuracies of interpretation associated with

44   See Seymour Menton, *La novela colombiana: planetas y satélites*, 2nd edn (México: Fondo de Cultura Económica, 2007) (first publ. 1978).

45   Menton, *planetas y satélites*, p. xiii.

46   Menton, *Planetas y satélites*, pp. 150–151.

47   For a comprehensive study of the historical contradictions germane to the criticism on these novels see Patricia Trujillo Montón, 'Problemas de la historia de la novela colombiana del siglo XX', in *Leer la historia: caminos a la historia de la literatura colombiana*, ed. by Carmen Acosta, Diógenes Fajardo, Iván Padilla and Patricia Trujillo Montón (Bogotá: Universidad Nacional de Colombia, 2007), pp. 61–107 (pp. 96–104).

the term La Violencia made the studies deficient in scope.[48] I agree with Juten that criticism on this group of novels has either been dismissive or perfunctory.[49]

The determinism with which these novels were seen through the years is evident in Gerardo Suárez Rondón's work. Studying some forty works published before 1966 he found these novels to be impressionistic and subservient to the 'power domination and the ideologies to which the writer is committed', since, as he argued, Colombian writers were generally 'hombre[s] de partido'.[50] Suárez Rondón showed that, during the 1950s and 1960s, these novels were 'documents' which were frequently used as 'historical' texts by historians, who reciprocated information between sociologists and writers, who, in turn, addressed the antagonistic bipartisanism in their work.[51] For Suárez Rondón political commitment was caused by pressure exerted on writers, by various actors including political parties and institutions such as the army and the Church. He contended that, in many ways, the novels tackled structural realities whose development depended on political issues, and writers' partisan inclinations were therefore evident.[52]

---

48   See Paul Juten, 'Notas críticas a la bibliografía de la literatura de La Violencia con algunas observaciones sobre una aproximación literaria'. Paper presented at II Simposio Nacional Sobre La Violencia en Colombia, Universidad Pedagógica y Tecnológica de Colombia, Chiquinquirá, 6 September 1986.

49   Another example of the sparseness of criticism on these novels is Alvaro Pineda Botero, *Del mito a la posmodernidad* (Bogotá: Tercer Mundo, 1990). For the matter of the paucity of literary criticism in Colombia, particularly informative views are found in Patricia D'Allemand, 'Silencios y reticencias de la crítica en Colombia', in *Bulletin of Spanish Studies*, 84, 4 (2007), 529–548. Available at <http://dx.doi.org/10.1080/14753820701452485> [Accessed 23 January 2009]; See also Oscar Osorio, 'Siete estudios sobre la novela de la Violencia en Colombia, una evaluación crítica y una nueva perspectiva', in *Poligramas, Revista Literaria*, 25, Cali, Universidad del Valle (June 2006), 85–108. Also available at <http://poligramas.univalle.edu.co/25/Osorio.pdf> [Accessed 29 March 2009]

50   Suárez Rondón, *La novela* (thesis, 1966), pp. 107–113, 125–127.

51   Suárez Rondón, *La novela* (thesis, 1966), pp. 4–6.

52   Suárez Rondón, *La novela* (thesis, 1966), p. 47.

His views and conclusions were driven by a reductionism and moralistic judgement that this book does not share.

García Márquez's role in the debate was crucial since Angel Rama dubbed him 'Un novelista de la violencia mericana'. Rama praised his ability to express the theme of violence underlining that Latin American man's common destiny was that of political struggle, which is the real 'plano de lo concreto'.[53] The assertion about the political manifestations as the material aspect of 'political oppression' suggested the actual preoccupations expressed by García Márquez in the 1950s: the resolution of a truth theorem capable of demonstrating the root cause of such assertions. Deep-rooted in the 'conglomerado social' this complexity articulated an 'anthropology' woven into a societal fabric in which, every 'threat' undermined the stasis of a network of power among social groups.[54]

The distinctiveness of García Márquez's works addressed by the Uruguayan poet Mario Benedetti brought forward a key point: that García Márquez was not a writer of obvious political message.[55] That suggestion gives us a hint about the presence of a coded political message. Benedetti's assertion concided with García Márquez's idea of the intrinsic 'political significance' inserted in the novels of the period in question; that is, a cryptic message that must be decoded. I follow these lines of enquiry since they help to demonstrate the ideological currents and eddies under the surface of these novels, as I attempt to show in this work.

Emphatically disputing the adequacy of the traditional view of the novel of 'La Violencia', Gustavo Alvarez Gardeazábal pointed to the importance of the writers' political commitment and acknowledged that novelists often gave priority to the expression of a tangled web of traditional bipartisanism. Alvarez Gardeazábal highlighted a few salient themes in these novels: a confrontational period of time between the 'two traditional parties, liberal and conservative', the evolving leitmotif surrounding 9 April

53   Rama, 'Un novelista', pp. 113–114.
54   Rama, 'Un novelista', pp. 106–125.
55   Mario Benedetti, 'Gabriel García Márquez o la vigilia dentro del sueño', in *9 Asedios a García Márquez* (Santiago de Chile: Editorial Universitaria, 1969), pp. 11–21 (pp. 13–14).

1948 and also a certain urban character perceived in them.[56] I agree with the points made by Alvarez Gardeazábal though my analysis differs in some key respects in that it explores, first, the historical roots of contingencies that he could not foresee at the time, and second, it uses historical sources and literary theory in order to arrive at different conclusions.

For his part, Román López Tamés interprets the Colombian novel within its social context but offers ideas without examination. He simply refers to a set of particular features that are often combined in the works, such as 'political parties disputes', 'landownership and rural work troubles', 'demographic increase', 'police and Church intervention', which are interpreted as a leitmotif at the core of this set of novels.[57] However, he does not explore these points in any depth.

Reaching virtually identical conclusions about the common denominators of four Colombian novels of this period were Luis Iván Bedoya and Augusto Escobar, who co-authored critical readings on *Viento seco*, by Daniel Caicedo; *La mala hora*, by Gabriel García Márquez; *El día señalado*, by Manuel Mejía Vallejo and *El Cristo de espaldas*, by Eduardo Caballero Calderón.[58] Bedoya and Escobar suggested that the novels focused on class struggle and simply communicated strategies designed to achieve political and economic power. They maintained that the works also combined conflict between characters such as priests and civil authorities in such a way that realism and ideology were made compatible. For

---

56 Gustavo Alvarez Gardeazábal, *La novelística de la violencia en Colombia* (BA thesis, Cali: Universidad del Valle, 1970), pp. 14–19.

57 Román López Tamés, *La narrativa actual de Colombia y su contexto social* (Valladolid: Universidad de Valladolid, 1975), pp. 33, 141.

58 See Luis Iván Bedoya y Augusto Escobar, *La novela de la violencia en Colombia. Viento seco, de Daniel Caicedo. Lectura crítica* (Medellín: Hombre Nuevo, 1980); *La mala hora, de Gabriel García Márquez. Lectura crítica* (Medellín: Hombre Nuevo, 1980); *El día señalado, de Manuel Mejía Vallejo. Lectura crítica* (Medellín: Hombre Nuevo, 1981); 'Religión y contexto social en *El Cristo de espaldas*', in *Ensayos sobre literatura Colombiana y Latinoamericana* (Compilación UNE), Biblioteca Banco Popular, vol. 137 (Bogotá: Biblioteca Banco Popular, 1989); see also Augusto Escobar Mesa, *Ensayos y aproximaciones a la otra literatura colombiana* (Bogotá: Universidad Central, 1997), particularly 'Literatura y violencia en la línea de fuego', pp. 97–153.

Bedoya and Escobar the link between religion and political networks represents an apparatus of ideological control which 'interferes' in the characterisation of individuals, leaders, family, education and culture as reflected in the novels. This combination potentially suggested the content of the novels as mechanisms for conveying a propaganda of social bonding, in effect a role-play to elicit emotional response. I do not disagree entirely with the points made by López Tamés, and Bedoya and Escobar, but they may be criticised on the grounds of the use of La Violencia itself, which for them appears as the *deus ex machina* controlling the plot of each novel.

Two bibliographies show the latent bias of the criticism on these Colombian novels. The first, Russell W. Ramsay's bibliography, focuses on the problems faced by critics in the study of social history matters.[59] Devoting a specific section to twenty-two fictional works – remarkably in what is a historical overview – Ramsay makes valuable comments about the conditions in which the novel was produced; he is particularly helpful, for example, on the issue of the role played by censorship. The second, Lucila Inés Mena's 'Bibliografía anotada', focuses on the idea of the novel as a reflection of social circumstances. This novelistic production, she considers, reflects the Colombian political situation whose analysis 'requiere una interpretación de años de historia en la vida política de Colombia'.[60] But these bibliographies say nothing about the plot of the novels or, indeed about structural elements therein. Gladys Lara Romero proposes a reading of the 'novela de La Violencia' from the perspective of the 'symbolic imagination'.[61] She focuses on the reconstruction of contradictions of the social universe in a few novels, which are read as sign objects ('objetos sígnicos') that offer imaginary solutions.[62] Yet the development of the social and communicational character within

59   See Ramsey, 'Critical Bibliography', pp. 3–44.

60   See Mena, 'Bibliografía Anotada', pp. 95–96.

61   Gladys Lara Romero, *Imaginación social y novela de la Violencia en Colombia* (Bogotá: Gráficos, 2006).

62   See Lara Romero, *Imaginación social*, pp. 30–39. The theoretical reading is based on Fredric Jameson, *La narrativa como acto simbólico* (Madrid: Visor, 1989).

the novels is restricted to articulations of violence. Her views on values and ideals ('valores e ideales'), that were transforming the Colombian society at the time, suggest the importance of many other values hidden within the stories, such as poverty and cultural differences, which are succinctly developed in the analysis. Despite the value of some aspects of her analysis, Lara Romero may be criticised for its reductive determinism on violence which aligns it with the traditional criticism with which this book does not concur.

Since I focus on the politics and ideology of these works my analysis and conclusions will be different to the criticism reviewed above. I pay attention to the delimited historical contingencies within which the novels were produced and apply a theoretical analysis to every case study. I pay attention especially to the role of 'letrados' in Colombia, as well as to the particular two-way connection of 'letrado' and politics that developed in the process of power reproduction, and the way it is articulated in the novels.

As I have underlined above, the way those works have been studied is in itself reductive if the works' political and ideological character is simply accepted at face value. My objective is to establish how a code of political significance mediated by an ideological discourse is articulated in the fictional narrative, together with its preoccupations with contemporary social, economic and cultural changes occurring in a politicised society. While assessing the variables of a changing genre within an evolving society, I focus my reading on the portrayal of political power, bipartisanism, alternative ideologies and the tensions of class struggle rooted in the works.

I offer close reading of the nine selected novels, which circumvent the narrow interpretation assigned to them by the criticism to date. My contribution is to move the study of this set of novels away from that reductive focus and I propose an alternative reading in which the historical contingencies of the novels are highlighted from a theoretical perspective. This close textual reading focuses on the literary devices, plot, symbols and themes found in each novel, and takes into account the literary criticism written about each novel. I deal with the novels separately and focus on the articulation of power relations, the need for reforms and social differences as they relate to bipartisan rivalry, opposition and insurgency.

I hope to show how these novels are far more important than suggested by traditional criticism. My contribution is also in line with the
aims of cultural Latin American studies that in recent years have pursued
a reading of the construction of the state, nationality and cultural identity,
such as in *José María Samper: nación y cultura en el siglo XIX colombiano*
by Patricia D'Allemand, who discusses the thought of Colombian politicians such as José María Samper in nineteenth century Colombia, as well
as his novelistic production within the process of construction of national
culture and literature.[63] It also relates to the lines proposed by Juan Pablo
Dabove in *Nightmares of the Lettered City: Banditry and Literature in
Latin America 1816–1929*, particularly in respect to the role of the 'letrado'
in Latin America and the construction of national cultures in Argentina,
México, Venezuela and Brazil.[64]

The Novels: Selection and Criteria

The works studied here have been chosen because each, in related but
different ways, throws light on the link between politics and ideology
in the Colombian novel during the period 1951–1987. Thus, pertinence,
significance and connectedness are the criteria that intrinsically relate to
the themes the novels explore which in turn are predicated on the ideological framework within which the author operates. Each of the works
focuses on contemporary social, economic and power issues, particularly those engendered by the need for radical social change and reform.
Because they were published over a period of thirty-six years, this set of
novels demonstrates how the need for social reshaping together with a

---

63   See Patricia D'Allemand, José María Samper: *Nación y Cultura en el Siglo XIX
     Colombiano* (Bern: Peter Lang, 2012).
64   Juan Pablo Dabove, *Nightmares of the Lettered City: Banditry and Literature in Latin
     America 1816–1929* (Pittsburgh: University of Pittsburgh Press, 2007).

sense of fairness was formulated in different ways. This choice foremost stresses the fact that – with the exception of *La mala hora* – there has been scant criticism on them, and the importance ascribed to García Márquez's work has often meant that the other eight novels have been assessed according to a yardstick predicated on that importance, thereby leading to a rather prejudiced and unbalanced view of the significance of these novels. In some cases these novels have been dismissed as a result of the fact that they do not measure up to the literary formula of magical realism.[65] Clearly this has had a pernicious effect on critical studies of the contemporary Colombian novel and the aim of this book is to attempt to offer a more balanced analysis of the evolution of the novel during the modern period.

Among these novels Pedro Gómez Corena's *El 9 de abril* (1951) is listed almost without exception in bibliographies and critical works as the first 'novela de La Violencia'. The critical approach adopted by critics such as Suárez Rondón and Alvarez Gardeazábal has tended to be rather reductive, or distorted, as it is in the case of Raymond Leslie Williams; often this novel has been seen as an explicative social document rather than as a novel per se.[66] In any study of the more politically motivated novel of contemporary Colombia, however, its presence is de rigueur given that it is generally acknowledged as the initiator of this cycle of novels. The justification for including *El día del odio* (1952) by José Antonio Osorio Lizarazo can be made on the same basis in that this work is typically included in any discussion of the genre, though, as with Gómez Corena's novel, *El día del odio*, it is often seen as a second-rate novel. As we shall see, though, Osorio Lizarazo was a prolific writer and journalist who dealt with a number of burning social and political topics during the 1950s in Colombia, and his approach to social and cultural matters as expressed throughout his creative works was innovative and

---

65   See R.L. Williams, *The Colombian Novel*, p. 49.
66   See Suárez Rondón, *La novela* (thesis, 1966); Alvarez Gardeazábal, *La novelística* (thesis, 1970); Mena, 'Bibliografía anotada', pp. 95–107; R.L. Williams, *The Colombian Novel*, pp. 49–51.

probing. *El Cristo de espaldas* (1952) by Eduardo Caballero Calderón, has been included as a result of the view expressed by a number of critics including Ramsey, Raymond Leslie Williams and also historians such as Marco Palacios, and Malcolm Deas that *El Cristo de espaldas* (1952) is the best of the novels which focused on bipartisan conflicts during the 1950s in Colombian society.[67] *Viernes 9* (1953) by Ignacio Gómez Dávila has been included in this study because of its controversial nature. While some critics such as Suárez Rondón have dismissed it as immoral, others such as Alvarez Gardeazábal have been rather more indulgent in their assessment.[68] It is, therefore, important to offer a more balanced view of the significance of Gómez Dávila's novel. Caballero Calderón's novel, *Siervo sin tierra* (1954) hardly needs any justification in a study of this kind in that it is universally regarded as a classic of the genre, and indeed it has for many years been a compulsory set text in Colombian secondary schools.

The presence of novels such as *La mala hora* (1962) by Gabriel García Márquez, *Años de fuga* (1979) by Plinio Apuleyo Mendoza, *Una y muchas guerras* (1985) by Alonso Aristizábal, and *Bulevar de los héroes* (1987) by Eduardo García Aguilar, included in this study, is justified for slightly different reasons. They were written some years after the real date 9 April 1948 and, in thematic as well as technical terms, are more reflective and in some cases less overtly political. These four novels combined a search for an appropriate literary form with a search for social truth and, for some critics at least, will be seen as having more lasting symbolic value. In these works the portrayal of historical contingencies has been tempered by a

---

67   The observation on the importance of this work is found in Russell Ramsey, 'Critical Bibliography on La Violencia in Colombia', *Latin American Research Review*, 8, 1 (1973), 3–44. Available at <http://links.jstor.org/sici?=0023–8791%28197321%298%3A1% 3C3%3ACBOLVI%3E2.0.CO%3B2–5> [Accessed 22 October 2007]; and Malcolm Deas, *Intercambios violentos* (Bogotá: Tercer Mundo, 1993), p. 56; R.L. Williams, *The Colombian Novel*, p. 51; Marco Palacios, *Entre la legitimidad y la violencia: Colombia 1875–1994* (Bogotá: Norma, 1995), p. 203.

68   On these different perceptions see Suárez Rondón, *La novela* (thesis, 1966), p. 16; Alvarez Gardeazábal, *La novelística* (thesis, 1970), p. 23.

closer attention to the symbolic aspects of the novel. Within this group of works García Márquez's *La mala hora* (1962) stands out. Angel Rama argued that this work was the expression of violence within Colombian society in that it portrayed the political violence which was not less real for not being visibly apparent. Political violence within Colombian society in García Márquez's work is expressed in Rama's view through the motif of stagnation and inertia, both of which become powerful metaphors of the aftermath of these issues in contemporary Colombian society.[69] *Años de fuga* (1979) by Plinio Apuleyo Mendoza, García Márquez's life-long friend, offers an interesting counterpoint to García Márquez's vision of Colombian society in that Apuleyo Mendoza developed his politics in the opposite direction to García Márquez. *Una y muchas guerras* (1985) by Alonso Aristizábal offers some important insights about the role played by generational change within society. In an arresting world-view built up of a collage of flashbacks it reveals the bipartisanism which characterises modern Colombian society, split between a decomposing rural society and a rampant urban environment. Finally *Bulevar de los héroes* (1987) by Eduardo García Aguilar is included because of the manner in which it subverts traditional views of the aftermath of a power struggle within society. It focuses on an urban subversive movement and the conflict between power and ideology which is born out of that dissent.

These works could, at first glance, be understood to reflect a wide range of ideological affiliations ranging from conservatism to liberalism to socialism, given the known political affiliations of the majority of the authors, e.g. García Márquez is identified with socialism and Eduardo Caballero Calderón was a liberal. The important issues raised by these novels are the politics and ideology they express as articulated by the main character, if used as a mouthpiece for the author's ideas, or the plot as it articulates a vision of the world.

---

69   See Angel Rama, 'Un novelista de la violencia americana', in *9 asedios a García Márquez* (Santiago de Chile: Editorial Universitaria, 1969), pp. 107–125.

Time Frame

With regard to the time-span, 1951–1987, it is important to point out that the period covers both the years of the actual predominance of liberal/conservative bipartisanism together with a later period characterised by the opposition of third parties, one which was influenced by global politics and ideology, i.e. the Cold War; and the years of amnesties and political trial or perestroika which prefaced the country's entry into a new era. That is the era that drove the country into a deep constitutional reform influenced too by global politics; but it was the point at which the Colombian novel shifted into a new phase which is beyond the parameters of this book.[70]

Pertinently, 1951 corresponds to the year of publication of *El 9 de abril* by Pedro Gómez Corena, the first piece of writing recognised as a novel referring in its very title to the crucial date that drew a line in Colombian politics after the assassination of the liberal politician Jorge Eliécer Gaitán, and the social uprising triggered by that event. Running parallel with the ideological dissension imposed by the Cold War occurrences such as the Cuban Revolution begun in 1959, the May 1968 student protests in France, the economic and financial embargo imposed on Cuba by the United States of America which started in 1962, the United States of America's invasion of the Cuban Bay of Pigs in 1982, the rise and fall of the socialist regime in Chile and, of course, the dictatorships across the continent, to mention just a few, all together were factors that left an enduring impression in the years these novels were written and published.

On the other hand, 1987 is the year *Bulevar de los héroes* by Eduardo García Aguilar was published, but furthermore, it belongs to a period of time when an old process was on its way out, while a new one was ushered

---

70 For an extended view on constitutional reform in 1991, see Palacios, *Entre la legitimidad*, pp. 267–291. Also Deas, *Intercambios*, pp. 65–66; also a well documented volume about changes related to the significance, progress and decline of revolutionary movements in Latin America after the 1990s is Jorge G., Castañeda, *La utopía desarmada: intrigas, dilemas y promesa de la izquierda en América Latina* (Bogotá: Tercer Mundo, 1994).

in. The year 1987 characterises an era prior to the country's subsequent period of dialogue between the old bipartisan structure and oppositional groups, in an amnesty process.[71] It also pre-dates the national democratic movement that, by the end of the 1980s, required the country to engage in a referendum on the writing of a constitutional reform, against the backdrop of the end of the Cold War. The post-constitutional reform era, however, saw the rise of right wing forces and a combination of factors, such as the ambiguity created as a result of assimilation between guerrilla groups and drug cartels, which gave way to a different world-view and a new phase in novel writing, that is beyond the limits of this work.[72]

This book addresses the notion of politics and ideology within the context of twentieth-century Colombia, probes its value within the debate on violence in the Colombian environment and discusses the development of the historical contingencies surrounding the articulation of power relations during the period 1951–1987.

Chapter One aims to provide an overview of Colombian twentieth-century power relationships by probing, first, the political practices and ideology of bipartisanism and traditional elite coalitions; second, the politics of populism together with the issue of La Violencia; and third, analysing the struggle between bipartisan representative government and guerrilla groups in the late 1980s. It also focuses on themes which are common to the nine studied novels.

---

71   Jaime Zuluaga Nieto, 'De guerrillas a movimientos políticos (Análisis de la experiencia Colombiana: el caso del M19)', in *De las armas a la política*, ed. by Ricardo Peñaranda and Javier Guerrero (Bogotá: Tercer Mundo, IEPRI, 1999), pp. 1–74 (p. 28).

72   For an extended treatment of how, after the 1991 constitutional reform, Colombia entered a complex process in which the political meaning of struggle for power and subversion was not as distinctive as it was in the previous decades, see Palacios, *Entre la legitimidad*, pp. 267–291. Also Deas, *Intercambios*, pp. 65–66; also a well documented volume about the significance, progress and decline of revolutionary movements in Latin America is Jorge G., Castañeda, *La utopía desarmada: intrigas, dilemas y promesa de la izquierda en América Latina* (Bogotá: Tercer Mundo, 1994). Also very informative on these matters is *De las armas a la política*, ed. by Ricardo Peñaranda and Javier Guerrero (Bogotá: Tercer Mundo, IEPRI, 1999).

Chapter Two examines the politics and ideology of bipartisanism, populism and anticommunism and study-related issues such as the Governing Bloc and conspiracy in *El 9 de abril* by Pedro Gómez Corena; exclusion, social immobility and state absence in *El día del odio* by J.A. Osorio Lizarazo; and capitalism at work and class struggle in *Viernes 9* by Ignacio Gómez Dávila.

The case of the Politics and Ideology of Landownership and Resistance is foregrounded in Chapter Three, which studies the portrayal of Local Network and Religion in *El Cristo de espaldas*; Landownership and False Ideological Cohesion in *Siervo sin tierra*, both by Eduardo Caballero Calderón, and Repression, State Absence and Clandestine Resistance in *La mala hora* by Gabriel García Márquez. 'The Politics and Ideology of Contradiction and Memory', Chapter Four, analyses the role played by political contradictions and voluntary exile in *Años de fuga* by Plinio Apuleyo Mendoza and the politics of partisan agency and disenchantment in *Una y muchas guerras* by Alonso Aristizábal.

The ideology at the core of the relationship between power and 'letters' is probed in Chapter Five, which is divided into two sections, first of which the Politics and Ideology of letters ('letras') and men of letters ('letrados'), which is a constant theme throughout the novels studied in the previous chapters. Chapter Five also explores the wider gap in the studies of these novels: the related topics of 'letrados' in Colombia and the connection to politics; the role of the intellectual within the period studied, together with cultural aspects linked to bipartisanism such as rhetoric and oratory, as well as the way writers connect to power and the notion of the revolution. The second section of this chapter studies the role played by intellectuals, Revolution and Utopia in *Bulevar de los héroes* by Eduardo García Aguilar, whose ideological and cultural factors are analysed.

CHAPTER ONE

The Context of Politics and Ideology of Bipartisanism and the Colombian Novel 1951–1987

The mid twentieth century in contemporary Colombia was a deeply disturbed era whose political disturbances which began with bipartisan (liberal and conservative) feuds, recording the 9 April 1948 uprising as its most representative expression, and culminated in the amnesty processes and a new outbreak of the conflict towards the mid-1980s, significantly influenced the development of the Colombian novel. Leading as well as little-known novelists began to attempt to portray the most salient of the events in a handful of novels. The most noteworthy encompass Eduardo Caballero Calderón's *El Cristo de espaldas* and *Siervo sin tierra*, and Gabriel García Márquez's *La mala hora* among others.

The purpose of this chapter is to provide a sense of how a system of power relations ideologically pervaded the Colombian social and cultural ambience and gave rise to the novels produced during this period. I attempt to explain, on the one hand, the significance of partisan relationships, and, on the other, to show how these relationships evolved as a particular process with a specific internal dynamic, distinctively different from the Colombian conflicts that arose later in the 1990s. This focus is justified as a means of clarifying the political and ideological relationships from which the novels read in this book directly derive.

This chapter looks at the understanding of facts in two related ways: partisan relationships and ideological orientation. With regard to partisan relationships, those aspects such as competition, alliances, disagreements, party presidential plans and reforms as well as the growth of alternative forces, will be considered. As for ideological orientation, issues such as partisan ideals, ideological cohesion as well as rebel insurgency will be examined.

In this approach a comparison and contrast of the views of scholars as to the socio-political process for the period in question will be carried out to explain the tactics pursued by respective political parties and their ideological similarities and differences. This is to test the hypothesis that the factual date of 9 April 1948 had a political and ideological impact on the Colombian cultural environment, so that its waves, replicating the contingencies articulated within it, rippled in novels such as *El 9 de abril* by Gómez Corena, *El día del odio* by J.A. Osorio Lizarazo, *Viernes 9* by Gómez Dávila and *Siervo sin tierra* by E. Caballero Calderón, in the earlier fictional expressions, and later as a memorialisation in *Años de fuga* by Plinio A. Mendoza and *Una y muchas guerras* by Alonso Aristizábal. Issues such as local and national power, linked to matters of landownership and religious interests, will also be assessed, as they are addressed, early on in *El Cristo de espaldas* by Eduardo Caballero Calderón and later in *La mala hora* by Gabriel García Márquez. Similarly, the bipartisan system of exclusion, the National Front, the bipartisanism of the 1950s, along with the guerrilla opposition brought with it, are probed in the later years' novels, *La mala hora* by Gabriel García Márquez, *Años de fuga* by Plinio A. Mendoza and *Bulevar de los héroes* by Eduardo García Aguilar; within this analysis, the transition from rural to urban society caused by a modernising process will emerge as a significant leitmotif.

The Politics and Ideology of Bipartisan Coalitions and the Rhetoric of Reforms

It is said that Colombia is the oldest democracy in Latin America, and there is a sort of boastfulness in the political tradition for being, in this continent, the country able to keep it that way, with no flourishing dictatorship and instead an electoral history that in the end legitimated a political civil system. In that sense Daniel Pécaut, a respected specialist in the subject, argues that: 'Colombia es uno de los pocos países de América Latina en los que el régimen político ha conservado casi permanentemente el carácter de democracia civil en el transcurso del siglo.'[1] It is true that, in building the state, the dominant classes drove society into a mixture of 'legalismos e ilegalismos', substantiated only by two political parties, liberal and conservative, that became traditional over the years. Imposing power over 'traditional' society in the Colombian context meant a two-party 'democracia excluyente' held by elite regular agreements and the maintenance of 'clientelismo cínico'; that is, a bureaucratic system whose quintessence, foisted onto society during the 1950s and 1970s, was the Frente Nacional, as shall be seen later.[2] Referring to the two-party strategy Jonathan Hartlyn defined the Colombian system as an elite-developed Consociational regime, i.e. a politics of coalition that put the Colombian case in an intriguing puzzle after its periods of hegemonic one-party rule, and even beyond its limited democratic political regime of two-party coalition governments.[3] Scholars agree that the complexities underlying this bipartisan relationship between the 1950s and the 1980s developed from their ideological differences and find their roots in the political atmosphere of the 1930s with the power shift and changes promulgated by liberal governments.

In principle, the year 1930 drew a line in the political arena to end the so-called conservative hegemony, and to signal the beginning of a period generally referred to as 'liberal hegemony'. As suggested by Pécaut, in 1930 the organisation of dominant classes in Colombia and its hegemonic

---

1   Daniel Pécaut, *Orden y violencia: Colombia 1930–1954*, 2 vols (Bogotá: Siglo XXI, 1987), p. 15.

2   Daniel Pécaut, *Crónica de dos décadas de política Colombiana 1968–1988* (Bogotá: Siglo XXI, 1990), pp. 21–28.

3   Jonathan Hartlyn, *The Politics of Coalition Rule in Colombia* (Cambridge: Cambridge University Press, 2008), (first publ. C. U. P., 1988), pp. 17–53; (published in Spanish as *La política del régimen de coalición* (Bogotá, Tercer Mundo, CEI Uniandes, 1993). See also in this respect Alvaro Tirado Mejía, 'Colombia: siglo y medio de bipartidismo', in *Colombia hoy*, ed. by Jorge Orlando Melo (Bogotá: Siglo XXI, 1995), pp. 103–178 (pp. 106–107). Tirado Mejía asserts that this 'liberal-conservadora' coalition ruled up to 1930 after having been established in 1885–1886. That coalition was managed by Rafael Núñez with the name of Partido Nacional, and it imposed a 'régimen autoritario, teocrático y centralista' based on two institutional pillars: the 1886 constitution and 1887 concordato with the Roman 'Santa Sede'. Scholars in general acknowledge the 'pluriclasista' character of the political parties in their composition but the representation of the dominant upper-class interests is imposed upon middle and lower social classes.

capacities was based on a pre-existing stabilised and unified oligarchic system.[4] Within that unified oligarchic system a dominant block grew progressively by means of a structural context expressed in the multiplicity of development zones, the heterogeneity of power-networks and the presence of a coffee-producing peasantry.[5] In 1930 Enrique Olaya Herrera won the presidency as a liberal, though supported in turn by a 'concentración nacional de composición bipartidista'.[6] Nevertheless, and in spite of the 'concentración nacional', the liberal triumph had deep significance for the common citizens who happened to support the liberal party as it brought with it ideas of change. Before concentrating on the paradigm shift proposed by the liberal party when it came to power it is important to look at the ideological contents of the liberal and conservative parties to get a clearer picture of the meaning and expectations of their power base, their potential allies and opponents.

Liberal ideology conveyed ideas of freedom, in the first instance, as in the past it had abolished slavery, and it also meant freedom of speech, agrarian reform, the possibility of industrial growth, commercial progress and educational reform. Such ideas bound together the interests of social classes. The upper class was involved in commerce or industry, and the ordinary people saw opportunities for belated economic and social growth and mobility which derived from the policies of the previous conservative government.[7] In this way, liberal ideas apparently represented the notion of change and therefore found support among popular sectors despite the fact that the liberal party had come to power by means of a coalition. The conservative party represented the status quo, which for those generations translated as stagnation and attachment to an old system empowered by landowners and the Catholic Church.[8]

Landowners possessed large extensions of half-neglected, half-exploited terrains and used to employ peasants known as 'arrendatarios,

---

4   Pécaut, *Orden*, pp. 27–28.
5   Pécaut, *Orden*, pp. 27–29.
6   Tirado, 'Colombia: siglo y medio', p. 140.
7   Tirado, 'Colombia: siglo y medio', p. 113.
8   Tirado, 'Colombia: siglo y medio', p. 113.

aparceros, agregados [o] peones' through different degrees of attachment to the land.[9] In addition, conservatives were seen as the staunch allies of the Catholic Church, thereby bringing into being what was known as the 'religious problem'.[10] The 'religious problem' was defined as the Church's interests in landownership and power which was articulated to its possession of a monopoly over education and its subsequent inclination to preserve a hierarchical society.[11] The Church's landownership had been maintained since colonial time and it was the most powerful and representative institution of the Spanish crown in Latin America, as well as the holder of the 'public and private' authority; as such it was the education controller.[12] Issues about the Church's landownership were raised in the past through liberal reforms stirring up the problems of having large extensions of unproductive land.[13] Abel sustains that religious orders such as the Jesuits, the Dominicans and the Salesians had dominated the education field in Colombia since the colonial times and that 'la opinión de la clase alta correspondía generalmente con la de la iglesia', since it was within this relationship that the upper class fixed the goal of its own reproduction.[14]

Religious aspects are prominent in the novels studied in this book. Works such as *Viernes 9*, *El Cristo de espaldas*, *La mala hora*, *Años de fuga* and *Bulevar de los héroes* portray religion in different but related ways, such as the influencing of opinion, education, social power networks or rebelling against the bipartisan system. These issues are expressed either

9　See Jorge Orlando Melo, 'La república conservadora' (1880–1930), in *Colombia hoy*, ed. by Jorge Orlando Melo (Bogotá: Siglo XXI, 1995), pp. 57–101 (pp. 59–60). Critical views on the unequal and 'diferenciación de clases' process experienced by peasant workers within this system are found in Salomón Kalmanovitz, 'El Desarrollo histórico en el campo colombiano', in *Colombia hoy*, pp. 257–307 (pp. 272–274).

10　Tirado, 'Colombia: siglo y medio', pp. 119–133.

11　Tirado, 'Colombia: siglo y medio', pp. 119–133.

12　See Christopher Abel, *Política, iglesia y partidos en Colombia* (Bogotá: FAES/ Universidad Nacional, 1987), pp. 25–26.

13　David Bushnell, *The Making of Modern Colombia: A Nation in Spite of Itself* (London: University of California Press, 1993), pp. 120–122.

14　See Abel, *Política*, pp. 41, 47.

in the form of characters who have a genuine affinity with the community's interests and seek social cohesion through faith, or otherwise are involved in double-dealing with moral values. These novels also portray the moral predicament inherent in the Church's role, as well as the significant role the institution plays in political networking. This paradigm shift becomes apparent in the later novels such as *Años de fuga* and *Bulevar de los héroes*, which show the emergence of the figure of the rebel priest in Latin America, later in the 1960s, as the representative of the Church that worked for the poor, such as Camilo Torres in Colombia.[15] The religious issues are important, both for the particular period that preceded the political process before 9 April 1948 as well as in the 1960s, as shall be seen later.

In the midst of the economic depression of the 1930s the ascent of the liberal party heralded massive changes for the entire country. The young urban population saw with hopeful eyes the potential for the growth of industry and commerce, as promised at the time, by liberals such as Alfonso López Pumarejo and Jorge Eliécer Gaitán. On the conservative front Laureano Gómez represented adherence to traditional values. I will analyse the differences between these politicians below, but not before I look briefly at some aspects of the economic growth which was changing society at that time since they are at the core of the ideological differences separating the liberals from the conservatives.

The key ideological dissimilarities that were changing society at that time were embodied by these leading politicians. But, by the same token, these were also ideological issues at the centre of the population's interests, which the politicians addressed. These two aspects – the economic and the political – are key in the novels published in the period 1951–1987 and they are expressed in different ways in the novels: either as the contrast between the rural and the urban structures of production, e.g. in *El Cristo*

---

15   For an extended view on the significance of the Latin American rebel priest and of Colombia in particular see, Jorge G. Castañeda, *La utopía desarmada: intrigas, dilemas y promesa de la izquierda en América Latina* (Bogotá: Tercer Mundo, 1994), pp. 209, 227, 243. Also for a comprehensible view on Camilo Torrres's life and the sociological conditions that surrounded his time see Germán Guzmán, *Camilo Torres*, trans. John D. Ring (New York: Sheed and Ward, 1969).

de espaldas and *Siervo sin tierra*, or as the transitional structure of values made visible through the portrayal of social organisation and characters, as in *El día del odio*, *Viernes 9* and *Una y muchas guerras*; although they were fictional, these novels represented the deep changes the society was going through at the time the novels were published.

Ideological differences are connected to the issue of the modernisation of the Latin American countries which began in the nineteenth century after Independence. First, modernisation pursued reforms towards an industrialised economy and a society structured around the goals of 'progress and development' characteristically similar to the 'naciones desarrolladas del mundo occidental', particularly the British and French models of industry and freedom after their respective revolutions.[16] By the 1920s the Latin American countries were in their majority 'already incorporated into the growth processes set in motion by the liberal world order of market capitalism'.[17] Second, the notion of 'dualism' defined Latin American and Colombia, namely the coexistence of two types of society: rural and urban, with the implication of a transition from the former to the latter, which imposed distinctive conditions on the development of the country, in terms of economy, society and culture. The nature of this transition in Latin American countries imposed an antagonism between archaism and tradition versus industry and modernity.

During the first decades of the twentieth century in Colombia, rural conditions predominated over the urban and the transition was driven by an economy which was still 'agraria y señorial, centralizada alrededor de la hacienda y el comercio' as inherited from the previous century.[18] Thus the economy equally exhibited a mixed and uneven rhythm of growth, dual in

16 See in this respect Rubén Jaramillo Vélez, *Colombia: la modernidad postergada* (Bogotá: Temis, 1994), pp. 22–50. Also Javier Ocampo López, *Colombia en sus ideas*, vol. 3 (Bogotá: Universidad Central, 1999), p. 936.

17 See Angus Maddison, 'Economic and Social Conditions in Latin America, 1913–1950', in *Long-Term Trends in Latin American Economic Development*, ed. by Miguel Urrutia (Washington: Inter American Development Bank and Johns Hopkins University Press, 1991), pp. 1–22 (pp. 1, 9).

18 See Ocampo López, *Colombia en sus ideas*, pp. 935–937.

its social characterisation, rural in its roots and still incipient in its urban
development, which as a whole was bringing about unequal progress in
different sectors. This uneven growth was pointed out in the media just
before the arrival of liberals to power. *Cromos* magazine, for instance, had
mentioned the disproportions existing within the educational system,
between expanding universities and declining primary schools, and drew
attention to the existence of orators alongside an astonishing illiteracy,
and the contrast between international airlines on the one hand and the
lack of communications infrastructure in small towns.[19] The asymmetri-
cal development propelled by the rural and urban economies was later in
1962 confirmed by the former president, Alberto Lleras Camargo, as he
referred to the 'desequilbrio entre ciertas estructuras pobrísimas y arcai-
cas de la sociedad y la afluente riqueza de otras' brought by this trend.[20]
This expresses graphically, however, the disproportionateness brought to
the country by that bipartisan leadership and its ideological input in the
project of modernisation during all those years.

Colombia's modernisation project had gathered momentum by the
1920s and 1930s. Analysts suggest that a sense of progress accompanied
capitalist market growth in the country at the time, based on a combination
of various economic factors such as a coffee bonanza, the funds provided
by North American indemnification for the loss of Panama, banana and
oil markets, and also external loans.[21] Nevertheless, modernisation was
mostly sustained by an agrarian capitalism and its primary export economy,
since Colombia was no exception to this particular type of Latin American
'progress', as scholarly opinion suggests. Gino Germani observes that Latin

19   Revista *Cromos*, January-June 1926, cited by Carlos Uribe Celis, *Los años veinte en
     Colombia: ideología y cultura* (Bogotá: Aurora, 1985), pp. 53–197; see also Simón
     Guberek, *Yo vi crecer un país* (Bogotá: Fundación Simón y Lola Guberek, 1974).
20   Cited by Ocampo López, *Colombia en sus ideas*, p. 936.
21   Palacios, *Entre la legitimidad*, p. 79. See also Bernardo Tovar Zambrano,
     'Modernización y desarrollo desigual de la intervención estatal: 1914–1946', in
     Gonzalo Sánchez y Ricardo Peñaranda (compiladores), *Pasado y presente de la vio-
     lencia en Colombia* (Bogotá: CEREC, 1986), pp. 167–181 (p. 169–171); Ocampo
     López, *Colombia en sus ideas*, p. 937.

American capitalism 'was not founded on industrial development but on the production of primary products (food, tropical crops, minerals, oil) for export'.[22] Maddison maintains that most of this trade was with the 'developed world, in particular with the United States and the United Kingdom', and that little trade existed among the Latin American countries themselves.[23] According to Melo, Colombia experienced a radical economic transformation by the 1930s, thanks to the impulse coffee gave to the country's development since its production became the headline economy and the most important export item.[24] Kalmanovitz suggests that the rise in the coffee export economy had multiplied profit returns by twelve at the time.[25] This profit created a stronger economic base allowing for expansion and consolidation of capitalism across the country since, thanks to the expansion in markets and industry, manufactured commodities were developed in many other areas. Textiles, breweries, shoes, clothes, cigarettes and other products for the building industry, among others, were manufactured giving vitality to main cities like Medellín, Bogotá and Barranquilla.[26] Industry speeded up in Colombia and generated a process of relatively rapid capital accumulation, making also the rural sector productive as a result of market demand.[27] However this process of industry and development was affected by external factors, such as the Great Depression in 1929, which, across the whole of Latin America, forced countries to become 'reoriented towards an internal market',[28] and the Second World War in the 1940s that led to

22 Gino Germani, *Authoritarianism, Fascism and National Populism* (New Jersey: Transaction Books, 1978), pp. 64–65.
23 See Maddison, 'Economic Conditions', pp. 1, 2.
24 Melo, 'La república conservadora', pp. 74–80; for comments with respect to crucial changes from old to new production regimes in the coffee economy see Kalmanovitz, 'Desarrollo capitalista en el campo', pp. 283–284. A key work on the process of coffee production and the economy is Marco Palacios, *Coffee in Colombia 1850–1970: An Economic, Social and Political History* (Cambridge: Cambridge University Press, 2002).
25 See Kalmanovitz, 'Desarrollo histórico', p. 284.
26 See Kalmanovitz, 'Desarrollo histórico', p. 268.
27 See Kalmanovitz, 'Desarrollo histórico', p. 263.
28 Palacios, *Entre la legitimidad*, pp. 135–136.

a decrease in exports and protectionism in the national industry through imports substitution.[29]

That progress necessarily led to new social and economic configurations and groupings. Large landowners and exporters gathered in financial organisations or interest groups such as the Sociedad de Agricultores de Colombia, SAC, the coffee producers society, the Federación Nacional de Cafeteros or the Industrialists National Association, ANDI. These economic groups supported the foundation of banking sectors representing their interests, e.g. the Caja de Crédito Agrario, a financial organisation created to serve agrarian (coffee particularly) and peasant development.

But if agrarian coffee economy gave the most important base to the capitalist consolidation at national level, it was not without a high degree of labour exploitation in which peasants and urban workers got the worst part of the distribution.[30] In that process, according to Melo, Colombia's population had also doubled and the prosperity promised by these developments was slow in coming.[31] Whereas in the rural parts of the country a population of small owners and peasant workers, mestizos or indigenous people, relied on agriculture destined to supply local markets, according to the national growth at the time, in the cities streams of workers were also growing.[32] In the 1930s and 1940s in Colombia, the increasing urban population – migrants from the rural sector – has been seen as the accelerating factor in the process of formation of the working class.[33] These matters are seen as conditions which are intrinsic to capitalist development that also entailed problems related to the urban life and the way the state had dealt with them.

Studies show that the state created a few institutions to supply the services required by the modern social organization, e.g. hospitals, schools and utility services such as water supply, sewage services, electricity, as well

29   Jesús A. Bejarano, 'La economía', in *Manual de historia de Colombia* (Bogotá: Procultura / ICC, 1984), pp. 54–55.
30   Kalmanovitz, 'Desarrollo histórico', pp. 263–264.
31   Melo, 'La república conservadora', p. 99.
32   Melo, 'La república conservadora', p. 100
33   Kalmanovitz, 'Desarrollo histórico', pp. 260–261.

as banking services for housing. Yet Colombian state achievements, Tovar Zambrano has argued, were far from the real necessities of the population, particularly the poorest sectors: 'las realizaciones del estado [...] estaban muy lejos de aliviar siquiera las penosas condiciones de vida de las clases populares [...] que tendían a agravarse con el mismo desarrollo capitalista'.[34] Furthermore, the state did not take effective measures to curb inflation, which contributed to the hardship of the poor.

The disproportion underlying social growth mirrored an economic increase that favoured one group above all else. Unevenness was expressed in everyday social life in a gap in education opportunities in which the upper class was privileged while the dearth of primary education persisted. Socio-economic analysis indicates that the 'disparities between the countryside and the cities were exacerbated by economical imbalances' and other contingencies such as the fact that the impact of the radius of the minister of education did not reach beyond the borders of Bogotá.[35] In other words, wealth did not trickle down towards the common citizen, while the two political parties 'expresaban la mentalidad y los intereses de la clase alta'.[36]

Echoed in varied ways, these economic and institutional asymmetries occupy a prominent space in the novels by Gómez Corena, Osorio Lizarazo and Gómez Dávila studied in Chapter Two. For example, in the novel *El 9 de abril*, 'social injustice' is reflected in the thoughts of a character who embodies a popular leader whose influence attracts representatives of a communist country that plans to topple a government during an anticommunist summit in Bogotá. On the other hand, social differences in the novel by Osorio Lizarazo, *El día del odio*, are not only vividly expressed to show the hardship experienced by its characters, but also the failure of the institutional services, such as health, in the moment of need, which thereby epitomises the absence of the state in the city they live in. The fictional characters express ideologically the inequality produced by modernising

---

34   Tovar Zambrano, 'Modernización y desarrollo desigual', p. 177.

35   Aline Helg, 'Education and Training in Colombia, 1940s–1960s', in *Welfare, Poverty and Development in Latin America*, ed. by Christopher Abel and Colin M. Lewis (London: MacMillan, 1993), pp. 239–255 (p. 239).

36   Melo, 'La república conservadora', p. 62.

structures in the urban environment of Bogotá. Gómez Dávila's novel, *Viernes 9*, points in a similar direction and shows capitalism both as a system that functions effectively through the commercial market within the transition from rural to urban environment, and also as a system which is shrouded by the class war.

Class struggle becomes apparent during the liberal period in the 1930s and 1940s, which analysts have seen as crucial in the design of a new country heading towards modernity. While reforms were not unprecedented in Colombia, Valencia Villa suggests that the López Pumarejo government introduced the most 'ideological' amendment to the 1886 constitution, and the proposed changes contributed to the old bipartisan strategy being reshaped into a class struggle.[37] Palacios notes that particularly during Alfonso López Pumarejo's first presidency (1934–1938), under the motto 'La Revolución en Marcha', important reforms were proposed, though not carried through, and, accordingly, what were thought by many to be radical changes turned out to be more rhetorical than factual.[38]

It is important, therefore, to see in some detail the particular characteristics embodied by Alfonso López Pumarejo as a politician as well as the ideas and reform proposals presented by him on behalf of the liberal party. López Pumarejo was the oldest child of a major Colombian banker and he had received academic training in London. His class background and education provided López Pumarejo with a pragmatic attitude. He knew the business world and was a successful banker with good rapport with North American financiers and investors.[39] But, for some, his capitalist vision was seen as subversive and bordering on communist ideals; radical conservatives called him a 'bolshevist'.[40] Bushnell asserts that López

37   See Hernando Valencia Villa, *Cartas de batalla* (Bogotá: Universidad Nacional de Colombia/CEREC, 1987), p. 159.

38   See Palacios, *Entre la legitimidad*, p. 143. Alfonso López Pumarejo was twice elected president. However, unlike his first presidency, he did not finish the second period in power. Nevertheless the ideological change of gear led by the liberals in power since 1930 lasted up to 1946.

39   Tirado, 'Colombia: siglo y medio', pp. 144–145.

40   Tirado, 'Colombia: siglo y medio', p. 145.

Pumarejo 'brought social and labour issues into the very centre of political debate for the first time, and in the process he stirred up intense opposition from traditional-minded political and business leaders'.[41]

The reform proposed in the political term led by López Pumarejo was mainly to do with land, education and religion. On land issues, as described by Bushnell, it 'increased the powers of the state in economic matters, spelling out [...] the doctrine that property rights must be limited by social rights and obligations'.[42] The mandate, through Act 200 of 1936, declared that pieces of land larger than 300 uncultivated hectares should revert to the state, which made large extensions have a social function since land would be redistributed to peasants. Research has shown that the issue of land reform has been considered the single most important component of the social unrest of the time, which led to clashes among the ordinary rural population. Land reform raises the issues related to the agrarian question and refer to the country-town dualism inherent in the Latin American societies, as discussed above.

These issues – i.e. the economy derived from the hacienda system, the socio-economic and political relations, together with the peasant protest – are some of the core historical contingencies which surface in *Siervo sin tierra*, by Eduardo Caballero Calderón.

Siervo sin tierra expresses the harsh contingencies surrounding land-ownership in Colombia of the time and some aspects particularly related to the hacienda system are portrayed fictionally. As we will see, from the upper-class point of view the novel articulates the vertical relationships maintained within a system that was not only economic but also political. The conflict rooted in land distribution and management, together with the peasants' interest in economic growth, and their own housing and shelter are brought to the surface of the work, while revealing the political obligations that hacienda life imposed. *Siervo sin tierra* shows the role of men and women within that system, disclosing the internal conflicts that masked the relationship between tenants and landlords. It offers, on the

---

41   Bushnell, *A Nation in Spite of Itself*, p. 185.
42   Bushnell, *A Nation in Spite of Itself*, p. 189.

one hand, a picture of a rural milieu with its own requirements to make land productive for a growing modern industry, and, on the other hand, the political subservience that tenancy demands of the powerless.

The matter of landownership in Colombia has given rise to a number of scholarly studies, not only concerning land distribution, but also its intrinsic relationship with economy, power reproduction and the bipartisan ideology involved in its operations.[43] The hacienda system grew exponentially during the colonial and republican periods and found itself established by the 1930s and 1940s, though with unsolved conflicts between owners and peasant workers. On the one hand, by the 1930s the wasteland granted to people by the government had contributed to the consolidation of large properties in fertile and productive areas in the country, according to a recent analysis.[44] At the same time, on the other hand, while there was a demand as well as supply of peasants, a labour system was created on the basis of an 'arrendador-arrendatario' (landlord-tenant) contract. As Palacios shows, the peasant 'en calidad de arrendatario entró en las haciendas establecidas', where he was paid a 'jornal' (a day's work), given a 'estancia' (a place to live) that he had to pay back with his own labour, and an area which he should keep for 'mejoras' (improving), planting and harvesting, according to the hacienda's terms and conditions.[45]

It follows that the demanding pressures imposed by the growing industry and the cities themselves, along with the landlord-tenant contractual system catapulted a peasant protest into existence. LeGrand has explained that by means of maintaining a monopoly of tracts of land that were difficult

43   See Catherine LeGrand, 'Los antecedentes agrarios de la violencia; el conflicto social en la frontera Colombiana, 1850–1936', in Gonzalo Sánchez y Ricardo Peñaranda (compiladores), *Pasado y presente de la violencia en Colombia* (Bogotá: CEREC, 1986), pp. 87–110; Paul Oquist, *Violence, Conflict and Politics in Colombia* (New York: Academic Press, 1980). Important views in this respect are found in Bushnell, *A Nation in Spite of Itself*, p. 79.

44   See Fernán González, Ingrid Bolívar, Teófilo Vázquez, *Violencia política en Colombia: de la nación fragmentada a la construcción del estado* (Bogotá: CINEP, 2003), p. 264.

45   Marco Palacios, *Entre la legitimidad y la violencia: Colombia 1875–1994* (Bogotá: Norma, 1995), p. 150.

to exploit, hacienda owners used various methods to infringe tenants' rights and in other cases dispossess small owners of their land, forcing them to become simply working tenants on the hacienda.[46]

This peasant attachment to hacienda, pressured by landowners, led to an agrarian protest carried out by 'diversos elementos de la población rural' with a firm interest in landowning, whose support was found in the Act 200 of 1936, since this reform derived from a legal concept of the social function of landownership.[47] Scholars such as Charles Berquist suggest that the political conflict was rooted in land exploitation and economy, particularly as concerns the coffee trade. Accordingly, initiatives on labour and landownership were designed to prevent a workers' insurgence.[48] Berquist argues that the working class was inevitably trapped between the selfishness of the capitalists and the democratic values forged in the struggle for progressive social change.

Issues of cultural relevance such as religion and education were also addressed by the liberal reforms of 1940s, as we will see, and these issues are some of the historical contingencies which are portrayed in the novels of 1951–1987. They are mirrored in characters representing hierarchical authorities such as priests, whose counselling is not without bias and, indeed, has a political edge, protecting the privilege of 'letrados', as shall be seen in *Viernes 9*, *El Cristo de espaldas*, *Siervo sin tierra* and *La mala hora*. In other novels they are portrayed as representative figures of committed collective conscience whose faith and vocation is put at the service of the struggle against social inequality, such as in *Años de fuga* and *Bulevar de los héroes*. In *El Cristo de espaldas*, for example, a priest reveals the political power of the Church and the role its representatives wield in the field of education. The novel shows the importance of knowledge and its transmission while

---

46   See LeGrand, 'Los antecedentes agrarios', pp. 87–110. Also compare Frank Safford and Marco Palacios *Colombia: Fragmented Land, Divided Society* (Oxford: Oxford University Press, 2002), p. 311.

47   See LeGrand, 'Los antecedentes agrarios', pp. 107–108.

48   Charles Berquist, 'Los trabajadores del sector cafetero y la suerte del movimiento obrero en Colombia 1920–1940', in Sánchez and Peñaranda, *Pasado y presente*, pp. 111–165 (pp. 121, 157).

suggesting that language itself is part of the skills set mastered by members of the Church. Language and its connection to rhetoric and oratory as a political apparatus is portrayed as the invisible yet powerful tool of the political arena. The articulation of these historical contingencies underlines their relationship with the political process, as well as the connection to cultural matters, as shall be seen later.

In terms of education and religion, 'La Revolución en Marcha', proposed the freedom of religious belief and schooling. The Church should share its monopoly on education with lay-oriented educators.[49] This tendency encouraged a demand for lay education across the country and also a constitutional reform to enforce the suppression of privileges owned by the Catholic Church. As Tirado asserts it, the power of the Church was based not merely on 'immaterial goods' but also on 'material goods' and the liberal discourse constituted a threat to its privileges since it was also the largest landowner in the country.[50] Research on the subject shows that the Church was highly politicised throughout this process and adopted a radical stance in many cases. Medhurst suggests that the Church and its 'political domain' was a source of intense controversy in Colombian politics.[51] He also argues this is a matter of values and practices nurtured since earlier stages of Colombian history, which persist later in other contexts in the form of outright rebellion. The close link between Church influence and conservative ideology has also been noted by other scholars. Bearing in mind the traditional political system, Fals Borda has argued that the reforms announced by the liberal party in power at the time

---

49   See in this respect Tirado, 'Colombia: siglo y medio', pp. 110, 148–149. See also
     Vernon Lee Fluharty, *Dance of the Millions: Military Rule and the Social Revolution
     in Colombia 1930–1956* (Pittsburgh: University of Pittsburgh Press, 1957). Citing
     Romoli, Fluharty notes that the López programme [was] 'radical enough in rela-
     tion to the people to whom it was applied' for the upper-classes it was daring and
     unconventional, although it made no basic reforms in the structure of society,
     pp. 51, 195.
50   Tirado, 'Colombia: siglo y medio', p. 110.
51   Kenneth N. Medhurst, *The Church and Labour in Colombia* (Manchester: Manchester
     University Press, 1984), pp. 32–33.

presented a challenge as a result of the secularism embodied in them and provoked serious resistance within conservative groups.[52] Abel for his part maintains that ecclesiastic reaction took place and clerics became involved in political arguments from their own pulpits, addressing personal verbal attacks against the liberal party. Church members accused the liberals of introducing communism to the country and turned the liberal party into a synonym of Satan.[53] Priests championed the conservative party and fuelled their sermons with an anti-liberal ideology, as this reform meant a split between the state and the Church.[54] Reform, indeed, brought with it an atmosphere of change leading to anti-clericalism in some small towns and localities.

But 'La Revolución en Marcha', scholars agree, ended in tears. López Pumarejo disappointed people since in his first presidency the rhetoric of revolution did not lead to deeds.[55] Nevertheless the policies of 'La Revolución en Marcha' allowed the liberals to create a political machinery and the right conditions to maintain the party in power.[56] The liberals won elections for Eduardo Santos who held the presidency between 1938 and 1942. Santos's government's motto was 'sin prisa pero sin pausa' ('no pause but no rush') combined with a policy of 'more administration, less politics'. Santos was in part supported by the communist party and took advantage of the abstention of the conservatives.[57] In 1942 Alfonso López Pumarejo

---

52   Orlando Fals Borda, 'Lo sacro y lo violento, aspectos problemáticos del desarrollo en Colombia', en *Once ensayos sobre la violencia* (Bogotá: CEREC/Centro Gaitán, 1985), pp. 25–52 (pp. 37–38).

53   See Abel, *Política*, pp. 179–189.

54   Palacios, *Entre la legitimidad*, p. 152.

55   See Abel *Política*, p. 121; Palacios, *Entre la legitimidad*, p. 143.

56   See Abel *Política*, p. 122.

57   See Palacios, *Entre la legitimidad*, p. 160. Santos was owner and director of *El Tiempo*, the most influential liberal newspaper of the day; his great-nephews, Francisco and Juan Manuel Santos, have been, the former, vice-president 2006–2010, and the latter, a member of the cabinet in the same term and elected president 2010–2014. See *El Tiempo*, archive, 'Luego de 72 años, otro Santos llega a la presidencia', 6 August 2010, at <http://www.eltiempo.com/archivo/documento/CMS-7847423> [Accessed 17 February 2011]

was elected for a second term but, as opposed to his previous presidency, this time he failed to complete the four-year term. López Pumarejo was opposed by APEN (Acción Patronal Económica Nacional), a pressure group formed by liberal and conservative landowners who were old opponents of the landownership reform, Act 200 of 1936. López Pumarejo resigned from office in 1945 in an attempt at reconciliation with the Colombian upper class.

The Politics and Ideology of Populism: Instigation and 'La Violencia'

The bipartisan Colombian agreement which kept either the liberals or the conservatives in power has been seen by Pécaut as a 'friend-enemy' relationship.[58] According to that analysis, López Pumarejo initially played the role of enemy and upset his class with the reforms of 'La Revolución en Marcha', but became a friend during his second truncated presidential term in which he was replaced by the liberal Alberto Lleras Camargo. Lleras Camargo in turn played the role of friend to share power with moderate conservatives during the period 1945–1946 and kept the conservative Laureano Gómez and his followers, who relentlessly disputed his political power, temporarily silenced.[59] Although within the top échelons of society the friend-enemy technique seemed to work well for power sharing, it did not function for Colombia's lower-classes. As much as in the conservative party, a polarity occurred among liberals too and groups of left and right-wingers grew within both parties. Anti-conservative factions, e.g. the Alianza Nacional Estudiantil Anti-conservadora, were formed within the

---

58   See Pécaut, *Orden*, pp. 14–15. That is what, according to Pécaut, defines the essence of politics in Colombia and its 'political regime' with which the country preserved its character of 'civil democracy' throughout the century.

59   Abel, *Política*, p. 140.

liberal party and right-wingers among the conservatives gathered in groups such as the Acción Nacional Derechista or Centro Primo de Rivera, drawing inspiration from the Spanish Falange.[60] According to the ideological spirit of the parties, flexibility allowing internal divisions, alliances and grouping were part of their strategic policy. As a consequence group fragmentation or re-grouping was not infrequent. The group UNIR, Unión Nacional Izquierdista Revolucionaria, for example, which was leading ideologically the countryside peasants' leagues, developed alongside the communist party. UNIR was founded in 1934 as a result of the internal rupture of the liberal party – its chair was Jorge Eliécer Gaitán.[61] In the presidential elections of 1946 the liberal party was divided between its official half, represented by Gabriel Turbay, and an independent wing commanded by Jorge Eliécer Gaitán. Thus the conservatives, while only in the minority, were able to get Mariano Ospina Pérez elected; he took office under the motto 'Unión Nacional' during the period 1946–1950. Gaitán, soon after he reached the liberal party's leadership as 'jefe único', was assassinated, on 9 April 1948. Before analysing the development of politics after 9 April 1948 it is important at this point to give a brief description of Gaitán and his ideology.

Gaitán has been described as a populist who embodied and expressed a large number of the population's aspirations at the time. Quite extraordinarily, he is said to have come from a very modest family and achieved an excellent education. Gaitán graduated as a lawyer with a thesis entitled 'Las ideas socialistas en Colombia' and took a specialisation in Italy under the guidance of professor Enrico Ferri. His experience abroad allowed him to develop a good understanding of many aspects about Europe and the political trends of the time such as Socialism and Fascism. By 1933, through UNIR, he followed the anti-imperialist political and philosophical Latin American trends inspired by the Peruvian APRA (American Popular Revolutionary Alliance) and the Mexican PRI (Institutional Revolutionary Party). According to Sharpless, 'Gaitán made much of his

60   Abel, *Política*, pp. 118–119.
61   See Richard E. Sharpless, *Gaitán of Colombia: A Political Biography* (Pittsburg: Pittsburg University Press, 1978), p. 29.

humble background [...] grew up close enough to real poverty to understand its consequences. The circumstances of his youth help to explain his
subsequent development into a champion of the poor.'[62] He was a 'political
agitator, educator, parliamentarian, jurist, party leader, and organizer of a
vast political movement', and personally a man of 'immense compassion
and genuine concern for the exploited and oppressed'.[63] All these facets
were not common in Colombia at the time, and even less so if his social
background is taken into account: Gaitán's parents were teachers and
had 'white-collar occupations' which positioned them socially as 'a lower
middle-class family'. However, 'they were seldom far from poverty', and
thus the needs of the poorer classes were not unknown to him, a fact that
made him champion the cause of the poor and the oppressed, as already
mentioned.[64] These social conditions shaped in Gaitán an ambitious character, 'an opportunistic politician seeking social acceptance and self-aggran-
dizement', but also 'a preacher of social democracy and a fighter for justice'
as he 'spoke a revolutionary rhetoric and practiced a bourgeois reformer's
politics'. He was 'a modern caudillo that combined a personal, paternalistic,
educative political style with the manipulative, sophisticated techniques
of the twentieth century'.[65] But the most important ingredient was his
personal drive: he studied law at the National University in Bogotá and
then obtained a postgraduate degree in Italy.[66] Gaitán's involvement with
the liberal party began in his early university years, but the organisation
of the populist movement took place in the 1940s, amidst the economic
pressures caused by the First World War: unemployment, inflation, which
had devastating effects on the lower classes in particular. One hypothesis
about his leadership and rise is that he had joined the liberal party as a
stepping-stone into the world of politics.[67] While he always kept the bond

62   Sharpless, *Gaitán*, p. 29.
63   Sharpless, *Gaitán*, p. 4.
64   Sharpless, *Gaitán*, pp. 31–33.
65   Sharpless, *Gaitán*, p. 4.
66   Sharpless, *Gaitán*, pp. 29–41.
67   In this respect see Gloria Gaitán, 'Orígenes de la Violencia de los años 40', in *Once
      ensayos sobre la violencia* (Bogotá: CEREC, 1985), pp. 325–360; and also Alfonso

of loyalty to the liberal party he gradually negotiated with the upper-class leaders – the oligarchs that he challenged – and shared with them positions in the government during his career.[68] As a leading politician Gaitán was minister of labour and mayor of Bogotá. Gaitán eventually emerged with a populist movement which transcended the liberal model of development and the oligarchic model of bipartisan power-holding. The liberal model of development was represented by economic groups formed by the elite who were close to the government, and the latter were represented by the two 'archaic' parties already obstructing the path towards national unity.[69] At the time populism was a thriving political movement that had gained momentum in some Latin American countries, e.g. Brazil and Argentina, during the first half of the century, as a sub-product of the growing middle classes. Gino Germani defines populism as a 'multiclass movement expressed in some sort of left/right heterogeneous ideology.'[70] As a multiclass movement it consisted of 'sectores populares' incorporating three typical components: 'la clase obrera, la masa popular urbana y la masa agraria'.[71] These particular conditions gathered in Gaitán's favour together with an accelerated migration to the cities and an increased urban marginalised population as a result of the lack of jobs. As Sharpless underlines:

> the entrance of peasants into the market economy and the conversion of many of them into proletarians provided them with new perspectives. As their hopes for better lives were frustrated and their feelings (and experiences) of exploitation increased, they slowly began to develop class consciousness and an awareness of their potential strength.[72]

The lack of opportunities for urban workers forced them into marginal economic activities adding to the unbalanced national income distribution,

---

López Michelsen, *Esbozos y atisbos* (Bogotá, Antares, 1980).

68 Pécaut, *Orden*, p. 455.
69 Pécaut, *Orden*, p. 363.
70 See Germani, *Populism*, pp. 67–95.
71 See Fernando Henrique Cardoso y Enzo Faletto, *Dependencia y desarrollo en América Latina* (México: Siglo XXI, 1987), p. 105.
72 See Sharpless, *Gaitán*, p. 18.

which at the time showed 58% of the active population receiving 31.5% of the national income, while 5% received 41%. Moreover, the poor standards of housing, and exclusion for the majority of the population 'from the benefits accrued by economic growth', together with the continued monopoly of the government by landowning and capitalist groups, increased the harsh conditions for everyday Colombians and led, subsequently, to social unrest.[73] Thus, class consciousness grew at a time when Gaitán was viewed as 'an articulator, a manifestation of the force of the mobilizing urban middle and lower-classes and a segment of the rural population'.[74]

The growth of class consciousness and the strength of Gaitán's support for the middle and lower classes are likewise part and parcel of the historical contingencies portrayed in the novels. What is more, beyond the death of Gaitán, these different ways the contingencies reverberate in the novels evince at the same time multiple perceptions as to the date itself. In effect, the date 9 April 1948 became a paradigmatic ideological leitmotif that found its way into novels such as *El 9 de abril, El día del odio, Viernes 9* and *Siervo sin tierra*. Gómez Corena, in *El 9 de abril*, uses the date as a metaphor of the bipartisan belief that there was a conspiracy plotted by communism which caused Gaitán's assassination, while encoding the element of class consciousness as informed by liberal populism. Osorio Lizarazo in *El día del odio* and Gómez Dávila in *Viernes 9*, bring into focus multiple aspects of a transitional society in which two world views clash and reflect the oppression maintained by institutionalised bipartisanism, while hinting at the need for socio-political reforms together with the political ability of the upper class to exclude numbers of the population thereby hindering social mobility.

As a peasant who favours bipartisanism but is excluded by its upper class the protagonist of *Siervo sin tierra* sees 9 April 1948 as a revolution to liberate land for the peasants. From two different perspectives in *Una y muchas guerras* and *Años de fuga*, 9 April 1948 is memorialised: as an upper-class liberal individual and a middle-class conservative bureaucrat.

---

73   See Sharpless, *Gaitán*, p. 18.
74   See Sharpless, *Gaitán*, pp. 16–18.

In every case the date is shown as the epitome of an ideological contingency embodying new forces challenging traditional bipartisanism as well as converting peasants into proletarians.

Seen with hindsight, 9 April 1948 represents in fact 'the collapse of the hopes of millions of [Gaitán's] countrymen for a better life'.[75] Some aspects of Gaitán's assassination are beyond the scope of this book. Suffice it to mention that the theories about his death vary from the fanaticism of his murderer, Juan Roa Sierra, to the idea that it was caused by a conspiracy associated with the anticommunism promoted across Latin America by the North American Government, as related to the events which were taking place in Bogotá on the day of his assassination, a matter that will be discussed in the analysis of the novel *El 9 de abril* in the next chapter.[76]

9 April 1948 has been described as a leaderless uprising in the capital Bogotá, later known as *El Bogotazo*, that happened immediately after Gaitán's assassination.[77] This spontaneous and leaderless insurrection was not fruitful since it did not eventually contribute to the achievement of a political leadership.[78] For Pécaut, the populism Gaitán embodied was disarticulated on that very day when a state of siege was declared and, indeed, retained for many years as a Colombian government rule.[79] The state of siege was a political state measure by means of which public order and social control were maintained under repressive circumstances provided by

---

75　See Sharpless, *Gaitán*, p. 3.

76　An essential work on the events of El 9 de Abril 1948 is Arturo Alape, *El Bogotazo: memorias del olvido* (Bogotá: Planeta, 1987), which provides a wealth of testimonies and information on this subject.

77　See Alape, *El Bogotazo*, pp. 169–192, and particularly testimonies from people such as Fidel Castro, to give an example, who in many ways lived the hours and intensity of that date.

78　See Palacios, *Entre la legitimidad*, p. 201. An exceptional witness says that that day there was a 'explosión espontánea completa [... que] careció absolutamente de organización'; see Fidel Castro's view among a great deal of eyewitness views on the events of 9 April 1948, in Alape, *El Bogotazo*, p. 192.

79　See Pécaut, *Orden*, p. 481. See also Abel, *Política*, p. 156. To Abel 'Gaitanismo was incapable of achieving a permanent movement'.

the state security apparatus. It involved the structure of justice and human rights in that it was a juridical instrument that allowed the system to take exceptional measures for national security and in relation to the threat created – the argument was – particularly by communism. According to Díaz-Callejas, the state of siege was routinely applied by governments in Latin America as an anti-communist measure; it was in effect a 'doctrina de seguridad nacional' engendered by the Cold War.[80] The state of siege is only one of the many political and ideological clues alluded to in García Márquez's novel *La mala hora*; we witness the political conspiracy of the elite classes while the people demand the right to participate and mobilise, though the novel does not directly refer to specific events nor the reverberations of Gaitán's death.

The subsequent disarticulation of Gaitanismo allowed the liberal upper-class to take advantage of the situation and unite with the conservatives in power, led by the president Mariano Ospina Pérez. Abel maintains that Gaitán's death in fact proved 'the pliability of the Colombian upper-class', since after 9 April 1948 the conservative party allowed liberal leaders to share positions within the national government in the cabinet re-shuffle that followed.[81] The cabinet was reconfigured so that liberals and conservatives were represented in equal numbers and on the Monday following Friday 9 April everyday life went back to normal, after an agreement of the 'Unión Nacional' that gathered the two socio-economic partisan elites together. As Pécaut describes it:

> Una semana después del 9 de abril, todo parece volver al orden. La Unión Nacional se ha organizado según su definición original, que es la de congregar las élites

80   See Apolinar Díaz-Callejas, 'Estado de sitio ante la Constituyente Colombiana', in *Nueva Sociedad*, 112 (March-April 1991), 66–72. Also available at <http://www.nuso.org> [Accessed 25 March 2009]
     An important aspect related to 'doctrina de seguridad nacional' engendered by the Cold War surrounding the events of 9 April was the anti-communist 'Novena Conferencia Panamericana' that was taking place in Bogotá at the time – fictional works such as *El 9 de abril* by Gómez Corena and *El día del odio* by J.A. Osorio Lizarazo place these events at the centre of their plots.
81   Abel, *Política*, p. 156.

socio-económicas de las dos comunidades [liberales y conservadores ...] la unión sagrada de las clases dominantes es considerada como una medida suficiente para hacer frente a la amenaza popular.[82]

However, the events of 9 April 1948 showed the upper class that their steadfast union was threatened. The fear of new political forces before and after 9 April 1948 came from a 'heterogeneous mixture' of demonstrations or 'anarchic mobilisation of disjointed and erratic hostilities with no other context and explanation than politics'.[83] Research shows that that 'heterogeneous mixture' or 'anarchic mobilisation' had also been perceived as 'La Violencia', although the only consensus about it relates to its nuclear connection to the political bipartisan system and its method of keeping the exclusive possession of power.[84] Hobsbawm suggests that this combination of factors was called 'La Violencia for the lack of a better term'.[85] That is, the term was 'a menudo inapropiado', 'ambiguo' and 'polifacético', given the intrinsic sense of ill-definition involved in the way it has always been used.[86] The term, as hinted above by Hobsbawm, was conceived as a 'sociological clue', a 'vocablo' or as a 'fraseología bipartidista', which rather obscures the meaning of 'criminality' deliberately promoted by the political 'sectarianism' promoted by the upper class.[87]

---

82 Pécaut, *Orden*, pp. 481–501. See also Abel, *Política*, pp. 155–156.

83 See Pécaut, *Orden*, pp. 491–492; Palacios, *Entre la legitimidad*, p. 207.

84 See in this respect Éric J. Hobsbawm, 'La anatomía de "La violencia en Colombia"', in *Once ensayos sobre la violencia* (Bogotá: CEREC, Centro Gaitán, 1985), pp. 13–23 (p. 13); also Gonzalo Sánchez and Donny Meertens, 'Political Banditry and the Colombian Violencia', in Richard W. Slatta, *Bandidos* (London: Greenwood Press, 1987), pp. 151–170 (pp. 151–153); Pécaut, *Orden*, pp. 491–492; Palacios, *Entre la legitimidad*, p. 207 are also relevant.

85 See Eric J. Hobsbawm, 'La anatomía', p. 13.

86 Pécaut, *Orden*, p. 22; see also Gonzalo Sánchez, 'Los estudios sobre la violencia: balance y perspectivas' in Sánchez and Peñaranda, *Pasado y presente*, pp. 11–30 (p. 12).

87 The inappropriateness of the term La Violencia is raised together with the imprecision of its chronology. For example, in defining the arbitrariness of its limits Daniel Pécaut asserts that '1930 es ciertamente un punto de referencia cómodo, puesto que coinciden la crisis mundial y el advenimiento del partido liberal al poder; 1953 no corresponde, en cambio, a ninguna ruptura' (*Orden*, p. 27). Regional studies show

Political sectarianism was promoted from the top levels of society to the rank and file, through conservative and liberal networks that operated as outlaw gangs for the conservatives and guerrilla resistance groups for the liberals.[88] Indeed, for Hobsbawm, most important was the light 'La Violencia' casts on the problem of 'unrest and rural rebellion' within a social grouping formed of liberal and conservative gangs, banditry, guerrilla actions and killings, and 'a communist sector not involved in the violence itself'.[89] These confrontations have also been equated with banditry though they have also been considered as a representative 'distinctive response' to the 'official terrorism' exerted by the conservative governments between 1946 and 1953.[90] Analysis shows that a combination of disturbances was predicated on an ideological antagonism that represented a more open confrontation between 'clases dominantes' and 'clases subalternas'.[91] Thus, the working class at an urban level was silenced, allowing 'the capital to gain, without obstacles, economic success and accumulate wealth', while

scattered periods: Quindío area 1945 and 1953, as in Carlos Miguel Ortiz, *Estado y subversión en Colombia: la Violencia en el Quindío años 50* (Bogotá: Fondo Editorial CEREC, 1985); Antioquia, two stages over a seven-year period: the first stage began in 1946 and ended in 1949, the second began in 1950 and lasted until the end of the conservative government of Laureano Gómez in 1953, according to Mary Roldán, *Blood and Fire: la Violencia in Antioquia, Colombia, 1946–1953* (London: Duke University Press, 2002), p. 43. This period 1946–1953 coincides with Malcolm Deas, *Intercambios violentos* (Bogotá: Taurus, 1999), p. 24. But it differs from 1945–1964, a span suggested by Palacios, *Entre la legitimidad*, pp. 189–190, who breaks down those years' processes in 1. 1945–1949; 2. Late 1949 and early 1953; 3. 1954–1958; 4. 1964. For Raymond Leslie Williams, *The Colombian Novel 1844–1987* (Austin: University of Texas Press, 1991), p. 11, the period goes from the 1930s until the 1980s. In some other cases 9 April 1948 as the beginning of the period is accepted, as in Arturo Alape, *La paz, la violencia: testigos de excepción* (Bogotá: Planeta, 1993), p. 29.

88   Sánchez and Meertens, 'Political Banditry', p. 153.

89   Hobsbawm, 'La anatomía', pp. 14–15.

90   Sánchez and Meertens, 'Political Banditry', p. 151.

91   See Gonzalo Sánchez, 'Las raíces históricas de la amnistía', in *Ensayos de historia social y política del siglo XX* (Bogotá: El Ancora, 1985), pp. 215–275 (pp. 218–219). Also important observations on the ideological character of this confrontation are in Sánchez, 'Los estudios', pp. 11–13.

at the rural level, 'an anti-liberal and anti-communist crusade uprooted the democratic aspirations of peasants denying them the share of land and power taken from the landowners'.[92] Furthermore, Pécaut argued that 'electoral clashes, political and military action, a spirit of religious crusade, individual revenges, economic extortion, emergence of guerrillas, social banditry', among others were all factors of political contention.[93] Within such a heterogeneous grouping a diversity of protagonists were involved, i.e. large and small landowners, peasants ('jornaleros'), tenants, the local petite bourgeoisie, politicians, police – the armed apparatus of the state – and political bosses, of all levels and members of the urban bourgeoisie who, accordingly, politicised the events.[94] There were conservative outlaws supported by the government whereas, on the liberal flank, resistance movements developed. Conservative outlaws were seen as a 'repressive machinery of state' while liberal resistance was seen as groups that gradually evolved into banditry with liberal and sometimes communist affiliations.[95]

Political sectarianism had a direct connection to two aspects of the ideological imperative: one was the language used by the leaders and the other the high level of politicisation of the population. The language of the politicians and the level of politicisation are two important elements in the disturbances which spread throughout Colombia before 9 April 1948 and afterwards. Issues related to speech reveal the direction politicians gave to the population and vice versa, the way people followed politicians, and will be discussed in greater detail in Chapter Five. Suffice it here to say that the level of politicisation was so intense during this period that it turned politics into a show. Palacios and Abel have argued that the intensity of speech was raised to such an extent that politicians played the role of entertainers.[96] But that intensity led to what Palacios called 'incendiarismo parlamentario', which influenced and became a catalyst in people's common quarrels.

---

92 Sánchez and Meertens, 'Political Banditry', p. 151.
93 Pécaut, *Orden*, pp. 491–492.
94 Pécaut, *Orden*, pp. 491–498.
95 Sánchez and Meertens, 'Political Banditry', p. 153.
96 See Palacios, *Entre la legitimidad*, pp. 201–202. Compare also Abel, *Política*, p. 142.

The conservatives backed by the Church championed right-wing ideas and exhibited Fascist tendencies. A radical conservative, Laureano Gómez, expressed his affinity with the ideologies of Hitler, Mussolini and Franco's dictatorship.[97] Research shows that conservatives encouraged their followers to take aggressive action, using expressions like 'acción intrépida', for instance; in some regions the clergy distributed Franco's photographs along with images of the Sacred Heart, and offered 'eternal salvation' to those who fought against the liberals.[98] Conservative rule ran in alliance with the Church. There was a mutual backing in which the Church, for instance, hallowed with a Te Deum the role of the president, on taking office, to legitimise his position and persona. Conversely, when the Church led common 'laico' events, such as Corpus Christi procession and the regular nation's consecration to the Sacred Heart, the president was acknowledged as having only a secondary role.[99]

Recent studies have suggested that this rightist alignment was influenced by the ideological polarity encouraged by the Cold War, together with regional politics calling for the 'control of workers and peasants' who constituted the social support of communist parties.[100] Laureano Gómez won the presidency in the 1950 elections, in the midst of rows in which liberals accused conservatives of kowtowing to 'falangismo internacional', whereas conservatives blamed liberals for being passive about the spread of communism.[101] Gómez's party succeeded in the polls as a result of the failed

97   Tirado, 'Colombia: siglo y medio', p. 158.
98   Abel, *Política*, p. 201.
99   Colombia consecration to the Sacred Heart of Jesus was made on 22 June 1902 and it is renewed every year by both civil and ecclesiastic authorities, with the celebration of a Te Deum service. In this respect see the Message of Jean Paul II to the President of Bishops' Conference of Colombia, Archbishop Alberto Giraldo Jaramillo of Medellín, Vatican, 9 May 2002. Available at <http://www.vatican.va/holy_father/john_paul_ii/speeches/2002/june/documents/hf_jpii_spe_20020606_conf-episc-colombia_en.html> [Accessed 17 September 2011]
100 See Palacios, *Entre la legitimidad*, p. 193; see also Nazih Richani, *Systems of Violence: The Political Economy of War and Peace in Colombia* (Albany: State University of New York Press, 2002), p. 21.
101 Abel, *Política*, p. 157.

liberal attempts to 'institucionalizar un gobierno de coalición partidista'.[102] Gómez was an engineer who achieved success in the political sphere in the 1930s with the support of the Jesuits; as a refractory rightist he became the arch-rival of the liberals, whom he labelled 'masones' or 'comunistas'.[103] Gómez, it is said, instigated a fundamentalist ideology that considered itself to be the 'avant-garde of the Colombian right-wing', as conservatives felt politically threatened by potential change as represented by the liberals. To be 'católicos, conservadores, nacionalistas y reaccionarios' was in essence their spirit.[104] Fluharty remarks that Gómez was

> a typical politician of the extreme right and we shall find one of him – with identical stigmata – in almost every South American country. He is strongly religious, strongly clerical, strongly Spanish [...] his ideas, his instincts, his sympathies, are all anti-United States.[105]

Gómez, whose presidential slogan was 'la revolución del orden', had a tough time in the presidency as a result of his bad health. This is reflected in the fact that a year later (1951) he transferred power to Roberto Urdaneta, although he continued to exert power from afar. This collaborative Urdaneta-Gómez government, however, did not reach the end of its constitutional term.

In 1953 General Gustavo Rojas Pinilla seized power in a *coup d'état* backed by Gómez's conservative opponents, the Church, as well as financial

---

102 See Palacios, *Entre la legitimidad*, pp. 202–203; also in this respect see Tirado, 'Colombia: siglo y medio', pp. 171–173.

103 According to Tirado, once in office Gómez verbally attacked the liberals and called them 'El Basilisco', which Gómez defined as a mythological beast or a 'masa amorfa, informe y contradictoria [...] con cabeza de un animal, el rostro de otro, los brazos de otro más, y los pies de una criatura deforme [...] se mueve con pies de confusión y estupidez, sobre piernas de brutalidad y violencia [con] barriga oligárquica, con pecho de ira, brazos masónicos y una pequeña, diminuta cabeza comunista.' See Tirado, 'Colombia: siglo y medio', p. 166; see also Abel, *Política*, p. 107.

104 See Tirado, 'Colombia: siglo y medio', p. 164.

105 Fluharty, *Dance*, p. 41, citing John Gunther, *Inside Latin America* (New York: Harper and Brothers, 1941). See also Adam Feinstein, *Pablo Neruda: A Passion for Life* (London: Bloomsbury, 2004), pp. 171–173.

and political groups.[106] Significantly, analysis shows that up until that moment in time the upper-class, both liberals and conservatives, had established a 'correlación de fuerzas' capable of preserving power, and the coup confirmed the existence of this pact.[107] Influential financial groups – such as ANDI (Asociación Nacional de Industriales), Fedegan (Federación de Ganaderos), SAC (Sociedad de Agricultores), Fedecafé (Federación Nacional de Cafeteros), among others – alongside the elites kept the military in power, while vindicating the dictating of their specific interests 'as if it were the whole society's interests', because they were looking for an 'ideología liberal de desarrollo'.[108]

The Colombian elite's pragmatism, which brought about economic growth and the rise of the urban middle-classes in Colombia was also evident in the extraordinary rapport the ruling classes had with the army: 'El ejército era sometido frecuentemente a chequeos de lealtad partidista [...] y a informes sobre la afiliación política de las tropas'. In addition, 'el requisito extra-oficial para ingresar a la Escuela de Cadetes era la adhesión política' and, according to some circumstances, there were 'concesiones al ejército', such as a double salary in some cases.[109] What is more, high-ranking officials were not immune to sycophancy with respect to elites and politicians.[110] Rojas Pinilla, on the other hand, had been a member of the cabinet as minister of communications in Ospina's government, the minister of 'obras públicas' in Gómez's administration, and he had participated in government decisions such as sending Batallón Colombia to Korea to fight alongside the North American army against communism, in 1951. Thus Rojas Pinilla's coup had general support from Ospinistas, conservatives and liberals, and from various economic groups. The Church also supported Rojas Pinilla and considered Gómez's ideology too extreme; thus it blamed him for the political troubles.[111] The convergence of opinion

106   Palacios, *Entre la legitimidad*, p. 211.
107   Pécaut, *Orden*, pp. 505–513.
108   Pécaut, *Orden*, p. 509.
109   Abel, *Política*, p. 253.
110   Abel, *Política*, p. 170.
111   Safford and Palacios, *Fragmented Land*, p. 322.

with respect to the idea that the coup was, at best, a convenient strategy to keep political power is almost unanimous. Pécaut, for example, argues that the coup fomented 'el entusiasmo general, salvo entre una ínfima minoría de conservadores "laureanistas".[112] The liberal politician Darío Echandía at the time suggested that it was nothing else than 'un golpe de opinión', a sentence that then became famous in Colombian politics as a masterful example of understatement. It has been argued that 'Rojas represented a political solution to the crisis and not a dictatorship in the usual sense'.[113] Pointing in the same direction is the argument that 'Este cuartelazo resultó en uno de los cambios de gobierno más pacíficos y festejados de la historia colombiana'.[114] Tirado, for his part, suggested it was a conspiracy plan in which Rojas Pinilla was chosen by Ospina – who at the time was opposing Gómez – as a 'salvador'.[115] In Abel's opinion it was the rupture of the upper-class consensus which caused the coup, though the military intervention implied that 'la facción en el gobierno logró conservar el poder'.[116]

Rojas Pinilla's downfall has been attributed mainly to the very reasons that caused his predecessor's collapse. He put power first because he wanted to be elected and gave little or no attention to factions and groups that had supported him at the beginning. The opposition was created fundamentally by an economic crisis and confrontation with the World Bank, which suspended credit to the country, and industrial and commercial recession followed by subsequent unrest and strikes in the cities.[117] Palacios points out that the resignation of Rojas Pinilla, in 1957, 'fue prácticamente negociada. Su suavidad retrata una dictadura blanda', if compared with the models of dictatorship at the time in other parts of Latin America and the Caribbean.[118]

---

112 Pécaut, *Orden*, p. 514.
113 Sánchez and Meertens, 'Political Banditry', p. 155.
114 Palacios, *Entre la legitimidad*, p. 211.
115 'Colombia: siglo y medio', p. 171.
116 Abel, *Política*, p. 171.
117 Palacios, *Entre la legitimidad*, p. 217; Safford and Palacios, *Fragmented Land*, p. 324.
118 *Entre la legitimidad*, p. 218.

The old friend-enemy relationship discussed above was revitalised and dressed in a new 'consociational' agreement known as Frente Nacional (National Front). Predictably enough – because it had happened for more than half a century – two old friend-enemies signed an agreement, as good friends, to alternate the presidency every four years for the next sixteen years. Before analysing the implications of the National Front it is important to underline that the military rule agreed by the elite offers another clue to the portrayal of the bipartisan ideology expressed in the novels examined in this book.

The military element lurking in this social contract while framing it within the conditionality of democracy is echoed in the novel *La mala hora*. That conditionality is suggested in turn as an articulation of bipartisanism, politico-ideological resistance and the guerrilla movement. The novel brings to the fore connotations of a tacit agreement between the upper class and a bipartisan rule that retains the military in order to preserve social order, while preaching democracy and practicing repression by means of legal instruments such as the stage of siege. While resistance and conspiracy are driven by a section of the community, class consciousness is revealed through the activities of resistance by a middle class that sees no change in a system controlled by the central government. Politico-ideological resistance and class consciousness are also found in the novel *Años de fuga*, though in a mixed way. The novel portrays important elements of liberal as well as communist ideology brought to the political arena of bipartisanism.

The Politics of Exclusion: National Front and Rebellion until the 1980s

The struggle for political participation articulated first by labour groups and second the peasantry paved the way for the gradual development of guerrilla groups that grew in strength from the 1950s until the 1980s, and became the nemesis of the exclusive club-like ruling style that the National Front adopted from 1958 onwards.

Inequalities in land distribution in many rural areas impelled migration to the cities, providing labour for urban industry, particularly in cities such as Medellín and Bogotá. This peasant migration led to the growth of lower and middle classes but also to an increase in urban poverty. Meanwhile trade unions and the communist party emerged as centripetal forces struggling to make their interests recognised. The emergence of labour unions in Colombia goes back to the early years of the twentieth century but the most significant organisation of the working class occurred alongside the industrial growth during the liberal term discussed above. The unionisation of labour occurred during this period in diverse industry sectors such as food, tobacco, drinks, textiles and oil, among others. Unionisation expanded into organisations such as the Confederación de Trabajadores de Colombia (CTC) and the Unión de Trabajadores de Colombia (UTC). Their cohesion nevertheless was often undermined by partisan interests and subsequently by the internal political divisions of their members. CTC counted leftist liberals, moderate liberals, communists and other political factions among its members which undermined the organisation from its inception, although at the same time it 'was vociferous in its support' of López Pumarejo.[119] On the other hand UTC was 'firmly sustained by the Church', and, taking the side of conservatism, adopted the same 'model of political negotiation' as CTC had taken.[120] These unionist political tactics caused weakness since their capacity for negotiation depended on their political activity and their relationship to the party in power. An example of this tendency is offered by the Confederación Nacional de Trabajadores (CNT), created during Rojas Pinilla's government and inspired by the Argentinian populist movement of Peronism.[121] The trade unions, as seen by Tirado, were political rather than economic institutions. That was because their effectiveness depended

---

119   Robert Dix, *Colombia: Political Dimensions of Change* (New Haven: Yale University, 1967), p. 333.
120   See Pécaut, *Orden*, pp. 435–438; and Hartlyn, *Politics of Coalition*, pp. 34–38.
121   Tirado, 'Colombia: siglo y medio', p. 172.

on their partisan action and their standing as groups of opposition too.[122] The growing opposition between the conservative party and the workers determined the unions' identification with the liberals, and likewise the liberals encouraged unionisation among workers. For its part, the communist party had the strongest influence among the labour unions and the rural peasant movement and, thus, the liberal party did not contribute to its strength. Diverse sources suggest that it was from within liberal groups from rural areas that guerrilla groups later emerged: they were considered as liberal hardliners or radicals that later became communists.[123] I have mentioned above that liberal guerrillas operated as a resistance movement that gradually evolved towards political banditry and communist cells. These groups were often characterised by fragmentation as a result of their ideological difficulties in 'projecting broadly social, rather than sectarian, goals to their programmes and actions'.[124] Research shows that liberal guerrilla resistance developed 'as a combination on a large scale of various political expressions and different levels of class consciousness' which in turn were also 'varied, on the level of common soldiers as well as that of leadership'.[125] Social studies of this period point to the emergence of two segments of social resistance. One led to the appearance of individuals who became outlaw bandits. The other led to rural movements that gradually evolved to become guerrillas with a political project opposing the system of social exclusion engineered traditionally by the two parties. The first, banditry, corresponds to a category that championed ideals of benefaction to favour the poor à la Robin Hood, but it did not evolve towards a political project, in spite of the political bonds with the rural communities wherein they acted. These rural areas suffered at the hands of the army and

122   See Miguel Urrutia, 'El desarrollo del movimiento sindical y la situación de la clase obrera', in *Manual de historia de Colombia*, vol. 3 (Bogotá: Procultura/Instituto Colombiano de Cultura, 1984), pp. 179–245 (p. 207).

123   See Carlos Arango Z., *Farc veinte años. De Marquetalia a la Uribe* (Bogotá: Aurora, 1984), pp. 28–32; also Eduardo Pizarro, *Las Farc (1946–1966): de la autodefensa a la combinación de todas las formas de lucha* (Bogotá: Tercer Mundo/IEPRI, 1991).

124   Sánchez and Meertens, 'Political banditry', pp. 153–154

125   Sánchez and Meertens, 'Political banditry', pp. 153–154.

the police, whose methods included the expropriation of 'harvests and forced sales of land at bargain prices'. As a result, 'partisanship and personal enrichment became confused'[126] as in many cases it developed as 'bandit entrepreneurship'.[127] The latter will not be discussed here as its characteristics go beyond the limits of this work. It suffices, though, to add that the simultaneous emergence of banditry and guerrilla groups derived from peasant protest.[128] By contrast, the guerrilla is relevant to the spread of different groups with a political consciousness though of diverse ideological orientation, e.g. MOEC, FARC, ELN, EPL, M-19, among others, as seen below. This is the historical context in which peasant protest took place, impacting on both rural and urban environments. Peasant protest and urban migration, indeed, are intrinsically linked, as the former 'became central to urban politicisation'.[129] Many of those who belonged to the peasant protest, in an act of self-defence, formed a small group which later became a guerrilla group which then adopted Marxist ideals, as argued below. Thus 'wealthy liberals' and 'the National Liberal Directorate' initially supported groups of armed opposition in the area of Llanos Orientales, particularly where the 'guerrilla liberal del Llano' emerged.[130] These armed opposition groups enlisted the help of peasants and the groups spread in the mountains and took refuge in other nearby areas such as Sumapaz and Viotá, small villages on the outskirts of Bogotá. Scholars have shown that this opposition which was initially supported from within by liberals in opposition grew exponentially as socio-political

---

126   Hartlyn, *Politics of Coalition*, p. 46.

127   Sánchez and Meertens, 'Political Banditry', p. 163.

128   The most important study on banditry in Colombia is that of Gonzalo Sánchez and Donny Meertens, *Bandoleros, gamonales y campesinos* (Bogotá: El Ancora, 1985). See also Eric Hobsbawm, *Bandits* (London: Weidenfeld & Nicolson, 1969). Banditry, in general, according to these works, refers to common crime veiled by the idea of 'heroism and benefaction' believed and attributed by people who benefited from it. At the time banditry was carried out by individuals who exchanged their acts of aid or threat for either support among communities or silence as a result of the fear they inspired.

129   Palacios, *Entre la legitimidad*, p. 149.

130   Hartlyn, *Politics of Coalition*, p. 45.

tension radicalised rural areas surrounding the capital Bogotá, such as Villarrica, El Pato, Riochiquito and Cunday, in the department (county) of Cundinamarca, but also in Tolima and in the oil refinery town of Barrancabermeja, in Santander. Oquist and Hartlyn suggest that these peasant groups then gained 'greater autonomy and organizational coherence' which enabled them to oppose the government. The perception of that political strength persuaded the Rojas Pinilla government to offer an amnesty, which many of the rebels accepted.[131] Nonetheless, in Hobsbawm's view, it was as a result of the growth of political consciousness among the peasants' leagues and the workers' socialist unions that more politicised groups sprang into being and many of them became radicalised. They were almost invariably communist followers rather than grass-root rebels.[132] An important theory to explain the emergence of political disturbances in this era is Oquist's notion of the 'partial collapse of the state'. Oquist maintains that, given the 'collapse of the state', the simultaneous appearance of bandits and guerrillas made their actions indistinguishable. This theory also explains that the 'collapse of the state' facilitated the erratic behaviour of 'the police and the army'.[133] In this sense, in areas such as old Caldas, Cauca Valle, Huila, Tolima, Boyacá and Santander, where the state was not present or where the local authorities barely had contact with central and state power, scattered clashes had taken place. In areas with a tradition of organised peasant struggles for land, conflict focused on the 'self-defence' of local communities; small-holding peasants were driven from their plots, thus intensifying urban migration. Political networks from the two partisan sides were run by individuals known as 'gamonales' who sought to divide local communities at lower levels and keep the bipartisan system intact.

---

131   See Oquist, *Conflict and Politics*, pp. 208–210; Hartlyn, *Politics of Coalition*, p. 45. See also Gonzalo Sánchez, 'Las raíces históricas de la amnistía', in *Ensayos de historia social y política del siglo XX* (Bogotá: El Ancora, 1985), pp. 215–275.

132   Hobsbawm, *Bandits*, p. 117.

133   Oquist, *Conflict and Politics*, p. 200. Oquist's theory is widely endorsed by scholars and has recently been taken as a sound base to explain the validity of power handling from top government to local networks found at the social base. See in this respect González, Bolívar, Vázquez, *Violencia política*, pp. 270–275.

Ortiz describes the 'gamonal' as 'el jefe político del municipio' who not only possesses political power but in all cases is a wealthy person.[134] The 'gamonal' is generally a landowner whose business and capacity to employ people makes it easy for him to intimidate by means of third parties.[135] The gamonal's capital and repressive methods were both enough to put pressures on the peasants and keep them at his beck and call, since every interest within the communities was under his control. Palacios suggests that, 'questions of religion [...] electoral system with its competition for access to bureaucratic spoils (the police, the schoolmasters, the judges)', were bound to the political process that secured the gamonal's pre-eminence.[136] The pressures exerted by this political and ideological process of exclusion over the rural and urban population, plus the above-mentioned growth of social consciousness, added momentum to ideological armed resistance. The first guerrilla groups began in 1949. These first guerrilla groups fought under the banner of the liberal party and were mainly made up of peasant groups.[137] However, a call for pacification made by Rojas Pinilla's government persuaded peasants to desist from guerrilla activity. Peasant movements and land reform played a crucial role in the political and ideological arena, as land was a principal factor of dissent. Thus agrarian reform was in the 1950s, 1960s and 1970s a key component in restoring harmony among the social classes. Agrarian reform was propelled amidst fears of the growth of peasant self-defence and the communist party's influence over the old peasant leagues. A secondary factor was the political pressures exerted by the United States during the 1960s on the Colombian government to prevent revolutionary outbreaks similar to that which had occurred in Cuba.[138] Agrarian reform programmes were launched through institutional

---

134 See Ortiz, *Estado y subversión*, p. 50.
135 Ortiz, *Estado y subversión*, pp. 50, 57. See also in this respect Gonzalo Sánchez and Donny Meertens, *Bandoleros, gamonales y campesinos* (Bogotá: El Ancora, 1985), p. 50.
136 Palacios, *Coffee*, p. 164.
137 See Pizarro, *Farc*, p. 57.
138 Leon Zamosc, *The Agrarian Question and the Peasant Movement in Colombia* (Cambridge: Cambridge University Press, 1986), pp. 34, 37.

organisations such as the Institute of Agrarian Reform (INCORA), the National Agrarian Federation (FANAL), a rural branch of the above-mentioned union UTC, and Asociación Nacional de Usuarios Campesinos (ANUC).[139] Nevertheless peasant organisations influenced by Maoist and Trotskyist ideologies fortified the 'ligas M-L', that is, the Marxist-Leninist Leagues. Analysis of the Colombian guerrilla reveals that these early groups combined a policy of self-defence with the ideological orientation of the communist party. Pizarro argues that these groups emerged as a result of the need for a peasant resistance but were later articulated as a political party even though they had essentially a social mission.[140]

Apart from liberal and conservative ideas, other streams of political thought circulated through the different levels of society by the mid-twentieth century. For example, communism was regarded as having a relatively strong ideological influence, especially in rural areas, and led to a process of deep social fracture with a consequent rise of radical political opposition. The stream of Marxism and Leninism was part of this ideological flow and conferences were held to argue for the need to create these forms of opposition. In the 1950s the Conferencia del Movimiento Popular de Liberación Nacional, for instance, addressed one of these specific problems and proposed a policy of social inclusion through alternative parties.[141] The idea of creating a democratic government for every sector of society with 'liberty for the grass-roots, freedom of expression and gathering, freedom for workers' organisation' was the keynote backed by the conference.[142] In addition, participants made clear the need for an agrarian reform. Principles such as 'la tierra para quien la trabaja' were part of a set of ideas for reform in rural areas and urban centres together with the need for reform of the social security system and education for every member of society. These principles gave rise to groups constituted by three important components of society: workers, students and peasants. These combined forces gave the

139   Zamosc, *Agrarian Question*, pp. 35–37.
140   Pizarro, *Farc*, p. 20.
141   Pizarro, *Farc*, p. 211.
142   See Pizarro, *Farc*, pp. 211–216.

name to a movement called Movimiento Obrero Estudiantil Campesino (MOEC), which increased in momentum after the successful Cuban Revolution in 1959.[143] The Cuban revolution became a strong ideological influence for new revolutionary organisations. The Ejército de Liberación Nacional (ELN) stands as the epitome of these ideological organisations that took off in the 1960s. The ELN started activities on 15 January 1965 in the Santander area at the Simacota assault. The ELN became an important case in point as to the movements and what they ideologically represented and particularly because of the debate it gave rise to.[144] Debate revolved around the relationship between ethics and the revolution once a member of the Catholic Church got involved. The Catholic priest, Camilo Torres, participated actively in the ELN, though briefly, since he was killed in 1966 during his first military incursion.[145] As mentioned earlier and as argued by Medhurst, religious intervention in the 'political domain' has been constant in Colombia. Camilo Torres's personal history constituted a *cause-célèbre* which significantly affected the course of the political debate. Medhurst suggests that Camilo Torres came from an upper-class background, and had trained in Europe where 'he was exposed to the most recent European currents of Catholic social thinking'.[146] Camilo Torres also had a high-flying career. He held a number of influential posts in the Church and in public institutions, which included the chaplaincy of the National University. His positions brought him into contact with a wide spectrum of national opinion and political activism. He became a charismatic figure and led projects of popular mobilisation, organised a movement called 'Frente Unido' (United Front) in opposition to the exclusionism and status quo of the Frente Nacional (National Front). The ideology of United Front championed social justice and Camilo Torres did social work and introduced ideas and plans for reforms in favour of the needy long before he decided to take a more belligerent path.

143   See Pizarro, *Farc*, p. 165.
144   For further developments on ELN see Jaime Arenas Reyes, *La guerrilla por dentro* (Bogotá: Tercer Mundo, 1975).
145   Medhurst, *Church*, p. 33.
146   Medhurst, *Church*, p. 33.

Another important figure of the 1960s was Alfonso López Michelsen (1913–2007), head of the Movimiento Revolucionario Liberal (MRL), and the son of the above-mentioned López Pumarejo, the president who had led the liberal 'Revolución en Marcha'. MRL put forward an ideological plan called SETT, 'Salud, Educación, Techo y Tierra' (Health, Education, Housing and Land), and even a nationalistic foreign policy designed to preserve national resources. Eventually MRL made an alliance with the communist party but it 'was clearly reformist rather than revolutionary in intent'.[147] This not at all revolutionary opposition was, as Dix wryly remarks, supported 'not for masses of the large cities nor from the proletariat but from liberal partisans', mainly those from the period which preceded the formation of the National Front – López Michelsen became president later on, and he represented the traditional liberal party as a whole in 1974.[148] Other movements appeared in the 1970s such as the Ejército de Liberación Popular (EPL) (Popular Liberation Army) and the group M-19, formed after the 1970 elections but made known in 1974. The M-19 movement developed as an urban guerrilla group and owed its origins to the disputed electoral results of 1970. The then recently formed third political party, Alianza Nacional Popular (ANAPO) (Popular National Alliance), whose leader was General Gustavo Rojas Pinilla, was led to a victory that was prevented by the government in order to comply with the National Front mandate.[149]

The National Front in essence was an alliance sealed by the two parties, the liberals and the conservatives, beginning in 1958, after the transitional

147   Robert H. Dix, 'Political Oppositions Under the National Front' in *Politics of Compromise: Coalition Government in Colombia*, ed. by Albert Berry, Ronald Hellman and Mauricio Solaún (New Brunswick: Transaction Books, 1980), pp. 131–180 (p. 135).

148   Dix, 'Political Oppositions', p. 135. See also Mauricio Botero, *El MRL* (Bogotá: Universidad Central, 1990); and Alvaro Tirado Mejía, 'El MRL y la cultura', in *Credencial Historia*, 3, March 1990. Available at <http://www.banrepcultural.org/blaavirtual/revistas/credencial/marzo1990/marzo2.htm> [Accessed 21 March 2009]

149   For important observations on political tensions developed within the context of ideological opposition of the Cold War and particularly those caused by the Cuban revolution and the Alliance for Progress promoted by North America in Latin America and supported by the National Front see Pizarro, *Farc*, pp. 203–204.

junta put in place after Rojas Pinilla's resignation, as mentioned above. In Spain, where Laureano Gómez had already set up home, two meetings took place to draw up the policy that, in effect, established a system of exclusive power to be held by only these two parties in Colombia. Alberto Lleras Camargo, on behalf of the liberal party, and Gómez as representative of the conservatives, met in the holiday towns of Sitges and Benidorm (Spain) in 1956, to reach an accord to bring down the military regime.[150] The joint message declared the need to bring the two parties together in agreement which called for the end of the military regime and the return of bipartisan civil rule. Later, in Sitges, in 1957, a referendum was put in place in a 'pacto de gobierno de coalición bipartidista' signed by Lleras Camargo and Gómez, and a transitional government military junta was established lasting until 1958.

The traditional bipartisan agreements were transformed into constitutional reform through a state of siege and a plebiscite.[151] Valencia Villa suggests that:

> Durante el breve gobierno de transición, los acuerdos políticos fueron transformados en un proyecto de reforma constitucional expedido por medio de un decreto de estado de sitio y sometido a la refrendación popular en el plebiscito de 1 diciembre 1957.[152]

However, while observing that the referendum was 'la única intervención directa del pueblo colombiano' in a constitutional decision, Valencia Villa also points out that the bipartisan pact was flawed for being 'antidemocrático' because it only legitimated a 'bipartidismo minoritario'. It was the same bipartisanism maintained by liberals and conservatives kept by the traditional same minority formed by the upper class and its networks, 'excluyente' by its own standards, which prohibited any other appeal to

---

150 See Leopoldo Villar Borda, 'El siglo de Aberto Lleras', in *Revista Credencial Historia*, 199 (2006). Available at <http://www.banrepcultural.org/blaavirtual/revistas/credencial/julio2006/siglo.htm> [Accessed 28 August 2010]

151 Valencia Villa, *Cartas*, p. 161.

152 *Cartas*, p. 161. See also 'La jornada que creó la segunda república', in *El Tiempo*, 1 December 1957, p. 7.

the population.[153] The return to civil power meant the imposition of an exclusivist system in which only the two old parties were able to participate and share the power for the following sixteen years. The friendly pact to rule the country determined that the presidency was to be alternated between the two parties every four years, though a presidential poll had to take place. Thus every four years the polls were there only to confirm either the liberal or conservative take-over following the protocol which had been fixed from the outset: liberal, conservative and so on. Only candidates whose turn it was for the presidency and from the bipartisan coalition for councils and congress were allowed to stand for election. Public office was shared half and half between the liberals and the conservatives in a distributive fashion known as 'paridad' (parity). In all, the bipartisan monopoly of power meant 'alternación presidencial, paridad burocrática y cooptación judicial'.[154] Valencia Villa argues that the National Front's first and second government terms pursued a rural pacification campaign and those operations, on the one hand, eliminated banditry but, on the other hand, encouraged the growth of an ideological guerrilla movement.[155] This view suggests, first, that 'founded on an exclusive bipartisan monopoly, a permanent state of siege [and] autonomy of the army for internal public order' the National Front stood at the beginning to confront the bipartisan feuds, i.e. outlaws and liberal guerrilla, which were still ocurring.[156] Second, that the National Front not only meant the reinvigoration of the old alliance to keep a restricted democracy – negating real spaces of inclusion and participation for political groups which were different from the imposed bipartisanism – but also contributed to the formation of new armed groups of opposition with a power interest agenda, i.e. communist enclaves, resistance and rebels.[157] An example of the latter is FARC,

153   Valencia Villa, *Cartas*, p. 161.
154   Valencia Villa, *Cartas*, p. 162.
155   Valencia Villa, *Cartas*, p. 163.
156   Eduardo Pizarro, 'La guerrilla revolucionaria en Colombia', in Sánchez and Peñaranda, *Pasado y presente*, pp. 341–411 (pp. 396–397).
157   Pizarro, 'La guerrilla revolucionaria', p. 397. It is important to note that peace talks between Farc and the Colombian government were reinitiated in Oslo, on October

Fuerzas Armadas Revolucionarias de Colombia (Colombian Revolutionary Armed Forces), which was transformed from peasants' self-defence into a communist guerrilla.[158] Although recent analysis acknowledges that the National Front, on the one hand, hoped for the modernisation of the state, it also suggests, on the other hand, that it came to be an obstacle in itself, as a result of its selective character. It was a coalition of the same bipartisan interests which did not allow the social, economic and political reforms required by a society that was rapidly changing and demanding new spaces for participation and inclusion.[159]

The fragility of this situation is illustrated by the last election within the National Front agreement held in 1970: there had been three clear results: a) Misael Pastrana Borrero, the conservative candidate who made it to the presidency, b) General Gustavo Rojas Pinilla, the leader of ANAPO, and virtual winner who was prevented by the government in order to comply with the National Front's mandate, and then banished to the United States, and c) the genesis of a new guerrilla movement, Movimiento 19 de Abril (M-19). M-19 was a guerrilla movement that took its name from the election which occurred on 19 April 1970, the date of the poll for the last candidate of the National Front to be elected to the presidency. Although M-19 did make its appearance on the 17 January 1974 ballot sheet, it had been organised precisely as a result of the rigged elections carried out in 1970 in order to comply with the National Front mandate. M-19 gave rise to a new trend in its language and style. More urban than rural the

---

2012 and since 2013 have been continued in Havana, Cuba, gradually achieving partial agreements on issues such as land reform and political participation, but by 2015 at the time this book has gone to press the process has not yet been concluded. See Arturo Wallace, 'Colombia and Farc Negociators Launch Norway Peace Talks', in *BBC News Latin America & Caribbean*, available at <http://www.bbc.co.uk/news/world-latin-america-19994289> [Accessed 19 October 2012] See also *Farc peace talks: Colombia unveils major breakthrough*, available at <http://www.theguardian.com/world/2013/may/27/farc-colombia-peace-talks> [Accessed 20 November 2013] *Peace Timeline* available at <http://colombiapeace.org/timeline2015/> [Accessed 7 April 2015]

158   Pizarro, 'La guerrilla revolucionaria', pp. 402–403.
159   González, Bolívar, Vázquez, *Violencia política*, pp. 292–293.

movement stressed the importance of democracy and argued that its goal
was to fight for power unless a genuine democratic option was allowed
in the country. Intriguingly, the influence elicited by this movement was
overwhelmingly political since part of its strategy was to generate opinion
among the population, and in the end, after some agreements, it became
a political party in 1989. Up to this point in time, although the bipartisan
alternation of power remained the same, an ideologically stronger society
was growing and what began as a student's idea for promoting the change
of the political constitution ended up effectively achieving what it had set
out to achieve. With the participation of representatives from the different interest groups in the country an 'asamblea constituyente' took place
in 1991 in order to write the new political constitution so as to construct
a fair and genuinely participatory society.

The novels published in Colombia between 1951 and 1987 not only
express the bipartisan power movements of this period but also the issues
of ideological rebellion within a society suffering the pressures of constant
exclusion. In the novel *La mala hora*, for example, the ideology of opposition is suggested by characters representing professional intellectuals
whose clandestine work questions the authority of the military town's
mayor and points to the need for politics by resistance expressed through
guerrilla movement. *Años de fuga*, for its part, mirrors the life of a nostalgic
upper-class intellectual in voluntary exile who recalls his intervention in
the formation of the guerrilla group, ELN, together with his friendship
with Father Camilo Torres. *Bulevar de los héroes* provides a broad-brush
depiction of Colombian bipartisan politics as expressed in the dichotomy
presented by writer-poets and a rebel, which has echoes of the story of M-19.

Up to this point I have discussed the complex ways in which the political apparatus and its bipartisan ideology were articulated in Colombian
society from the 1950s until the 1980s. I intend to show how those structures
permeated the novels written during that period. In order to find a fairer
balance and do justice to the fictional works I look now at the politics and
ideology as expressed in each of the novels selected in this book.

It is clear from the outset that these works could be, at first glance,
understood to reflect a wide range of ideological affiliations ranging
from conservatism to liberalism to socialism, given the known political

affiliations of the majority of the authors, e.g. García Márquez is usually identified with leftism or socialism and Eduardo Caballero Calderón was a liberal. The important issues raised by the novels studied in this book are the politics and ideology they express as articulated by the main character, if used as a mouthpiece for the author's ideas, or the plot as it articulates a vision of the world.

According to the criteria of pertinence, significance and connectedness, in the following chapter I begin with the study of these issues from the perspective of three novels of the early years, namely, *El 9 de abril* (1951) by Pedro Gómez Corena, *El día del odio* (1952) by José Antonio Osorio Lizarazo and *Viernes 9* (1953) by Ignacio Gómez Dávila. I shall focus in particular on the articulation of politics and ideology and the historical contingencies which led to the insurrection of 9 April 1948 after the murder of Gaitán. The plot of these novels often reflects the liberal-conservative bipartisan relationship, the need for reforms, as well as a class struggle that gradually becomes more visible, as the novels progress from the early to the later years.

CHAPTER TWO

The Politics and Ideology of Bipartisanism, Populism and Anticommunism

Many novels of the period at work in this book share common characteristics of bipartisanism, populism and anticommunism: *El 9 de abril* (1951) by Pedro Gómez Corena, *El día del odio* (1952) by José Antonio Osorio Lizarazo and *Viernes 9* (1953) by Ignacio Gómez Dávila, all three present the best example of them in that bipartisanism and populism are expressed either transposing the name of Gaitán or using it in connection with the interests of the dispossessed. These novels in different ways show inequality as their common denominator with slight variants in which a class struggle becomes evident. The novels show either the profligate way of life of the ruling and upper class or a noticeable absence of the state in which institutional structures are perceived as trampling on the needs of the lower classes.

In these works a stock character is either a lawyer, a poet, a con man, or a priest advising members of the upper class in opposition to the middle or lower classes. The middle and lower classes are often perceived in the form of a nameless multitude or only represented by a transitional member of the society, that is, a peasant coming to work in the city, whose social mobility is hindered by government structures or by the very upper class for whom they work. Contemporary power, social, economic and cultural issues are portrayed in each of the works and, in particular, the need for radical socio-political reform. The works also reflect the authors' own political affiliations or ideological tendencies as outlined in the previous chapter.

In order to broaden the analysis and focus on the articulation of the power relations in these novels my focus now is on the politics and ideology as they are reflected in these narratives. I analyse the hypothesis that in these novels there lies a hidden ideological motivation. I draw on Jane

Tompkins's notion of the novel as the 'product of historical contingencies', as fictional works are bearers of a set of 'national, social, economic, institutional, interests', considering the 'complex circumstances' in which the novels were written.[1] Other theoretical views, such as Terry Eagleton's notions of politics and ideology are implemented in this analysis.

The Governing Bloc and Conspiracy: *El 9 de abril*[2]

Gómez Corena's novel was the first fictional production to recreate the multiple significations brought about by the most representative date of the disturbances of mid twentieth-century contemporary Colombia: 9 April 1948. Pedro Gómez Corena was an outstanding figure within Colombian society at that time. His photograph appeared in a 'Galería de Notabilidades Colombianas', and he was a member of an upper-class family which achieved social recognition through publishing a number of literary works. Gómez Corena was a member of the renowned Bogotá 'tertulia', 'La Gruta Simbólica', and as such he met well-known 'bogotano' authors such as Clímaco Soto Borda, Luis Eduardo Nieto Caballero and Luis María Mora 'Moratín', among others. Members of this 'tertulia' usually adopted nicknames and pseudonyms. Gómez Corena was known as 'Pulgarcillo' or 'Rodrigo de Rahavánez', particularly when co-writing with Daniel Bayona Posada.[3]

1   Jane Tompkins, *Sensational Designs: The Cultural Work of American Fiction 1790–1960* (Oxford: Oxford University Press, 1985), p. xii.

2   Pedro Gómez Corena, *El 9 de abril* (Bogotá: Iqueima, 1951). Further references to this novel are taken from this edition and given only the page number after quotations in the text.

3   Many of Gómez Corena's works were co-authored. With Bayona Posada he wrote *Contrastes* (1905) and *Pasiones* (1911), among other novels. A brief commentary on the novel *Pasiones* appeared in *El Tiempo*, 23 April 1967 authored by Raúl Jiménez

Reviewed by Gerardo Suárez Rondón in 1966, *El 9 de abril* was seen overall as a highly ideological piece of work. Suárez Rondón regarded it as a valuable source of information about the state of the nation, but not much more. It was, to quote him, 'un ensayo de explicación a los sucesos del 9 de abril'.[4] In 1970 Gustavo Alvarez Gardeazábal mentioned that the novel was chronologically the first novel to deal with the events of 9 April 1948 and echoed Suárez Rondón's judgement that it was a monolithic 'ensayo' (an essay or thesis).[5] In 1978 Lucila Inés Mena included *El 9 de abril* in a bibliographical contribution, which gathered references to seventy-four novels, and argued that Gómez Corena's novel was largely an historical piece.[6] A few years later Raymond Leslie Williams echoed this view to describe *El 9 de abril* as a novel with a documentary impulse which was better read 'as historical document and essay than as novel'.[7] I disagree in many respects with R.L. Williams's assessment of *El 9 de abril* as a novel which may be read 'as an essay'. In his evaluation clearly resonates Suárez Rondón's view on the novel which reads as follows: 'Como su nombre lo indica, se trata de un ensayo de explicación a los sucesos del *9 de abril*'; a reading that derives from a linguistic misinterpretation.[8] What Suárez Rondón describes as an attempt to explain the events, R.L. Williams mistakes for an 'essay' (or thesis) about 9 April. More surprising is, however,

---

Arango. See at <http://www.banrepcultural.org/blaavirtual/historia/notabilidades/notabilidades67.htm> [Accessed 18 November 2008]

4   See Gerardo Suárez Rondón, *La novela sobre la violencia en Colombia* (Doctoral thesis, Bogota: Pontificia Universidad Javeriana, 1966), p. 12; in the context of Suárez Rondón this meaning of 'ensayo' refers to a sense of the word in its linguistic meaning in Spanish 'attempt to', and not as an essay in its literary significance, e.g. a piece of writing on a specific subject.

5   Alvarez Gardeazábal, *La novelística* (thesis, 1970), p. 91.

6   Lucila Inés Mena, 'Bibliografía anotada sobre el ciclo de la Violencia en la literatura colombiana', *Latin American Research Review*, vol. 13, 3 (1978), 95–107. See at <http://links.jstor.org/sici?sici=00238791%281978%2913%3A3%3C95%3ABASECD%3E2.0.CO%3B2-J> [Accessed 22 October 2007]

7   See Raymond Leslie Williams, *The Colombian Novel 1844–1987* (Austin: University of Texas Press, 1991), p. 50.

8   Suárez Rondón, *La novela* (thesis, 1966), p. 12.

R.L. Williams's argument that the events in *El 9 de abril* occur 'in a land called Risolandia', which is clearly a misreading of the novel, since he takes literally what is meant as an ironic anagram.[9] As we shall discover, *El 9 de abril* deserves a more sustained analysis in that it problematises historical contingencies involving not only bipartisanism but the emergence of new ideological forces.

The Ruling Class and the Politics of Anticommunism

The action of the novel is set in Bogotá city in 1948, the week beginning 9 April. The structure of the story-line is based on the life of its main character, a young man called Oscar Mendeira, a lawyer who finds himself at the peak of his own political career as a 'prime advisor', a position created by the government to work with the 'Ninth Interamerican Conference', an international event taking place in Bogotá (8). Mendeira's wife, Hortensia, stands beside him as his right-hand aide, as she is a highly trained woman, due to the elevated social class to which they both belong (15). Oscar, for his part, is determined to achieve personal, financial and political success: he wins elections as representative for his own province and successively is elected as a 'member of the parliament', and later as a senator of the republic (15).

The portrayal of success, on the other hand, is counter-balanced by an obscure world of malevolence emanating from Hortensia's step-uncle Policarpo Galuso, and their friend, Tito Bauzar, a poet. A difficult relationship among them triggers a lawsuit against the two latter individuals and the legal matter is then the device on which the plot of the novel hangs, and which will later involve a prestigious forensic lawyer (18). Eleázar Gahiala (a thinly disguised portrayal of Gaitán) is a lawyer who is not only famous for his successful judicial manoeuvres but also for his position as a popular political leader who is likely to become the country's president.

9   R.L. Williams, *The Colombian Novel*, p. 50.

The backdrop of this social scenario is a large, unprecedented international event which is to take place in Bogotá: the 'Conferencia Interamericana'. The event addresses the concern felt in certain circles about the growing communist threat in the Americas, a matter of current interest at the time, and its urgency led to the presence of international delegations. A central presence within the diplomatic mission in Bogotá is Risolandia, a fictional European country whose representatives' secret interest is to boycott the conference, cause massive disruption and bring about the government's downfall (48–49).

Mendeira's position of authority makes him acquainted with Marfa Fedora Nadia Ogareff, the Risolandia ambassador's wife, but the couple set him up, by virtue of Fedora's honey-trap, to steal state documents. To carry out this mission a second plan becomes necessary: Eleazar Gaihala's assassination. Gaihala had been managing Mendeira's wife's inheritance and thereby he came into conflict with Galuso. Risolandia's representatives, Alejandro Ogareff and Marfa Fedora Nadia Ogareff, who are masterminding the plot, find in Galuso the right person to help them to put their plans into practice since they know he hates Gahiala for being the man in charge of Mendeira's legal business. According to the Ogareff's plan, Gahiala's assassination will bring about a massive upheaval as promoted by activists who had arrived in the country apparently in order to attend the conference, but whose presence is in fact intended to maximise the political chaos right across the country. Galuso brings along Jacinto Riosierra whose mission is to kill Gaihala. The novel closes the circle with its subsequent account of a social upheaval that erupted after the gunshots rang out, killing Eleázar Gahiala (138). The 'revolt' that follows shows people shouting accusations against the government which they blame for killing their 'caudillo'. The poet, Tito Bauzar, Galuso's friend, takes up his position in the radio station – as agreed previously with Mrs Ogareff – and broadcasts his politically revolutionary message, inviting the crowd to make a stand against the president and his cabinet. Galuso urges the mob to set the 'palace of justice' ablaze; his real secret interest is, however, to destroy the criminal files against him, which were drawn up by Gahiala.

The most significant source for the novel was clearly provided by the historical events of 9 April 1948 centring around Jorge Eliécer Gaitán's assassination in the commercial area of the city of Bogotá. The assassination took place at 1:05 pm, a few steps away from the intersection between Avenida Jiménez and Avenida carrera Séptima, where Gaitán's office was located. Gaitán, a lawyer and a nationally renowned liberal politician, was campaigning at the time for the presidency of the country. The week of Gaitán's assassination coincided with the meeting of Latin American leaders who had gathered in the Ninth Panamerican Conference in order to discuss the ideological threats posed by communism.[10] Gaitán had not been invited to participate in the event because of his political credentials; though a liberal, he was regarded as a communist by many of his ideological opponents, as emerged in the previous chapter.

One theory about the motive for this murder rests on the notion of conspiracy and, as shall be seen, the political intention of Gómez Corena's novel is clearly linked to the conspiracy theory which spread soon after the events occurred on 9 April. Recent journalistic documents have shown that, even before 9 April 1948, conspiracy theories were rife within the country and internationally. These versions were caused by the tensions gathering around the Ninth Panamerican Conference that took place in Bogotá, during 30 March–2 May 1948, i.e. the week the assassination occurred. The Ninth Panamerican Conference was an international summit representing the existing ideological tensions between the two economic systems, capitalism and socialism, that rose in the aftermath of the World War II. Its keynote was the national security for the western countries and as such it was an anti-communist event sponsored by both the conservative government presided over by Mariano Ospina Pérez and led by General George C. Marshall, Chief of Staff of the U.S. Army.

The Ospina Pérez government, accordingly, embraced the suspicion that the country was threatened by international communism and planned to boycott the conference, and 'arrested foreigners though it never revealed

---

10   See Herbert Braun, *The Assassination of Gaitán: Public Life and Urban Violence in Colombia* (Wisconsin: University of Wisconsin Press, 1985).

neither the names, nor the evidences for which they were held responsible'.[11] Christopher Abel in this respect has argued, for example, that 'los conservadores y *El Tiempo* culparon a la Embajada Rusa, al comunismo internacional y a la Acción Democrática por El Bogotazo'.[12]

This theory was based also on the fact that a representative of leftist ideas was in the country at the time representing the Federación de Estudiantes Universitarios (FEU), together with others of its members, and apparently distributing propaganda for their congress, for which they were arrested.[13] There is also evidence of an arranged meeting between a young Cuban student of law and politician, and Gaitán that Friday afternoon. Because of this meeting the idea arose that the assassination was in some way associated with a conspiracy in which international communism – epitomised by Fidel Castro – had an important though murky role to play.[14]

The Atmosphere of a Conspiracy

The main way in which Gómez Corena addresses political ideology in the novel is by focusing on the idea of conspiracy. Closely based on historical accounts of the uprising of 9 April 1948 the fictional story focuses on the idea that *El Bogotazo* was the result of an international conspiracy engineered by communist insurgents.[15]

---

11 Miguel Angel Flórez Góngora, 'El círculo de conspiraciones sobre el 9 de Abril de 1948', in *El Espectador*, 9 April 2012. Available at <http://www.elespectador.com/noticias/politica/articulo-337056-el-circulo-de-conspiraciones-sobre-el-9-de-abril-de-1948> [Accessed 10 October 2012]

12 See Christopher Abel, *Política, iglesia y partidos en Colombia* (Bogotá: FAES/Universidad Nacional de Colombia, 1987), p. 155.

13 See Fidel Castro's testimony, in Alape, *El Bogotazo: memorias del olvido* (Bogotá: Planeta, 1983), pp. 168–192.

14 See Abel, *Política*, p. 155; see also Richard E. Sharpless, *Gaitán of Colombia. A Political Biography* (Pittsburgh: Pittsburgh University Press, 1978), p. 172; and Alfredo Guevara and Fidel Castro's testimonies in Arturo Alape, *El Bogotazo*, pp. 168–192.

15 The idea of conspiracy surrounding the events of 9 April 1948 has been suggested in many ways, see for example Abel, *Política*, p. 155; Richard E. Sharpless, *Gaitán of*

The opposition posited by the story in terms of class struggle can be productively revised on the notion in which ideology is a set of 'beliefs which coheres and inspires a specific group or class in the pursuit of political interests judged to be desirable'.[16] That is what *El 9 de abril* suggests at first, a scene in which democracy appears to be the system that keeps the government in power, as inspired by a specific group: the upper class. But it also points to how power interests clash at the level of the social superstructure, that is, within the upper layers in which power is manoeuvred.

First, democracy appears as a political system which is repeatedly referenced in the story, through allusions to Mendeira's successful career: a charismatic lawyer-politician, well connected within the society he lives in. Secondly, his own powerful position makes it clear that he is not only authoritarian but also anti-democratic: though not stated in the novel, Mendeira is a conservative, a fact deduced from his position as the prime advisor for the international conference charged with preventing the infiltration of communism in the country. His role revolves around the superstructure of power in order to reproduce it, as we will see.

The ideological clash is not explicitly stated either, but it emerges implicitly when, voiced by the narrator, he comments on the events which take place in the story, around the main characters. From a reflective conservative perspective Gómez Corena portrays a foreign diplomat, Alejandro Ogareff, the commissioned diplomat of Risolandia's Embassy who visits Gahiala in order to invite the politician to support a protest against the 'Conferencia Interamericana' and the government, as well as his plan to disseminate propaganda through Gahiala's popular journal (87–89). The extent to which the narrative is conditioned by its political ideology is highlighted through the interest demonstrated by the foreigners in spreading Ogareff's country's 'political doctrine'.

This reference also becomes an indirect hint at the presence of a Russian intervention as the 'Conferencia Interamericana [... que] trata

---

Colombia, p. 172; Alape, *El Bogotazo*, pp. 168–192. More recently see Flórez Góngora, 'El círculo de conspiraciones', *El Espectador*, 2012.

16   Terry Eagleton, *Ideology: An Introduction* (London: Verso, 1991), p. 44.

de la defensa contra la intervención comunista en las Américas' (48–49), in Gómez Corena's fiction. The idea of the 'Conferencia', in the novel, is suggested as an event that apparently does not appeal to the Risolandeses and they may attempt to boycott it: 'tal vez no les haga mucha gracia esa reunión y traten de sabotearla' (48–49). Chronicling everyday events, two months before the Conference began 'el 13 de febrero de 1948', *La Patria*, a Manizales city conservative newspaper – which we will find in the context of the story *Una y muchas guerras*, in Chapter Four – reported that 'Gaitán había recibido dinero de la Unión Soviética para organizar actos de sabotaje contra la cita continental de mandatarios'.[17]

Gahiala, however, is portrayed as standing for his 'patria' and democracy, as he suggests: 'es suficiente que los ciudadanos de Colombia se enteren de mi propósito de formarles una patria grande y democrática' (88). The foreign diplomatic mission shows naked political ambition when they claim that they do not want to openly encourage rebellion, since they are aware of Gahiala's potential to seize power. This is why Gahiala's response is in the end unequivocally determined: 'quiero Gloria [...] sin compromisos esclavizantes. Tengo ideas distintas a las del gobierno actual [...] No seré yo quien se solidarice con el sabotaje a la Conferencia Interamericana' (91). Thus the hidden agenda of the 'Conferencia Interamericana' is demonstrated clearly in the novel since it is widely believed that the conference had in reality an anti-communist purpose intensified by the international political contingencies posed by the Cold War.[18]

The tension of the two international powers resonates in the novel in a clash of forces as understood in Eagleton's terms, i.e. that ideologies 'exist only in relation to other ideologies', and thus a 'dominant ideology has continually to negotiate' with its opponents in a sort of 'open-endedness' in order to recognise an 'other'.[19] This effect will become apparent as the form of a class struggle, as we will see in a moment.

17   Flórez Góngora, 'El círculo de conspiraciones', *El Espectador*, 2012.
18   See Alape, *El Bogotazo*, p. 603.
19   Eagleton, *Ideology*, p. 45.

The foreign representative forces Gaihala to reflect on the erroneous belief foreigners have about Colombia, that is, that it is full of 'salvajes e ignorantes' only lacking a 'taparrabo' (loincloth). According to Gaihala the people need improvement, instruction and civilisation: 'yo he tratado de dignificar al pueblo [...], he querido que se instruya y se civilice; sacarlo del ambiente ignaro en que vive' (92–93).[20] The problem of the abysmal social difference is expressed by one character, Macario, Gaihala's close aide, whom we see once before the crowd shows up. Gahiala says to him: '¿Pero qué entiende usted, Macario, de todas estas cosas?' (93). This question, and the secondary character to whom it is directed, are both related to central issues of ideology and politics in the novel. It is true that Colombian society is depicted as a democracy; indeed the foreign diplomat sees Gahiala as '[el] hombre más demócrata del país' (87) and is aware of the politician's strong position to seize power in the coming electoral contest.

On the other hand, it is the class struggle that is central to the structure of ideas conveyed by the novel via the character that Gaihala embodies in the work, that is, Gaitán. The ideological clue with respect to class struggle is suggested by Ogareff at the time he talks to Gaihala about the former's interest in inserting his doctrinaire propaganda in the latter's newspaper. Ogareff remarks that his propagandistic interest is based partly on the common knowledge that Gaihala propagates and defends ideas that empathise with his country (88), a clear echo of Gaitán and his association with the Bolsheviks, as suggested by his opponents, both conservatives and liberals, as seen in Chapter One.[21]

The social dilemma underpinning the political system becomes clear within the narrative in two main ways: a) the depiction of the ruling class and diplomats, 'el alto mundo oficial' (31), often attending lavish parties, above all Mendeira and his friends, and b) 'el pueblo', which is depicted as a marginal character which, only until before the denouement, is barely

20   About Gaitán's interest in civilisation matters see Sharpless, *Gaitán of Colombia*, pp. 131–136.
21   Also, as noted in Chapter One, Gaitán's degree thesis was on the socialist ideas in Colombia.

visible, and only seen as a bystander at the luxurious parties (38), as epito-mised by Macario, Gahiala's aide. The class represented by Gaihala and Macario is the invisible, silent social class which will grow unexpectedly in importance as the novel progresses, as we shall see in a moment. A number of these ideas are present throughout the story, though not in an over-obvious manner.

The class struggle emerges within the general ambience of the story which depicts an enormous social divide between the lower and the upper classes in Colombian society. Firstly, the narrator describes the lives the privileged classes lead within a political structure that sustains power-class relations. For example, the beginning of the novel depicts a party whose attendees celebrate Mendeira's new appointment as an 'asesor primado' for the 'Conferencia Interamericana', a position created by the national con-gress; the extravagance of the event is suggested by carefully chosen details: 'espejos' adorning the walls and matching 'óleos de bodegón' besides 'trajes y las joyas de las damas [...] smokings y las pecheras de los caballeros' (29). This event is followed the next day by another party, 'el baile de estilo' offered by the 'legación checoeslovaca'; this time in an 'elegante cabaret aderezado por el gobierno para agasajar a las diputaciones Interamericanas', where 'finos licores' and 'platos delicadísimos' are available, together with a great orchestra (29–30). Typically, this high life is depicted as one of corruption when we see Mendeira allowing Nadia Ogareff to steal state documents. On the other hand, moral values, but more particularly the lifestyle of the rank and file, are shown as at the opposite extreme to that of the powerful.

People and Deprivation vs Upper Class and Opulence

El 9 de abril typically depicts 'el pueblo' as actively involved in the upris-ing that followed Gahiala's assassination. We see a highly distressed crowd rioting, letting off their frustration and demanding the government be held responsible for their destitution as they shout: '¡Pérfido gobierno!' (138). Thus the novel shows the face of an enormous section of society which had never been seen before by the Mendeira couple and their friends who lived in an apparently safe and perfect world. The crowd are materially and culturally deprived people, 'hombres y mujeres astrosos', a large multitude whose actions give them only a fleeting sense of justice. The crowd's actions are not aimless because they 'know' that the government is responsible for the death of Gahiala and, thus, they give birth to a new anti-bipartisan ideology. Moreover, the character Tito Bauzar, a poet, plays his role as a haranguer who invites the crowd to stand up for 'reivindicaciones justicieras [...] para echar a rodar la infamia encarnada en el presidente de la República' (139–140). The poet's words epitomise on one level the ideological message at the centre of the novel, though this episode needs to be set against the conclusion of the novel which, given that it depicts the main character, Oscar, as emerging unscathed from *El Bogotazo*, suggests that the novel expresses an anti-liberal, pro-conservative political point of view. Although the political party is not named either as liberal or conservative, within the plot, this clearly knitted environment of cronyism provides clues as to how the political system works for a man like Oscar. The system allows him to obtain positions such as 'ministro de educación, comercio, obras públicas' and finally as 'asesor primado' through his 'amistades dentro del partido político', that is, a political network of 'amiguismo'.

The novel becomes a reflection of a Colombian society radically divided into two poles. The divisiveness within society is expressed by the split between a world of fantasy as epitomised by the grandeur of legal language and the metaphors of Rubén Darío-esque *modernismo* on the one hand and the ugliness of everyday life for the lower classes on the other. *El 9 de abril*, thus, expresses the clash between the fantasies of a non-existent world where everything is perfect and opposes this to the ugliness of the social misery experienced by the lower classes. This opposition between fantasy and reality evinces from the early part of the novel in which the protagonist feels 'afortunado, protegido por el hada de los cuentos azules' (7).[22] A fairy tale whose world of plenty needs no more

---

22   Many other passages in the story use the word 'azul' in the same sense of idealism and 'fantasy' proper of the modernism, but also its stylistic resources, such as the excessive use of adjectives, and foreign references such as 'el cuerpo grácil de odalisca' or 'el koll de las ojeras' (sic), 'el bigote cortado a la inglesa', 'el calembur', etc.

than a recurrent 'preciosismo' that blindly separates itself from reality: 'la hermosa muchacha, con su contextura de amazona', 'La mesa resplandecía de plata y cristalería' (p. 8), 'cabellos dorados' and 'la perfección de su rostro' (10), to give but a few examples. That fantasy is, of course, possible in the protagonist's world, always confirmed by an explicit presence of 'perfection', which appears on numerous occasions throughout the novel, e.g. 'la muchacha tenía el sentido de las cosas perfectas', their adopted son possessed an 'ángulo facial perfectamente recto' (24). That perfection brings the metaphor of power showing that in a country where there is no monarchy, princes are replaced by high dignitaries and princesses by perfect women: A high government representative such as Mendeira is in charge of the arrangements for a special event at the Interamerican Conference, and therefore he is usually surrounded by 'representativos de los círculos políticos y diplomáticos del alto mundo oficial' (31), and, to top it all, his wife is perfect (7).

The Crowd as Character

At the opposite end of the social spectrum is the rarely seen character, 'el pueblo', who appears in a revolt and is named pejoratively as 'la chusma' or 'hombres y mujeres astrosos' (141). They are Gahiala's followers and are maligned as being helped by 'manos ignoradas de individuos cautelosamente llegados al país y vinculados con el comunismo internacional' (138–154).

On the other hand, the allusion to a triumphal past alongside fantasy, a leitmotif of *modernismo*, is clearly not devoid of ideological meaning, as evident in the reference to 'el paseo Bolívar; ese sitio que soñó la imaginación fecunda del "hombre del quinquenio" [...] algo semejante a los chalets que adornan la ciudad Rosa de la Costa Azul' (33–34).[23] The subtle reference to a president and the party he represented, but also the

---

23   This is a subtle reference to General Rafael Reyes, a conservative who held the presidency for five years between 1904 and 1909, for which he is called 'presidente del

mention of symbols suggesting wealth and power – 'la ciudad del águila negra y las granadas de oro', the Bogotá coat of arms and the 'chalets' of the Côte D'Azur – become expressive of a social class whose raison d'être is predicated on the delusion borrowed from *modernismo*.

The novel typically works in terms of transposition: Eleázar Gahiala, of course, portrays the successful lawyer and politician Jorge Eliécer Gaitán, whose second family name was Ayala, resulting in the novel's character name of Gahiala (Jorge Eliécer Gaitán Ayala – Eleázar Gahiala). The narrator tells the story of a successful 'jurisconsulto especializado en lo criminal' (criminal barrister), 'eloquent' to an extent that he expounded the truth with 'silogismos contundentes' and 'como un Dios Olímpico' able to run linguistic rings around his political rivals. The narrator informs us that Gahiala was able to speak as 'el soberbio Vargas Vila: "¡No pertenezco a ningún partido! ¡Los partidos políticos me pertenecen! Voy solo como el águila y como el león; porque solamente los carneros y los cerdos van en manada"' (80). The metaphor of power is clear, though, as the images of eagle and lion represent power, whereas rams and pigs offer the image of running in flocks, which itself becomes an omen of the actions of 'el pueblo' or 'la chusma', as the narrator qualifies.

The novel also has a number of omens, though these are not predicted by Gahiala but instead by Colombia's famous pamphleteer, the above mentioned 'soberbio Vargas Vila'. Pamphlets are also alluded to in the story, though not strictly speaking in the way they are seen in García Marquez's *La mala hora* – see the discussion below in Chapter Three – but rather as 'anónimos', i.e. blackmail. It is Bauzar, the poet, who writes 'anónimos' to Mendeiras, supported by Galuso, connecting the omen of the Colombian 'letrado' to the omen of oratory epitomised by the above mentioned eloquence of Gahiala.

Transposition works in the same way for characters such as Niplio Sendoma and Pancho Gaipar as Gahiala's friends, transposed from Plinio Mendoza and Francisco Gaitán Pardo respectively, Gaitán's friends in history, and Jacinto Riosierra, the character embodying Juan Roa Sierra, the

---

quinquenio'. This is important because constitutionally the presidential period was and still is a four-year term.

man held responsible for Gaitán's historical assassination. Tito Bauzar, the poet involved in the conspiracy plan, in whose house 'tertulias' are held and who takes part in the uprising as a haranguer instigating the crowd to hold the flag of 'reivindicaciones', is a rather unique societal incarnation. The details of his character present two peculiarities: firstly, he too is drawn from reality since he is based on the poet Jorge Zalamea Borda (Bauzar is a compound from Zalamea and Borda) and, secondly, he is a caricature. Zalamea Borda, it is said, went on the national radio to instigate resistance against the government during *El Bogotazo*. Historical accounts coincide with the depiction as occurs in the novel. James Henderson, for example, wrote that on the radio 'se oyó la voz familiar del liberal Jorge Zalamea Borda' announcing that he 'había hablado con el expresidente Santos [quien venía] a dirigir "la revolución del pueblo", que había triunfado sobre "el odiado régimen"'.[24] On the other hand he is satirised when he is called 'el poeta laureado' (there is no poet laureate in Colombia) (10). Presented as the host of 'reuniones con visos literarios' whose attendees 'leían artículos emotivos, se comentaba el último suceso intelectual' (10–11), although 'en puridad de verdad' the 'tertulias' are simply designed to applaud Bauzar's success. Moreover, Bauzar is a sycophantic follower of Gaitán whose radio speech is 'pintoresco' and pejoratively linked to 'piedracelismo' (139).

Authorial Ideology and Cynicism

In conclusion, *El 9 de abril* clearly offers a story built around the depiction of a conspiracy in which a class struggle is unveiled and ends in the triumph of an ideal. That is, the ideal expressed at the beginning of the novel: a fortunate man protected by a fairy godmother, 'el hada madrina de los cuentos azules' (7). From the outset the reader encounters a protagonist enveloped in a world of political power and the dispensations it offers. It is an idealistic world, symbolised by the colour blue (azul), based on social privilege

---

24   See James Henderson, *Cuando Colombia se desangró* (Bogotá: El Ancora, 1984), p. 149.

which brings a perfect marriage and lavish parties. Yet it is clearly a naïve upper class world that is depicted as casually threatened by a conspiracy, one which seems unaware that a ruling class, in Eagleton's terms, 'must engage with genuine wants, needs and desires' of the 'other' and thus inscribe this otherness, a 'potentially disruptive force within its own forms'.[25] Medeira's blue world, in Bogotá city, symbolically reveals the party he belongs to – though not explicitly declared – that is, the blue of the conservative party in power hosting an anti-communist event threatened by a foreign power. But that world conspiracy with its disruptive effect proves not enough to destroy the political power represented by the protagonist, who typifies a privileged social class. Conspiracy, on the other hand, emerges as the antithesis of power as expressed by a social class described pejoratively by the oligarchy as simply a 'revuelta populachera' (146). It is clear that in *El 9 de abril* authorial ideology coincides with the ideology of the work, for Gómez Corena brought to his novel a conservative world-view which was that of a 'notable' in the *bogotano* society to which he belonged. At times the conflict between the social classes leads to parody. The names, for example, given to the characters or the very idea of calling an embassy by an anagrammatic name such as 'embajada de Risolandia' (a neologism formed of 'risa' [laugh] and 'landia' [land]) is highly parodic, and disguises not only the author's mockery but also the unvoiced arrogance of Bogotá's upper social classes with which Gómez Corena clearly sympathises. That parody, on the other hand, is evocative of the author's generational tendency to 'chispazo' or 'chascarrillo' (cracking a joke), characteristic of 'La Gruta Simbólica', the Bogotano 'tertulia' to which he belonged.[26] This connection becomes another important omen, for 'tertulias' were part of

25   Eagleton, *Ideology*, p. 45.
26   The 'tertulia' in Colombia has been a vital component of intellectual environments and La Gruta Simbólica is the bogotano classic in its genre. For an extended discussion on this tertulia, see Luis María Mora, *La gruta simbólica y reminiscencias del ingenio y la bohemia en Bogotá* (Bogotá: Biblioteca Banco Popular, 1988). See Enrique Santos Molano, 'La novela y los novelistas' in *Revista Credencial*, 203, 2006. Available at <http://www.banrepcultural.org/blaavirtual/revistas/credencial/noviembre2006/novela.htm> [Accessed 9 July 2012]

a cultural environment in which upper class intellectuals gathered to show their erudition and skills combining language with wit in order to mock and amuse the political audience.

In summation, despite its overwrought parody, *El 9 de abril* offers an intriguing example of the ways in which politics and ideology intersect, particularly in that its triumphalist ending vindicates the patrician viewpoint of the protagonist, Oscar, while at the same time undercutting the validity of that very same gesture given that it is based on a politics of fantasising which the rest of the novel shows to be cynical.

Exclusion, Social Immobility and State Absence: *El día del odio*[27]

José Antonio Osorio Lizarazo was a well-known journalist who worked widely in the field of fictional literature. In both his journalism and his fiction he depicted the complexities of Colombian politics and society. Osorio Lizarazo's interests in social issues grew from the early years of his training as a journalist. The son of a carpenter, Osorio Lizarazo joined the generation of writers such as Luis Tejada and particularly the poet Luis Vidales, with whom he shared an interest in Marxist ideology. Many of these ideas were later transmitted to workers with whom the writers used to socialise. Osorio Lizarazo's novels are closely linked to his journalistic observations and his political convictions. Osorio Lizarazo's journalistic work was focused on revealing the dysfunctional aspects of society and the relation the power structures had to this dysfunctionalism. Examples of his journalism are chronicles such as 'Mansiones de pobrería' and 'La usura en

---

27   José Antonio Osorio Lizarazo, *El día del odio* (Buenos Aires: López Negri, 1952). Further references to this novel are taken from this edition and given only the page number after quotations in the text.

Bogotá'[28] which comment on the severe problem of poverty in Colombia and the immoral exploitation of the poor in Bogotá in the 1940s. He also wrote on matters related to the liberal party and Gaitanismo which illustrate his political interests at the time. Among these are 'La aventura de un Gaitanista' and 'Fracaso de una política'. In the former Osorio Lizarazo expresses both his support for the liberal ideals and his criticism of the way politicians had become professionals seduced by their own success within the power machine; in the latter article he criticised the bipartisan governments' policies on prices, production and consumption in Colombia.[29]

The events on which *El día del odio* are based are distinctly dramatic and might be traced through three paths: a) the author's proximity to poverty, especially during his formative years, b) the author's own journalistic chronicles, and c) the events of 9 April 1948. Journalistic biographical notes attest to the difficulties and limitations Osorio Lizarazo experienced during his youth. Gustavo Samper portrays Osorio Lizarazo in those early years as a boy who helped his father at his carpentry workshop; he was a 'muchacho diminuto, con apariencia constante de hambre y debilidad permanecía junto al banco mirando trabajar [...] su padre trabajaba de sol a sol pero no ganaba casi nada'.[30] Osorio Lizarazo's own family life as a young man and his experience of the areas where the city's poor – who were becoming poorer – lived acquainted him with the intrinsic traits of that social fabric together with its exclusion from the structures of power. Furthermore, interestingly, Osorio Lizarazo also had the opportunity to get to know the growing middle-class section of society created by rural immigration as well as members of the elite, during his youth. As a young boy his father managed to get his son into the Jesuit school San Bartolomé right in the city centre where he met upper and middle-class classmates, but also – keeping his foot in both camps – before starting his journalistic career, he went to work as a miner and as a coffee plantation worker.

28   See 'La usura en Bogotá', in *Novelas y crónicas. J.A. Osorio Lizarazo*, ed. by Santiago Mutis Durán (Bogotá: Instituto Colombiano de Cultura, 1978), pp. 376–382.

29   See *Novelas y crónicas*, pp. 569–576.

30   Gustavo Samper, 'Osorio Lizarazo', cited in *Novelas y crónicas*, p. xxvii.

Thus Osorio Lizarazo had the opportunity to see the different faces of a population seeking change, when 'la ciudad estaba en pleno crecimiento exhibiendo los nacientes encantos de las primeras construcciones modernas' along with the arrogance of the privileged and the difficulties experienced by the poorer classes.[31] In this respect it is also important to take into account the time-frame within which Osorio Lizarazo lived, 1900 to 1964, which was a crucial time for the social changes that paved the way for the country's entrance into modernity. It was during the first half of the century that important structural changes occurred in the country, as seen in Chapter One. Osorio Lizarazo's own chronicles point to the changes he witnessed at the time, as he suggests in reference to the first three decades: 'En sólo treinta años ¡cuán profunda transformación! Vino el automóvil [...] se ensanchó el radio urbano, la gente vivió más aceleradamente.'[32] Osorio Lizarazo had great admiration for the influential Russian writer, Maxim Gorky. In a noteworthy article entitled 'Un nuevo aniversario de Máximo Gorky', he underlines Gorky's significance for his work in that he took 'la literatura como un instrumento para despertar conciencia [...] de rebelión, de lucha, de justicia', and singles out the Russian author as inspirational for his commitment with the 'masas populares'.[33]

Osorio Lizarazo's interest in political and social structures brought him into contact with Marxist reading groups, which he combined with Gaitán's views on socialism blended with his convictions about liberalism. Osorio Lizarazo did not become a communist; he was rather a liberal supporter, which is evident in the non-fictional works in which his liberal ideals are expressed, an example being his essay *Liberalismo, partido de izquierda* which has been described as a thesis of 'redención social y económica para el proletariado.'[34]

Osorio Lizarazo's preoccupation with the proletariat evinces also in the description of the marginality of new urban groups, their difficulties

---

31   Samper, 'Osorio Lizarazo', in *Novelas y crónicas*, p. xxxii.

32   Osorio Lizarazo, 'Los bohemios bogotanos de principios del siglo', in *Novelas y crónicas*, pp. 337–342.

33   *Novelas y crónicas*, pp. 546–555.

34   Samper, 'Osorio Lizarazo', in *Novelas y crónicas*, p. xxix.

in finding housing and health care, combined with the daily ordeals of their living conditions, in the above-mentioned chronicle 'Mansiones de pobrería'. It is with a poignant realism that he portrays the poor districts of Bogotá as places where extreme poverty lives like a 'monstruoso dios mitológico', gathering 'en repugnante promiscuidad, los productos multiformes de la máxima pobreza'.[35] Osorio Lizarazo's first-hand acquaintance with the city's 'vecindarios', in his journalism, came to form the backdrop for novels such as *Casa de vecindad* and *El día del odio*. In the novel *Casa de vecindad*, Osorio Lizarazo created a work that mirrored the social pressures and 'anguish' experienced by the lower class before 9 April 1948, and in *El día del odio*, his interest in social problems as well as the articulation of the larger structure of politics and power-sharing is revealed. Osorio Lizarazo's preoccupations surface in *El día del odio* in a portrayal of the trauma experienced by people arriving in Bogotá from the countryside looking for jobs, overwhelmed by circumstantial absurdities largely driven by a dysfunctional state's structure.

The incidents recounted in *El día del odio* revolve around the last weeks in the life of a girl called Tránsito Hernández, aged sixteen, a housemaid working for a small middle-class family in Bogotá. Brought to Bogotá city by her mother, a peasant trader who works at an open market, Tránsito goes to work for the Albornoz family in the hope that her salary will help support her parents' livelihood in the countryside. Tránsito is sacked after being accused of stealing a small jewel that belonged to the Albornoz family's landlady. Tránsito, an ingenuous girl, is thrown out on the streets with only a third of her salary (two pesos) since her employer, Alicia Albornoz, did not have enough money to pay her monthly salary of six pesos. Tránsito attempts to get back to her parents' home in a small town close to the capital, but is unable to do so for lack of money and, arriving late at the train station, she finds herself on her own. Tránsito is trapped and then raped by a policeman. To make matters even worse, and thinking she should try to get back to her ex-employer, Tránsito is arrested on suspicion of theft because of the sack in which she is carrying her personal belongings.

---

35 See 'Mansiones de pobrería', in *Novelas y crónicas*, pp. 302–308 (p. 305).

In spite of her efforts to explain that she is a maid, Tránsito is brought by the police to be registered as a prostitute and given a red card that identifies her as such, and is also recorded as a thief and gets her belongings and money confiscated since nobody believes her story as to why she is walking the streets late at night. In Colombia it was common to view a woman on her own on the streets late at night in the 1950s as a prostitute looking for business, and this is reflected in Lizarazo's novel.[36] When she returns to the Albornoz family she is exonerated as not having stolen the missing jewel but she is not given her job back at the house because of the red card she has been given at the police station. The family does not believe Tránsito is innocent and believes she may even be dangerous to the family. As things get worse, she find herself homeless, alone and unable to get another job for lack of references; Tránsito inevitably falls into a vicious cycle of poverty and prostitution when she meets a man called Teódulo Peralta, better known by his nickname, El Alacrán, and also Alfredo Pineda known as Manueseda; they are low-life Bogotá types. Alacrán courts Tránsito and brings her to live with him with the promise he will help her to return to her rural home-town. The men meet Forge Olmos, who helps them, but there is a sting in the tail since Olmos is also someone who indoctrinates people about politics. Arrested by the police, Tránsito's partner, Alacrán, is taken to jail, which makes Tránsito homeless and unprotected again but later she meets a builder (whose name is not provided) who invites her to live with him. Tránsito's bad luck strikes again when her new man is killed in a 'chichería' as a result of a drunken quarrel over politics; she is found by the police and taken to the station on suspicion of murder of the man she lived with. After being detained and nearly dying of starvation Tránsito then bumps into her ex-partner Alacrán and she is taken to a place to live with him. Alacrán's intention is to work and settle down with Tránsito and, after a brief stint working in a brick factory, he leaves the job for fear he will be caught in the raids carried

---

36   There is an important reference to no women on Bogotá's streets, 'ni una mujer en la calle', in Germán Castro Caycedo, interview with García Márquez, 'Gabo cuenta la novela de su vida' (1), in *El Espectador*, 16 March 1977, p. 5-A.

out by the police in preparation for the Conferencia Panamericana. The next day, hungry, Tránsito and Alacrán see a large fire burning in central Bogotá and they decide to go and find out what is happening. They are overwhelmed by the riot in which Tránsito loses her life, not without spelling out her rage screaming '¡muera!' The analysis of a few contingencies surrounding Tránsito's death may help us to visualise the impact and significance of her scream, as we will see below.

Ideology and Transitional Society

The ideological substratum of the novel *El día del odio* transpires from the social disarray and the gradual rise of new forces within society. *El día del odio* is clearly situated at the juncture between the old rural hacienda way of life and the slowly emerging capitalist urban structure of a dualistic society in which development is based on primary products, as I have explained in Chapter One. *El día del odio* refers to people arriving in Bogotá from all over the country looking for opportunities that allow them to improve their quality of life. Many come from peasant families whose economy is based primarily on basic products sold in the city's open markets. Tránsito's newly acquired urban identity comes with her employment as a housemaid in a middle-class family. What Tránsito is expected to do is to serve 'señora' Alicia's family; in this sense she epitomises the young woman coming to the city to work as a maid for social arrivistes who struggle even to pay their servant since they depend on the salary of a precarious breadwinner who is generally the husband. This was a family barely surviving on the husband's salary; their 'privaciones' were, indeed, common in the 'clase media' of the time. These 'privaciones' meant that occasionally they did not have enough money to pay Tránsito's mother when she came monthly to claim her daughter's salary; indeed, Tránsito was given only two pesos, a third of her salary, when kicked out of the house. They were a family 'sin hogar fijo', homeless in a sense because they did not possess a property and therefore were obliged to pay rent, 'abrumada bajo el fracaso económico, sujeta a las contigencias que perturbaban la posición y el sueldo del marido' (11), with 'problemas

insolubles' and 'ambiciones frustradas' (14). Despite the harsh conditions of her employment Tránsito was an honourable and loyal servant,
and mistakenly accused of theft she was unfairly sacked from her job and
thrown to her fate in the streets as mentioned above. Falling first into the
chasm of homelessness, it is Tránsito who provides the reader insight into
the ideological traces of *El día del odio*.

'Social Temperature' and 'Structure of Feeling'

Criticism on the novel in its heyday pointed to the social significance
conveyed by this novel's main character. Téllez, for example, asserted that
the novel essentially addressed 'el destino de la clase social más desvalida
frente a los poderes del estado y de las clases privilegiadas'.[37] Téllez thereby
implied that there was a deep social division between the have-nots and
the rich reflected in the novel. That rupture was also the material expression of a deeper intrinsic social 'structure of feeling' evincing a 'desajuste
social'. Such a 'desajuste social' suggested by Téllez emerges in the course of
the novel along Tránsito's route to death. The events of her life highlight
what Téllez calls the 'temperatura social' of Colombian life in the 1940s.
This 'temperatura social' is similar to the 'structure of feeling' referred to
by the Marxist critic Raymond Williams, which is defined as a 'particular
sense of life, a particular community of experience hardly needing expression' or a 'social character' that is not trivial or marginal and rather quite
central within a social process.[38] What is intended by the term 'structure
of feeling' within a society might be read in Eagleton's terms as a 'largely
concealed structure of values which informs and underlies factual statements', a unity in the 'shape of political solidarity and comradely feeling'.[39]

---

37   See Hernando Téllez, 'El día del odio', *El Tiempo, Lecturas Dominicales*, 25 October
     1953, p. 1.
38   See Raymond Williams, *The Long Revolution* (London: Hogarth Press, 1992),
     pp. 48–49.
39   See Eagleton, *Ideology*, p. 45; also *Literary Theory: An Introduction* (Oxford:
     Blackwell, 1996), p. 13.

In *El día del odio* this concealed 'structure of feeling' emerges as the people's combined frustrations caused by an absurd destiny linked to a structure of institutional power that denies them every opportunity to be respected or heard or given the chance to thrive in their social environment. Tránsito's trajectory reveals that state institutions are not there to help but to bully the powerless; the absurdity which characterises her life is not a philosophical problem but revealed to be a societal absurdity. For one thing Tránsito is never 'heard' by anyone who represents either superiority, e.g. her employer, 'señora Alicia', who accused Tránsito of a theft that never occurred, or by the authorities such as the police and the staff in the judge's office from whom she routinely experiences abuse and disrespect. Thus Tránsito, like the grassroots society with which she identifies, resiliently survives until her final demise and becomes a symbol of the subaltern in the novel. It is thus that the story describes the central issue of social exclusion, while simultaneously showing a latent threat posed to the ruling class and its order based on privilege by the newly emerging population expecting social mobility. In Osorio Lizarazo's time the population growth gave rise to important debates in congress, as Samper highlights: 'los periódicos y el parlamento discutían sobre la situación angustiosa de la clase media'.[40] Parliament saw the main problem of the time as the impoverishment of the middle class, whereas the novel points to a deeper concern: the gradually increasing insurgency of a significant part of the population.

The 'Poor Upper Society' and the Lower Class's Degradation

Read according to Eagleton's principle, *El día del odio* will be interpreted as a novel which discloses the state's incompetence in creating a viable social structure that allows individuals to thrive; in effect the state distributes 'lack' rather than social structures. In this respect Gutiérrez Girardot pointed out that *El día del odio* was a novel 'adecuada al objeto que se propuso describir', that is, what Colombian society was felt by some to be like at Osorio

---

40   Samper, 'Osorio Lizarazo', in *Novelas y crónicas*, p. xxix.

Lizarazo's time.[41] In a clear reference to its characters and that atmosphere of social bullying Gutiérrez Girardot affirmed that 'tan degradadamente pobres eran las clases populares'.[42] This is a clear reference to the popular classes depicted in the novel as 'obreros de ínfima categoría, jornaleros de centavos, detritus sociales, chusma rechazada por la sociedad, gentuza sin categoría humana' (153). They were groups who included even Tránsito's ex-employer; social layers whose 'significancia no merecía que jamás una autoridad se preocupase por su higiene, su dignificación ni su cultura' (153). As Gutiérrez Girardot suggests, the novel *El día del odio* sought to 'lift the veil' that covered the eyes of Colombian 'poor upper society' on its powerful capacity to degrade their own people, while being blissfully unaware of the actual growing discontent experienced by the lower classes.[43] Such references practically explain the 'desajuste social' referred to by Téllez, and shed light on the conditions of the lower class, that society which according to Gutiérrez Girardot is 'menuda y real', the same that assembled informally, while drinking, to talk about politics and its impact on their own lives. As mentioned above, Marxist ideas were crucial in Osorio Lizarazo's formative years when he attended meetings hosted by a Russian immigrant called Silvestre Savitsky.[44] However, Osorio Lizarazo did not become a communist but rather a leftist liberal with socialist inclinations and an interest in social reforms. Politically he was, as Samper maintains 'un temperamento de izquierda' since he champions 'las tesis más audaces y francas de redención social y económica para el proletariado'.[45] More importantly, it was the content of Osorio Lizarazo's literary production that reflected a world-view in which such ideas were expressed as he was conveying an 'interpretación de las angustias colectivas' as well as ideas about

41   See Rafael Gutiérrez Girardot, 'La literatura colombiana en el siglo XX', in *Manual de historia de Colombia*, vol. 3 (Bogotá: Procultura/Instituto Colombiano de Cultura, 1984), pp. 447–536 (pp. 517–518).

42   Gutiérrez Girardot, 'La literatura colombiana', pp. 517–518.

43   Gutiérrez Girardot, 'La literatura colombiana', pp. 517–518.

44   Samper, 'Osorio Lizarazo', in *Novelas y crónicas*, p. xxiv.

45   Samper, 'Osorio Lizarazo', in *Novelas y crónicas*, p. xxix.

people's demands for social justice.[46] Osorio Lizarazo held the belief that the novel must denounce but also penetrate into the imaginative potential of the social mass and its problems, by creating 'un personaje o una síntesis símbolo del equilibrio imperante que abarque todas las actividades de la vida en conjunto'.[47] Thus *El día del odio* offers insight into its author's own social class on the one hand and, on the other, of the world of power he managed to infiltrate as a result of his career. The novel in effect creates a social consciousness via the use of contrasts between characters. Alacrán – Tránsito's partner – had been an orphan and had grown up on the streets, starving and intimidated by the police (95). Another character, Manueseda, for example, had also been an orphan, though with a heightened consciousness about society and the problem of marginalisation (150). In this way the novel gives a picture of how political ideas were instilling a class consciousness in the population. Osorio Lizarazo was keen in his novels to express a 'sensibilidad colectiva', which he understood to mean a vision of the way in which different parts of society integrate including 'el rufián' denied 'entidad moral'; 'el campesino [...] estrangulado por sus explotadores'; and 'el obrero' in his way of life which is 'monorrítmico y sin alegría'.[48] This news on the 'sensibilidad colectiva' included also the input of the bureaucrat, as Osorio Lizarazo himself suggests, 'hasta el funcionario que arrastra una existencia vana y artificial que llega a ser inútil por su escaso valor contributivo [...] a la riqueza común'.[49]

The Penpusher and the Power Network

El día del odio mimics the ways in which the 'sensibilidad colectiva' coalesces to form various social levels made up of individuals with interests and aims which are shared in various ways. It is through a character such as Olmos

46   See *Novelas y crónicas*, p. xxxv.

47   Osorio Lizarazo, 'La esencia social de la novela', in *Novelas y crónicas*, pp. 422–425 (p. 425).

48   'La esencia social de la novela', in *Novelas y crónicas*, pp. 422–425 (p. 425).

49   'La esencia social de la novela', in *Novelas y crónicas*, pp. 422–425 (p. 425).

that Osorio Lizarazo articulates the political and bureaucratic aspects of society within the novel. Olmos 'provenía de una familia de obreros de mejor categoría'. Olmos's father had been a cobbler and had received education in a 'escuela' and 'colegio'; though economically unable to attend the faculty of law he became a 'tinterillo' (penpusher), who drafts all sorts of legal documents and is transposed in this novel to serve as the jack-of-all-trades to his friends.[50] Olmos's trade is precisely one that entails all the characteristics associated with the letrado. He is a quasi-lawyer whose job is partly to 'redactar memoriales o contratos' and partly to be in touch with judicial employees; he stands as an intermediary between official matters and private interests (154–155). Olmos's friends are also his private clients for whom he has to make all sorts of connections within the official institutions where he has his contacts, which are varied. Osorio Lizarazo, as a journalist and writer knew at first hand the system of patronage on which the political parties and government were based. The criticism expressed by the narrator was what Téllez termed as the 'desajuste social', a term that encapsulates the portrayal of a society split from top (government) to bottom (lower social class). The schism within Colombian society is expressed in a passage in which Tránsito finds herself arrested in a police station and a doctor says to the inspector: 'es que no hay conciencia con esta pobre gente [...] alguna vez esta gente se revolverá [...] y arrasará la justicia que la persigue' – unusually the doctor complained about the deprivation 'que descubría en su empleo' (232–233). This institutional mismanagement is articulated explicitly in *El día del odio*, particularly in the character of Olmos, as we shall see.

Olmos's job brings him into close contact with the bureaucracy and 'directorios políticos' who are involved in 'relaciones políticas capaces de cooperar en el encubrimiento de sus intrigas judiciales y sus perjurios' (164).

---

50   The 'tinterillo' is a very important character as a result of the role he plays in this particular society. The term defines someone who is educated to a level that allows him to deal with bureaucratic errands, but who is not legally entitled as a professional. We will see the role of the 'tinterillo' in Chapter Four, in the novel *Una y muchas guerras*, surviving as a former bureaucrat and eventually writing for a newspaper. 'Penpusher' is, the more approximate English term for 'tinterillo', according to the *Oxford Spanish-English Dictionary*.

Controversial issues such as corruption within government institutions are expressed through the narrator's voice and bureaucrats are depicted as 'todopoderosos con los humildes, serviles con los grandes' (powerful with the powerless and servile with the powerful); thus the bureaucrats 'pobres empleados, mal remunerados, aceptaban con júbilo los billetes', and in that way Olmos 'prestaba invaluables servicios a muchos desamparados' (155–156). As a result vote rigging in the polls becomes apparent. Olmos becomes an intermediary on behalf of politicians to help them negotiate more votes, being himself a minor league politician. Olmos resents the lack of opportunities he had as a result of being the son of a poor cobbler and he considers participating in a riot against the upper class and the political 'dirigentes'. He believes that an anarchical uprising had been the essence of the French Revolution (165), which mirrors in the fictional work the anger experienced by the lower classes in Colombia as a result of their exclusion from power. Olmos believes that all politicians were no more than gamblers in a game called politics. These 'tahúres de la política' (172), Olmos thinks, progressed because of the lack of ideals and their servility to complex economical interests with the result that only the 'intrigantes' became 'ciudadanos probos y ejemplares'. The system appears to suggest that 'crime pays'. As a result Olmos becomes rather cynical and sceptical: 'no le preocupaba quién ganara en los tramposos comicios cívicos, porque todos eran [...] tahúres de la política' (164–165). Nevertheless Olmos thinks that among the politicians only Gaitán embodied the reforms that were needed for people to be included as citizens within Colombia's body politic. He believes that Gaitán could make a difference because he was winning the population's trust. Olmos's conviction about the justice of Gaitán has in effect been transferred to his friends with the purpose of pricking their conscience about social inequality and exploitation.

By talking to his friends Olmos 'ayudaba a fomentar la ansiedad revolucionaria, a promover la conciencia del poderío multitudinario, a reunir gente en las plazas' (170). He informed them about inequality: 'no se hace el progreso, ni trabaja la ciencia, ni florece la civilización'; about when a crime was not a crime: 'robar un pan para saciar el hambre que los ha[bía] atormentado desde la infancia'; about the 'divide and conquer' law of the oligarchy: 'mientras ustedes se matan por la pasión política ellos reparten dividendos y se apoderan de la tierra', or 'ustedes son las víctimas de la organización social que hicieron los de arriba para aplastar a los de abajo' (170–173). Olmos expressed the hope that, one day, he and his friends would have a fulfilling social life and that their families would be treated with dignity. Thus Olmos informed people about the chasm that separated the rich from the poor and about the reforms they need to allow them to 'reincorporarse a la vida colectiva y ser ciudadanos útiles'; it was not true, he argued, that 'nazcan hombres condenados a la ignominia por el solo hecho de provenir del pueblo' (172). During these meetings a class consciousness is created, which at times even prompts a level of distrust towards lawyers and politicians. For example, in one meeting Olmos said that 'lúnica vaina es que [Gaitán] es abogao – y eso qué tiene? Interrogó otro, – mejor pa que no se deje enredar de los doptores' (173). The pun implies reference to the cultural structure that connects 'letrados' to lawyers since members of the latter profession populated the world of politics, and legitimated the meaning of 'doctor'. We have already seen the world of the 'doctores' in the above-mentioned novel *El 9 de abril* and we will see it portrayed in other novels such as in *Siervo sin tierra* and *Bulevar de los héroes*. Here in *El día del odio* Olmos represents the social critique of a self-serving society of lawyers ('doctores') and politicians (also 'doctores'). This criticism is expressed via the explicit allusion to broken trust between voters and the powerful. For example, Olmos tells his friends: 'yo […] sé que las leyes las hacen [los] de arriba pa afianzar sus privilegios' and comments that it would be better 'partir de nada como en la revolución francesa' (134).

It is thus that *El día del odio* arrived, the day when Gaitán was assassinated. That day, visibly desperate and starving, Tránsito also met her death. Tránsito walked into the path of a time-bomb that was spontaneously exploding, which she and her partner never understood. Tránsito's partner had been caught in the raids made in the government's clear-up preparations before the Conferencia Panamericana (269) and they were, as a result, unemployed and starving.[51] In terms of the visible plot – Tránsito's death – the novel expresses

---

51   On the political aspects of the Conferencia Panamericana see Alape, *El Bogotazo*, p. 603.

despair at the deprivation in a society in disarray. At a deeper level, *El día del odio* points to two important aspects of political concern, a) the incapacity of the state to offer opportunities and social inclusion to their members and b) the anti-communist repression directed at the society of the time, as epitomised by what happened to Tránsito's partner particularly, and as expressed by the tangential reference to the Conferencia Panamericana. Thus *El día del odio* addresses the issue of social exclusion promoted by oligarchic power structures while showing intense sympathy for the lower levels of society within which the people become ideologically politicised and thereby created social consciousness.[52] At this level it is appropriate to get back to the 'structure of feeling' suggested by Raymond Williams, which refers also to the 'changed organisation enacted in the organism', the response the new generation gives to the 'world it is inheriting [...] shaping it into a new structure of feeling'.[53] In this very sense the 'structure of feeling' might appropriately be applied to the Osorio Lizarazo's term, 'sensibilidad colectiva', which links in turn to what Téllez named as the 'desajuste social' that could be perceived in the fictional ambience portrayed in *El día del odio*. This novel prompted fierce debate about the gap existing between power and powerlessness in Colombia at that time. In this novel the author was representing in fictional form the pressures on an old and worn-out system of new social forces; *El día del* odio is about a rural and the new urban generation that expressed their innermost feelings in a day of rage: 'Es un hecho evidente que el pueblo colombiano tiene hambre y está mal nutrido', as Osorio Lizarazo underlined in a newspaper article, and Tránsito was the transitional representative model of that crisis.[54] That she is part of the transition is suggested by her name, Tránsito.

That transition embodied by Tránsito and her own life in need was closely related to the anti-communist policy promoted by the Conferencia Panamericana, and the repression targeted at her society, as Tránsito's partner experienced it; these links allow the reader to understand the political

---

52   Awakening of a class consciousness in the novel might be compared with the upper class and ruling class worries which were that 'Gaitán in reality was a socialist disguised as a liberal', according to Sharpless, *Gaitán of Colombia*, p. 124.
53   Raymond Williams, *The Long Revolution*, pp. 48–49.
54   'Fracaso de una política', in *Novelas y crónicas*, pp. 569–576 (p. 570).

and economic factors that conditioned the novel. The novel, seen from Eagleton's point of view, is 'determined by ideological and economic factors by the spiritual emptiness and exhaustion of bourgeois ideology which springs from the crisis of capitalism' of the 1930s and the ideological effects of the Second World War, as seen in Chapter One.[55] That is to say, 'the reflection of those conditions' takes into account the level of 'mediation' played by the novel itself, in that it mirrors the social, political and economic conditions of the author himself. In that sense the novel expresses general forms that ideology imbricates, that is, general forms evinced in the internal complexity of society and shows how 'all these are produced by the extremely complex class relation' of that society at the time.[56]

The Scream

We have already seen that Tránsito and her partner were unemployed and starving on the day she, unexpectedly, met her death. They both walked into the city centre looking for something to feed themselves with but instead they encountered an explosive situation they never understood. In fact, for having been close to the city centre, they felt attracted by an unusually big smoke plume clouding over the sky that they were able to see from a distance. The date 9 April 1948 is not mentioned at all in the novel, but it is loudly expressed in the shout '¡muera!' pronounced by Tránsito right at the moment of her own death. The shout is none other than the utterance of the 'sensibilidad colectiva' and 'desajuste social' indicated by Téllez, and is equivalent to the notion of 'structure of feeling' in Williams's terms. *El día del odio*, as we have seen, portrays much more than rage, rather it describes a situation in which two actors clash: the masses and the political system. First, the masses, the social multitude symbolised by Tránsito, that collectively had experienced deprivation, the lack of opportunities and the negation of the dignity naturally deserved

---

55   See Eagleton, *Marxism and Literary Criticism* (London: Routledge, 1989), pp. 13.
56   Ibid.

by a member of a society, given the oppression exerted by the government system. Second, the political system that, in the novel, bullies the members of its society and fails to provide public institutions to preserve the dignity of the members of the society and social reforms to give them opportunities for social mobility.

The question is, does the novel provide an account about what happened on 9 April 1948? The answer to this question is no; the novel concentrates on the build-up to the day for the lower and middle-class 'bogotanos' alike. Thus the story symbolises the oppression in which people looking for opportunities within their own society were kept. The need for reform is made visible in the life Tránsito is obliged to lead in a society which contrives to destroy the destitute class for whom Tránsito herself stands as the synecdoche. She is the part that represents the whole: the masses that shared Tánsito's needs, exclusion, social immobility and the presence of an absent state that does not represent her. *El día del odio* conveys a deeper ideological message than a simple representation of the situation which a society was living through, since it announces the politics of a state which is either absent or deficient. Tránsito's scream becomes the metaphor of her desire to kill a system (the society that employed her, the institutional structure that raped and pushed her into prostitution, the uselessness of the health service that rejected her when in need) that slowly promotes the destruction of the lower class which struggles to achieve basic human dignity, to no avail.

Capitalism at Work and the Class Struggle: *Viernes 9*[57]

The novel *Viernes 9* by Ignacio Gómez Dávila seemed controversial at the time it was published because of its love motif. It was seen by Suárez Rondón as an outrageous novel that gave a bad example of social behaviour because

---

57   Ignacio Gómez Dávila, *Viernes 9* (México: Impresiones Modernas, 1953). Further references to this novel are taken from this edition and only the page number appears after quotations in the text.

it addressed the subject of adultery and for that reason it was not 'recommended reading'.[58] Alvarez Gardeazábal saw *Viernes 9* as more complex novel, a 'novela psicológica' mixing elements that could make it 'policiaca' though, in the final analysis, it was 'cursimente romántica'.[59] Nevertheless Alvarez Gardeazábal detected 'algo de parcialidad política' that, according to him, goes unnoticed since the romantic primary them absorbs the whole narrative. Raymond Leslie Williams for his part describes *Viernes 9* as 'a story of human relationships among the members of an urban family, but with the assassination of Gaitán the second half becomes an account of human carnage and death'.[60] R.L. Williams' view is very important since the criticism on *Viernes 9* has been rather sparse, but his interest in dismissing it as a novel of violence prevents him from perceiving the clear social differences the novel addresses. In contrast, a recent study of this novel, though in relation to *El Bogotazo*, adopts a broader frame, highlighting that it 'recreates the fixed ideas those who do not consider themselves members of "el pueblo", have about it'.[61] This idea implies the existence of two differentiated layers of society and therefore it suggests that *Viernes 9* offers a more complex environment than R.L. Williams's reading which simply scratches the surface. As we will see, this is a valuable novel to work on in that it is different from other novels of this period in its fusion of love and politics.

Little is known about Ignacio Gómez Dávila apart from the fact that he wrote two novels, one called *Viernes 9* and the other entitled *El cuarto sello* (1951). Gómez Dávila belonged to a wealthy family and was educated in Paris and later in México where he lived most of his life. During his life-time Ignacio Gómez Dávila was overshadowed by his more famous

58   See Gerardo Suárez Rondón, *La novela sobre la violencia en Colombia* (Doctoral thesis, Bogotá: Pontificia Universidad Católica Javeriana, 1966).

59   Gustavo Alvarez Gardeazábal, *La novelística de la violencia en Colombia* (BA thesis, Cali: Universidad del Valle, 1970), p. 23.

60   Raymond Leslie Williams, *The Colombian Novel* (Austin: University of Texas Press, 1991), p. 50.

61   See María Mercedes Andrade, 'Ciudad y nación en las novelas del Bogotazo', in *Literatura y cultura: narrativa colombiana del siglo XX*, ed. by M. Jaramillo, B. Osorio and A. Robledo (Bogotá: Ministerio de Cultura, 2000), pp. 184–213 (p. 189).

brother, the philosopher Nicolás Gómez Dávila. It was Ignacio who encouraged his brother to publish his philosophical works and seemingly printed his own in small numbers to be distributed in a private circle.[62] As we shall see, the right-wing ideology permeating *Viernes 9* shares some similarities with the rightist thought found in the philosophical treatises of his brother, Nicolás Gómez Dávila. The Gómez Dávila family enjoyed an elitist life-style as intellectuals who regularly hosted exclusive 'tertulias' in Ignacio's brother's house. Nevertheless – or perhaps as a result of this – Ignacio Gómez Dávila's novel is barely known.

The novel *Viernes 9* describes action which occurs over a three week period. It is the story of two lovers who are preparing to leave Colombia on Friday 9 April 1948; their attempted flight is frustrated by the disturbances caused by the assassination of a politician called J.E. Gaitán in the novel. The main plot of *Viernes 9* may be summarised as follows. A business man Alfredo, a trader and shop owner, is having an affair with Yolanda, a prostitute who is twenty years younger than him. Alfredo has planned to leave his wife and his homeland with his lover although he feels some hesitation as a result of Yolanda's complicated private life. Yolanda confesses to Alfredo her apprehensions about a former lover, Manolo, a Spanish dancer who is coming to Bogotá for a seasonal performance and has made known his hostile intentions if she is involved in a relationship with another man. Though puzzled by these threats Alfredo is determined to get ready for their departure on the long-awaited day of Friday 9. Alfredo's life revolves around his doubts about what is best for him: either Yolanda, his lover, or Blanca, his wife. He experiences moral guilt regarding his wife, not least because of his social class – he comes from a very wealthy family. Alfredo feels proud of his wife's social origins and the education only women of her social condition could afford (30), while he feels that Yolanda's background

---

62   Family information has been generously provided to me by Ignacio Gómez Dávila's niece, Rosa Emilia Gómez. It is important not to confuse Ignacio with Nicolás whose work of a philosophical character has attracted much scholarly attention in recent years.

is problematic, which makes him acutely aware of 'las diferencias de las clases sociales' (43).

Two more people are crucial to the plot: the priest Ricardo Quevedo, who is Blanca's cousin, and Jaime, Alfredo's business associate. They discuss family, marriage and children with Alfredo at different times and attempt to persuade Alfredo of the dangers involved in leaving his wife with their two school-aged daughters and the disadvantages faced by a single woman (48). But Alfredo ignores their advice and is even intent on killing his rival Manolo, Yolanda's ex-lover, before their departure. On Friday, while poised to go ahead with his arrangements, Alfredo finds that things do not go as planned. At the precise moment he is waiting for Manolo, his victim, to come out of the church at two o'clock in order to run him over, Alfredo notices that people are gathering around his car, making him think that perhaps they have discovered his plan. Soon afterwards Alfredo finds out that Gaitán has been assassinated, and he concludes that everybody, Gaitán included, is in league against him to ruin his planned happiness of living abroad with his lover. Immediately after Gaitán's assassination the news begins to spread and people start walking towards the place it happened. Thus the city changes its mood, and life in a few moments turns upside-down as a result. The crowd soon become hell-bent on wanton destruction, and Alfredo witnesses in the following hours mayhem that destroys downtown Bogotá. In the end, Alfredo returns to his wife but, to his dismay, she tells him she is prepared to fight back to support the political system; thus Alfredo walks out onto the streets and, while trying to help someone who had been attacked, he gets arrested by the police for a crime that he has not committed.

Unlike *El día del odio* and *El 9 de abril*, *Viernes 9* offers a broader ideological portrayal of class struggle and the way in which it is perceived from the upper-class perspective.

The Politics of the Governing Bloc

The articulation of politics and ideology is approached in this case via the characters' dialogue, the narrative on how people organise social life together and how their beliefs connect with the power-structure and power-relations underlying the society depicted in the novel.[63] *Viernes 9* focuses on the life of a man whose double life makes him an ideal illustration of social inequalities in Colombia. The underlying class struggle, however, becomes gradually apparent in the cogitations of the protagonist who, initially, is blind to the division within Colombian society. Useful to the analysis of this articulation is Eagleton's view on the 'relations between governing and dominated classes in society'.[64] Accordingly, a dominant ideology 'cannot be deciphered from the consciousness of the governing bloc taken in isolation, but must be grasped from the standpoint of the whole field of class struggle'.[65] I argue that the protagonist, Alfredo, becomes aware of the class struggle and this coming-to-consciousness has five stages, as follows: a) the protagonist is confident of his high-class social status, b) the protagonist recognises a divided society, c) the protagonist sees with his own eyes the class struggle, d) the protagonist sees the revolution as a failure, and e) the upper class is intolerant of the revolution. Within these five stages the transition from rural to urban society is highlighted.

Stage a) *the protagonist is confident of his high-class social status.* Alfredo's reflections permanently irritate him when he is trying to find an explanation for his double life which is, however, coming to an end because of his decision to abandon his wife. Although Alfredo feels himself to be a man with no political interests, because he is only 'un simple comerciante sin enredos políticos' (25), his elevated social status means he is enmeshed in politics.

Alfredo's family life shows him as a self-satisfied man who is often pictured in the newspapers' 'páginas sociales' beside the 'ex-presidente' (38), proud of his wife's outfits and jewels, served by a 'sirvienta' while he reads the paper in the morning, offering his home as a space for 'reunión de políticos y literatos' (68). This opulence, however, traps Alfredo in a life of bourgeois contradictions somewhere between boredom and comfort. For one thing boredom invades him because of his constant 'deberes sociales ineludibles' (15) which include his wife's own parties together with family

---

63 See Eagleton, *Literary Theory*, pp. 169–170; also Eagleton, *Ideology*, pp. 13–14.
64 See Eagleton, *Ideology*, pp. 101, 122.
65 See Eagleton, *Ideology*, pp. 101, 122.

conversations about drinks' bills, or his wife's antics regarding the servants (15, 28). For another, material comfort allows Alfredo to contemplate the tranquility of a peaceful neighbourhood in which servants do their tasks or people of his similar social class indulge in the commodities of a rich life-style (38). Alfredo's wife is obsessed by the servants: 'las adoraba y las odiaba, eran sus confidentes y sus enemigas'; she also 'las aconsejaba' and more than that 'las insultaba', and even 'las encerraba'. She is richer than Tránsito's 'patrona' in the novel *El día del odio*. Her husband's riches are such that he could easily live abroad with a lover while at home someone else could run his business.

Alfredo's lover is a prostitute but even she is trying to climb the social ladder. Conversely Blanca is a decent woman educated in a school where 'conocían a la mejor gente' and where 'no trataban con los "parvenus"', a finishing school which prepared them to be members of charity organisations (30) and even politicians. These characteristics complement her conservative religious spirit as she attends mass every day, which is, surprisingly enough, also a habit of Yolanda's ex-lover (36). Despite his wife's spirituality Alfredo feels quite sceptical about the Church because he sees it as an institution completely obsessed with political power. Alfredo believes that the Church has forgotten its spirituality and instead its priests are 'tiranos políticos' (41–42).

Stage b) *the protagonist recognises a divided society*. Many other ideological views gradually emerge when Alfredo begins to think about something he has never thought about before: the difference between the social classes (43). It is Yolanda's life stories that force him to reflect and understand that there is social injustice in Colombia (44). Those aspects of poverty already noted in the analysis of *El día del odio*, such as the plight of single women or single mothers, are also visible in *Viernes 9*. In *Viernes 9* it is Blanca who is about to be estranged and abandoned as the single mother of two children; despite having economic power she fears repudiation by society once she is on her own. These facts are brought home to Alfredo by his business associate, Jaime, who tells him that Blanca will be rejected because the society they live in is 'Colombia, el país más atrasado del orbe' and more precisely 'una sociedad cien años atrasada' (48). Alfredo also comes face to face with social injustice when he finds out about Gaspar, his employee.

Gaspar is a peasant who, despite being an employee in Alfredo's shop in the middle of Bogotá, still stays close to his roots. Similar to Tránsito, in *El día del odio*, Gaspar in *Viernes 9* speaks in an unpolished Castilian, he uses words such as 'hora' for 'ahora' or 'su merced' or 'patrón', or talks to his boss 'tímidamente' and always thanks him saying 'gracias, que la virgen se lo pague' (119), and he still wears 'alpargatas'. Gaspar was inherited by Alfredo, he had been 'el Viejo sirviente de confianza de la finca' but then came to work in Alfredo's shop in the city and was promoted, as we shall see in a moment. Again like Tránsito, in *El día del odio*, Gaspar came to Bogotá first to be a servant. The difference, otherwise, is that Gaspar was lucky enough to have been the servant of his patrón's father in their hacienda.

Characters' speech is typically used as a pointer for social class in the novel. In *Viernes 9* language expresses not only social difference but is the cause of the general scorn with which the upper class see the worse-off. This scorn is demonstrated when Gaspar is referred to as 'el indio' who was suitable for the job, who 'se acomodó a cuanto trabajo le pusieron', at which point he was promoted to 'muchacho de almacén' (51–52). The words 'indio' and 'muchacho' are still to this day pejorative terms which imply class difference and menial social position, e.g 'muchacha del servicio', as in effect Tránsito was in *El día del odio*. *Viernes 9* highlights the bad habits that the urban classes question. Gaspar, for example, is told off for carrying dirty 'alpargatas' (55) though he is attempting to raise with his 'patrón' the matter of the loan for the payment of his 'rancho', a small part of which will be to buy a pair of shoes.[66] Nevertheless Gaspar is rebuffed by Alfredo's contemptuous comment: '¡Zapatos a tu edad! Pero si no podrás usarlos ¿Para qué tanta elegancia?' (55).

Alfredo's perception of the lower class at this point in time is based on a crude social determinism: 'Esta gente era pobre e infeliz porque no podía ser otra cosa; no era por falta de oportunidades'. Thus Alfredo's conclusion was that poor people were 'una raza distinta' and 'una especie aparte; nada

---

66   'Rancho' in this context refers to a modest house built by the poor working class in urban areas as well as by peasants in rural settings, as shall be seen in the analysis of the novel *Siervo sin tierra*.

se podía hacer con ella; pertenecía a un mundo muerto, a una civilización abortada o extinta. Viven como bestias salvajes' (51). Because of this, in Alfredo's view, the poor cannot 'entender ningún aspecto de la vida moderna' and the only thing that attracts them about modern life is the motor car: 'quizás tan sólo el automóvil les fascina tanto como a sus antepasados el caballo de los conquistadores'. Thus, Alfredo sees no solution: 'Viven sumidos en la miseria, la mugre y las supersticiones, con mentalidad de siervos' (51–52). As the novel progresses, however, Alfredo gradually begins to see the truth, i.e. that politics and politicians are to blame for what he sees as an 'odio de clases'.

Stage c) *the protagonist sees with his own eyes the class struggle.* The class struggle becomes more visible when Alfredo thinks that 'El pueblo andaba inquieto, insatisfecho con sus dirigentes y desde años atrás venía fomentándose un odio de clases' (136). All these things were happening by and large because of the cost of living: 'El costo de la vida había subido' (136). As a result there was a growing uneasiness about 'el hambre'. As the narrator points out: 'la clase obrera se quejaba de hambre y la frase "ricos y pobres" más que nunca era parte predominante en el léxico' in the society at that time (136). This division between 'ricos y pobres' was signalled by 'La palabra "oligarca", grito de guerra del caudillo Gaitán'. The word 'oligarca' was part of common parlance and it was used as a catchword for everything: 'la aplicaban sin diferenciación a cualquiera que fuese dueño de un automóvil o de una casa' (136–137). These views are in stark contrast to Alfredo's views expressed when driving through the city, that Bogotá was leaving behind its 'aspecto pueblerino [...] El tránsito era a ciertas horas como el de Nueva York o el de Londres' (135). Alfredo's thoughts subtly allude to the architectural changes and new developments carried out by the conservative government in order to achieve the 'éxito que ha tenido la conferencia' (141) against communism. Alfredo initially expresses support to the city's grandeur: 'quizás después de todo, las obras que había emprendido Gómez no eran tan absurdas' (136). The city needed 'grandiosidad' though 'esas sumas inmensas gastadas en inútiles lujos' spent by the government on celebrations and parties 'en el estado actual de la situación podrían provocar algún descontento' (136). A subtle reference to Gaitán as a social reformist is made by Alfredo as he ponders the idea that government security was being threatened by 'los reformistas sociales que pedían la distribución de la riqueza: "que los ricos sean menos ricos y que los pobres menos pobres"' (130). For Alfredo the negative outcome was that people who did not work wanted to get what others had achieved by dint of much effort in order to secure their future: just like Alfredo, who had a business and a building to rent and lived off its profits and his bonds' yield in the banks (130). He sees, however, that 'las desigualdades económicas de la población eran extremadas' (131) and he believes that the government only spoke of inequalities but did nothing to 'poner remedio a la zozobra del proletariado que día a día crecía' (131). Alfredo begins to find a social conscience. He thinks that the government has forgotten the 'clases obreras' and is 'simplemente preocupado por mantenerse en el poder ya que su situación minoritaria era incierta y débil' (131). His conclusion is that the government provoked the people's animosity because it wanted only to affirm its position in power since it wanted to maintain its 'privilegio de clase' thereby strengthening the position of 'las altas capas burguesas apoyadas por el capitalismo internacional' (131) which Alfredo knew well as he was a board member of three companies (131).

Alfredo's musings drive him to discuss the real threat to the privileged class, that is, the new generation which had become less respectful to their superior social class (52). The new generation, aware of the social inequality note only that 'unos son ricos' and 'otros son pobres', they now dare to talk about social revolution (52). Alfredo's thoughts bring him to the conclusion that the wave of communism has infiltrated the world like a virus: 'este mal es mundial, el virus del comunismo que por todo lado se infiltra, con esa absurda teoría de que todos los hombres son iguales y que no debe haber ni ricos ni pobres' (52).

Stage d) *the protagonist sees the revolution as a failure.* The news about Gaitán's assassination persuades Alfredo at first that this 'no podía ser más que una "bola" callejera' (151). While disguised as a chauffeur (as part of his plan to run Manolo over), Alfredo finds himself in the middle of an angry crowd. In his ransacked shop he finds Gaspar who explains to his 'patrón' he was powerless to stop people breaking in; he says he knew Gaitán had been assassinated by the conservatives because he wanted to 'hacer la revolución' (167). Realising that everything is turning topsy-turvy

Alfredo now dreams of getting back home to escape the nightmare and return to a world of playing golf, going to the club on Saturdays, and even 'discutir otra vez política en el café asegurando que "en Colombia nunca pasa nada"' (177). In the middle of the mayhem Alfredo then bumps into Gaspar carrying many pairs of shoes. Gaspar tells him: 'ahora todos somos ricos, ya no es solamente el patrón y los suyos' (198). And Alfredo asks Gaspar '¿Pero nos odian? ¿Por qué?' To which Gaspar answers: 'No, patrón, no los odiamos; más bien les tenemos susto' (199). As if Gaspar's answers were not clear to Alfredo a new language now comes to the surface. This was the language of a new generation, i.e. Gaspar's oldest son asking with outrage, '¿por qué le dices patrón a este individuo? ¿No te das cuenta que esas humillaciones ya se acabaron, que este capitalista ya no te volverá a explotar?' (201). A generation gap seems to emerge as Gaspar replies to his son that nothing wrong has done the patron ('nada malo ha hecho el patrón') to which his son replies confirming that an old society has been left behind: '¿Te parece poco explotar al pueblo, explotarte a ti como lo ha hecho durante tantos años? ¡No entiendes nada! Esta es la revolución' (201). As a result Alfredo wakes up politically: this is '[un] paso hacia atrás para lograr dos hacia adelante', since after all they had 'un gobierno retrógrado y corrompido' and perhaps that wild behaviour if turned out to be triumphant it could create later on a new popular state (202). Alfredo's conjectures lead him to posit that this was a 'mistaken' revolution, a sui generis case because people seemed to be celebrating something which had not yet been attained. Alfredo could not see how that crowd could win in the end. But Alfredo is in two minds and his thoughts revolve around the support any government would need from a majority, otherwise, however military strong it would inevitably collapse (202). This collapse would not happen in the context of 'la histeria de los odios partidistas' because that could not lead to the people winning power by a massive opinion. Thus Alfredo justifies the protest that he sees in front of his eyes, the people were doing nothing different than imitate what their masters and leaders had done during their lives (203). In this way he compares Gaspar and himself and asks the question: '¿Quién era más culpable?' Either Gaspar who had been looting that day or himself who thought only a few days before that Gaspar was no more than a being without conscience or understanding;

he had seen him as a wearing machine which better replaced. Alfredo thus blames himself since he never ever cared about the welfare of his employee, 'nada le habían importado sus angustias y sus afanes, sus tribulaciones y sus deseos por mejorar su condición' (203).

Stage e) *the upper class is intolerant of the revolution.* An important facet revealed by the novel is the protagonist of the ruling class in the society it depicts. It is through Alfredo's wife, Blanca, who was a conservative, that the novel shows a strongly rooted, powerful social class ideology which is not willing to give way to reforms that might improve the people's living conditions. Blanca 'entendía de negocios y sus consejos eran certeros; sus opiniones políticas no fallaban, y lo había probado con el triunfo de su partido' (71). For Blanca more important than men and women were the political parties: 'En política, jamás había vacilado entre uno y otro partido [...] para ella no existían hombres buenos y malos sino partidos' (127). But that way of thinking was, according to Alfredo, a characteristic of all Colombians; he thought that 'así eran la mayoría de los colombianos' (127). Alfredo thought that his wife would back anything as long as her party managed to stay in power: 'cualquier atrocidad que cometieran los de su partido para afianzarse en el poder, Blanca la consideraba justificada'. Thus Alfredo meditates on the sectarianism and intransigence typical of his wife's party: 'era sectaria e intransigente [...] pues era una de las características de sus copartidarios'. The conservatives wanted to return to the 'estado feudal, a los Siervos y a los Señores, a las brujas y a los santos; gobernar a los hombres por la fuerza y no con la libertad' (127–128). They did not want a government in which people were included and reforms that could improve their lives, as Gaitán was recommending. Gaspar himself said as much to Alfredo: 'sumercedes los ricos tampoco querían al difunto [Gaitán] porque les decía muchas verdades' (163). That is what Alfredo will confirm later when he manages to talk to his wife and her cousin, the priest. Blanca confirms to Alfredo that the government is taking control of the situation and with God's help she is prepared to fight back while supporting a political system: 'esta pesadilla pasará y tendremos entonces, con la ayuda de Dios que mostrarle a este miserable pueblo de qué metal estamos forjados' (207).

That the novel effectively concludes with Blanca's words suggests that *Viernes* 9 possesses a conservative ideology. Ignacio Gómez Dávila's novel offers a useful counterpart to the ideology of *El día del odio*. *Viernes* 9 shows the society from the perspective of the upper class and shows its desire for domination at all costs, whereas *El día del odio*, as we have seen, shows the same society from the subaltern perspective. Even though *Viernes* 9 expresses a pro-conservative ideology, it points to the widening divide between rich and poor in Colombian society as well as the cracks which were beginning to appear in conservative ideology. The language used by Gaspar and his son makes this clear.

As we have seen, the point made by Alvarez Gardeazábal about the novel's 'parcialidad política' going unnoticed as a result of the romantic primary theme was a good one since the novel does, indeed, express a pro-conservative agenda hidden behind the scenes of a love story, which is woven over the moral matter of adultery, while drawing attention to the cracks in that political façade. It is through the voice of Alfredo's wife that the author reveals the plan of a political party that promises 'they will fight back' to preserve the order (207). However, it is through that woven story of love and intolerance that the social consciousness of the growing masses emerges. It is thus that, as shown above, *Viernes* 9 reflects a social consciousness growing within the urban population alongside the determination of the ruling class to keep hold of its power.

CHAPTER THREE

The Politics and Ideology of Local Networks, Landownership and Resistance

The novels analysed in this chapter show politics and ideology in a more complex way. In these novels matters of local network and religion, landownership and false ideological cohesion, repression, state absence and clandestine resistance are woven together in, respectively, *El Cristo de espaldas* (1952), *Siervo sin tierra* (1954) and *La mala hora* (1962). These historical contingencies are articulated within the logic of landowning and political resistance, announced in the chapter's heading which are the nexus of these narratives.

Within these works the issue of the 'letrado' gains more prominence in the way his presence is portrayed. He stands tall within a provincial environment making a crucial political difference whether embodied as a priest or as an orator, as in *El Cristo de espaldas*. Rather like in a crime novel, the narrative discloses at the same time how a political network operates in a small town, connected to the ruling class in the city where the centre of the structures of power lies. This network of power is also articulated in the second novel *Siervo sin tierra*, in which the issue of Gaitán comes to the surface, revealing the impact it had not only in Bogotá but also in small provinces. *Siervo sin tierra* focuses on the significance landowning had for the peasant who wished not only to own a piece of land but to become a producer for the capitalist market. Here the role of the 'letrado' is also evident in the term of address, 'doctor', used for bureaucrats or people of superior social standing. *Siervo sin tierra* also portrays the network as it operated within the particular structure of the hacienda system.

Thirdly, sharing common characteristics such as bipartisanism, *La mala hora* weaves in a very dense and symbolic structure the portrayal of a binary system that calls itself a democracy but in fact is a dictatorship. Issues of upper class tacit accords, inequality and discontent are shown as a common denominator that reveals a class struggle and a conspiracy led by middle class intellectuals in a small town. Thus the 'letrado' becomes a crucial figure, together with the legal instruments used by a democratic system to exert oppression and maintain corruption and deficiency.

In these novels contrasting characters such as priests and politicians exhibit eloquence and writing skills in opposition to the lower or middle classes, who are identified with the rural population, and who are aware of the transition that is materialising in the society they live in, within which some gradual social mobility is perceived. Those historical contingencies related to power, social, economic and institutional, as well as cultural issues present in each of the novels are moulded such that they express the particular need for reforms.[1]

Local Network and Religion: *El Cristo de espaldas*[2]

Noted by Hernando Téllez as pivotal in the 1950s Colombian novel, *El Cristo de espaldas* together with *Siervo sin tierra*, which is also studied in this chapter, prompted a particular reaction first as a result of who its author was. The fact that Caballero Calderón was a person who belonged to an oligarchic family made his novel more remarkable, as Téllez observed.[3] Caballero Calderón's works came from a specific social and political ambience which signalled a 'poderío burgués no discutido ni amenazado' as well as the author's own 'herencia intelectual'.[4] It was particularly his

---

1   Jane Tompkins, *Sensational Designs: The Cultural Work of American Fiction 1790–1960* (Oxford: Oxford University Press, 1985), p. xii.

2   Eduardo Caballero Calderón, *El Cristo de espaldas* (Buenos Aires: Losada, 1952). Further references to this novel are taken from this edition and the page number is provided after quotations in the text.

3   See Hernando Téllez, 'Literatura y testimonio', *El Tiempo, Lecturas Dominicales*, 27 June 1954, p. 1.

4   Téllez, 'Literatura y testimonio'.

intellectual inheritance that made of Caballero Calderón the epitome of the Colombia 'letrado' in the 1950s. Raymond Leslie Williams, for instance, depicts Caballero Calderón as 'the perfect embodiment of the highland letrado'.[5] Caballero Calderón dedicated himself to letras, wrote about 'letrados', and was also a dedicated liberal representative of the ruling class who held bureaucratic positions.[6] It is for all this significance embodied by the author that in the 1950s *El Cristo de espaldas* and *Siervo sin tierra* were seen as a rebellion happening within Colombia's national literary landscape. An educated man, a member of the ruling classes with large landholdings in the interior highlands of the country and connoisseur not only of the rural traits of that society but also of the emerging urban environment, Caballero Calderón hinted of changes to come.[7] *El Cristo de espaldas* depicts bipartisanism operating as well as political practices and intolerance.

In this particular reading I argue that *El Cristo de espaldas* anticipated the Colombian novel's tendency during this period to tell a tale in which a political network functions as a sub-elite to either keep power or create disruption within the local society in which it operates. Such a political network is characterised by members who are 'letrados'. Other novels such as García Márquez's *La mala hora* share this characteristic – the presence of a political network – although not as part of political bipartisanism but as an oppositional force fighting against it, as shall be shown in the final part of this chapter. As for *El Cristo de espaldas*, it portrays a town in which politics is the only dynamic network operating and one which is manoeuvred by 'letrados'. Including members of the local upper class or the middle class the network functions by means of a hearsay system which reproduces the political ideology generated by a powerful individual belonging to the

5   Raymond Leslie Williams, *The Colombian Novel 1844–1987* (Austin: University of Texas Press, 1991), p. 77.

6   See Marco Palacios, *Entre la legitimidad y la violencia: Colombia 1875–1994* (Bogotá: Norma, 1995), p. 203.

7   For further information on social and political articulations related to Eduardo Caballero Calderón see Ricardo Silva Romero, 'De ayer a hoy: año Caballero Calderón 1910–2010', document, 23 April 2010. Available at <http://www.bibliotecanacional. gov.co/recursosuser/documentosbnc/catalocaballeroe.pdf> [Accessed 23 April 2011]

party in power. Ideologically managed, the network gives its members important bureaucratic positions, thereby creating in the small town an anomalous government with incompetent civil servants who maintain the status quo and impede societal progress.

The Politics of Twisting the Truth

El Cristo de espaldas is an account of a murder carried out for family reasons and which is then transformed into a political killing. The story is mediated by a young priest who firmly believes faith, justice and charity may be taught to people in the small town. Unexpectedly, however, the priest finds a strongly politicised town where old family feuds are combined with political intolerance. The story lasts five days, from Thursday night to Monday and might be summarised as follows:

On Thursday night the young priest arrives in 'el pueblo de arriba' (the upper town) to replace 'el cura viejo', the old priest who has gone to the 'pueblo de abajo' (the lower town). The town has experienced a) a family feud and b) the sale agreements involving a business between the 'gamonal', don Roque, the notary and the town's mayor. The family feud happens between Pío Quinto Flechas from the 'pueblo de abajo' and don Roque Piragua, from the 'pueblo de arriba', where the young priest arrived coincidentally on the very same day Anacleto, don Roque's son, had returned from the capital to arrange formalities relating to his inheritance. He was living in the capital and involved in the transport business, and wanted his share of the money to carry on with his urban trade. Anacleto, however, is allowed no more than two days in the town for the legal arrangements by mandate of don Roque who is working in collusion with the town's mayor and notary, as they have prepared a scam to rob Anacleto of his material assets. Involved in don Roque's tricks is the notary, who is also godfather to Anacarsis, don Roque's illegitimate son. On Friday morning after mass when the young priest introduces himself as the 'good shepherd', the town has discovered that don Roque had been assassinated the night before and Anacleto is held as the perpetrator since he had been allowed to sleep that night in don Roque's house. The young priest pleads for Anacleto not to be condemned before an appropriate judicial procedure determines whether he is or is not responsible 'según las leyes' (according to the law). Anacleto, however, has been beaten up in the mayor's premises (71) where the crime has already been declared 'a political crime' (85). Helping Anacleto in this town makes the priest unpopular among don Roque's supporters, not least because he is a liberal. Tension is created as liberals fear they will be attacked by conservatives as a result. As the tension grows the mayor gets drunk and threatens to kill Anacleto. The young priest then goes to the 'pueblo de abajo' to conduct an agreed exchange of liberal for conservative prisoners. In the 'pueblo de abajo' the young priest meets the outspoken old priest he replaced. On their way back to the 'pueblo de arriba' there is a confrontation between Pío Quinto Flechas and the policemen accompanying the mission, and as a result, the acolyte is badly injured and confesses to the young priest that he had been paid to kill don Roque, though he dies before being able to say who paid him. A stage of siege is declared in the 'pueblo de arriba' and the notary's wife, Ursulita, confesses to the priest about her husband's guilty conscience when she learns of the acolyte's death; she also tells him about their relief as a result of don Roque's death despite his promise to appoint the notary to the 'juzgado superior del distrito' (high court jugde) (153). Five days after his arrival in the town the bishop orders the young priest to return to the city because the 'miembros del directorio nacional conservador' (members of the national conservative party) (161) complained about him. He is assigned to teach language in the seminary (160–163).

The Politics of the 'Friend-Enemy'

El Cristo de espaldas is focused on those political practices carried out in rural areas and, unlike the majority of the works studied in this book, the 9 April 1948 uprising does not form part of its plot. Nevertheless it addresses the theme of a rural society keeping its traditional ways of life and government together with the political and ideological control imposed from the central government, as we shall see. Very importantly, this novel depicts historical contingencies concerning governance mismanagement as well as rebel behaviour connected specifically with the two parties at issue as well as transitional rural-urban social changes.

Drawing on Eagleton's analysis of societal power structure and power relations I shall discuss the theme of the rural society maintaining its traditional ways of life and governance together with the imposition of new political structures as ordered from central government. In addition together with this view I support my analysis on Macherey's perspective in order to show what happens behind the entire narrative structure. This analysis of ideology in the novel shows how elements of 'letrado' culture are imbricated in the culture as a whole.

As I have described above *El Cristo de espaldas* is a crime novel about a case that needs to be solved by finding the murderer, but only one individual is found guilty, and he has little objectively to do with the crime. The crime has more to do with the political affiliation that crucially defines the ideology behind bipartisanism. This political affiliation is what makes Anacleto guilty for a crime he did not commit. Anacleto's political affiliation is liberal despite being the son of a conservative father. I have shown in Chapter One that in the 1940s and 1950s in Colombia people were either liberal or conservative according to the family they belonged to.[8] As the novel develops this issue becomes crucial when it refers to the matter of how two brothers chose different political parties. Anacleto became a liberal and Anacarsis a conservative according to the family within which they grew up respectively. Despite having a conservative father (as don Roque was) Anacleto became liberal since the Flechas, his mother's family, by whom he was raised, were liberal, whereas Anacarsis, quite the opposite, won his father's affection for being as conservative as don Roque (55). It is intrigu-

---

8   This particular cultural characteristic was part of the mid-century generation as confirmed by Plinio A. Mendoza in an interview with Spanish television. As Mendoza says: 'en Colombia nacemos liberales o conservadores y yo soy de una familia liberal de abuelo y padre liberal aunque hoy ya no pertenezco a ningún partido ni siquiera a ese partido liberal que se me volvió socialista. Ingresó a la Internacional socialista'. See interview with Víctor Gago, in *Contemporáneos*, televisión española, 28 March 2008. Available at <www.youtube.com/watch?v=EpY7pmqRy4> [Accessed 17 February 2009]

ing to see how the family embroilment develops in the novel. The Flechas shared 'el poder con su cuñado y enemigo don Roque Piragua' (54). The peasants were also born with their political affiliation ready-made according to the political allegiance of the farm where they live. It is thus that 'los campesinos eran liberales si habían nacido en la finca de don Pío Quinto Flechas y conservadores si en la hacienda de los Piraguas' (54). These peculiarities revealing the origin of political affiliation show how networks in small towns operated under the rule of bipartisanism. The novel reveals how the peasant workers worked for the 'gamonal' who also demanded of them other appropriate activities such as elections 'cuando los requerían para que se matasen unos a otros' (54). Otherwise peasants were required to take the harsh conditions of their work, 'Mientras no había elecciones [...] fueran godos o liberales no dejaban por eso de mirarlos como bestias de carga' (54).

I have explained in Chapter One the meaning of the category 'gamonal' in Colombian politics and also the 'friend-enemy' power-sharing strategy intrinsic to the bipartisan system. That relationship is reflected in the novel as a system of power-sharing which permeates the whole socio-cultural environment of Colombia. It is for this reason that don Roque, a conservative 'gamonal', and Pío Quinto Flechas, a liberal 'gamonal', both used to be friends and share 'el poder' as 'cuñados y enemigos' (54). This was until Anacleto's father, don Roque, abandoned his wife. *El Cristo de espaldas*, as we have seen above, mirrors thus a territorial division in what is called 'el pueblo de arriba', a town dominated by the conservative 'gamonal', don Roque Piragua, and whose population is predominantly conservative; and 'el pueblo de abajo' which is mainly liberal and led by Pío Quinto Flechas. The latter is described as a rebel losing unluckily 'unas elecciones manejadas desde la ciudad por sus enemigos', that was in other words when 'se le volvió el Cristo de espaldas' (57). The centrality of this subterfuge to the plot of the novel is suggested by the fact that the expression 'se le volvió el Cristo de espaldas' (suggestive of treachery) becomes the title of the novel. Subsequently, the novel shows that the powerful 'gamonales' in these two small towns work within an interactive network system in which stratagem and fabrication as well as the distortion of truth is the norm. In *El Cristo de espaldas* the network consists of 'notables' led by the 'gamonal' who manages his power on the basis of the capitalist rural economy of the hacienda or farm. These 'notables' are the mayor, the notary, the judge, the chemist and also ancillary rank and file such as the acolyte in this case. These politically well-connected characters show how the social network operates locally and point to the synaptic strength of the network when linked to central power.

These characteristics are informed as follows: a) within this circle a deceptive ploy is fabricated not only to rob Anacleto but to negotiate the asset, which is a property in this case, among themselves; b) the business is carried out, first, by selling the trust deeds to the mayor so that the property may be transferred subsequently to the notary; and c) within that power bargaining other subtle agreements are revealed which disclose that powerful people in government are also involved. Thus the novel informs us that 'Don Roque le tenía prometido al notario el juzgado superior del distrito, que sería la coronación de su [...] carrera' (153), that is, the notary would keep Anacleto's property and also be appointed 'magistrado del Tribunal Superior', a post superior in importance to that of the mayor or the 'diputado del departamento' (28). That position had been offered by someone in the national government once the election was rigged with their help and by means of fake IDs (15–17). However, it was the notary who paid for don Roque's murder and not exactly for political or ideological reasons, as shown above. The notary nursed a bitter historical resentment towards don Roque because the latter refused to marry his daughter, Belencita, though he had made her pregnant, and she had delivered don Roque's child in the nuns' convent, all of which outraged the notary's family pride. Thus, social and political position as well as economic profit are what prevail in this society; typical of this ethos is the notary who expected a higher post as a magistrate as well as the most desirable house in town so as in turn to get his daughter Belencita married off to anyone they might wish (29). These frustrated expectations of marriage suggest that kinship was a particular way of strengthening political networks. Kinship is shown in the novel particularly in the category of 'godfathering' which allowed network members to become even closer through the 'compadre' relationship. The 'compadre' relationship is shown in the novel to be highly valued as it is created by a religious link. In *El Cristo de espaldas*, for example, the notary is a 'compadre' of both the mayor and don Roque (47). A closer examination of the novel suggests that within this network the notary is indeed the main cog in the machinery. Firstly, because of his job (although it is not clear if he is really a lawyer or no more than a 'tinterillo' (penpusher), that is, in any case, an expert in legal documentation) and, secondly, because his role implicitly depicts him as the man who deals with the property deeds and legal statements; there is the suggestion that his role also includes dealing tactfully with the young priest who is called back by his Church's superiors, as shall be shown later. It is the notary who, in fact, deals with the legal matters related to Anacleto's inheritance, the deeds and his agreements with don Roque and the mayor in this respect; and, in the final analysis, the acolyte's confession together with Ursulita's worries about his behaviour reveal him as the criminal mastermind. This characterisation of the acolyte as the murderer is evident in scattered moments of the plot. Because it is not made explicit, this allows a level of mystery to emerge in the novel, evoking Macherey's notion of what is left unsaid in the novel. Macherey argues that the relationship of literature to ideology replicates that of signifier and signified, and suggests that criticism should seek to discover the laws which lie at the root of the articulation of a given literary text. Thus, 'in the book not everything is said', and 'to reach utterance, all speech envelops itself in the unspoken'.[9] In this sense the 'silence becomes the centre and principle of expression'.[10] That evanescent point expresses itself in a particular character and his singularity.

The Ideology of the Literate

The notary as a lawyer tacitly implies that he is a man of 'letras' and it is this role that clearly presents him in his best light. The 'letrado' character in this novel is reflected, first, by the notary behind the scenes, who manipulates the political network and secondly, from outside the network, by the priests.

---

9   See Pierre Macherey, *A Theory of Literary Production* (London: Routledge, 2006), pp. 92–95. See also Terry Eagleton, *Ideology: An Introduction* (London: Verso, 1991), p. 46.

10   Macherey, *A Theory*, p. 46.

The notary, for example, uses his superior knowledge in order to assert his power over the ignorant. For instance, extolling don Roque's virtues he says to Anacarsis 'no lo dudes tu padre tenía madera de procónsul' (p. 70), to which Anacarsis innocently asks: '¿Pro qué? Procónsul [...] ¿esos empleados que el gobierno manda al exterior para que conozcan París? [...] [notary:] No ahijado, esos son los cónsules. Los procónsules eran [...] todos los don Roques que tenían los romanos en sus pueblos' (70). This sort of pun in which the novel delights, expresses the rhetorical ability of the 'letrado' class which is not without a measure of hypocrisy. The use of knowledge as a tool of repression is also evident within the dialogues between characters: it is known that the acolyte is illiterate; 'no sabe leer' (26), and, on another occasion, the notary says to his wife, 'qué maravilla sería si tú supieras algo más que leer!' (29), to which she replies: 'sé leer letra menuda, que es lo difícil'. Nevertheless she acknowledges that the notary is canny as well as being literate – that is, he knows about law and this gives him the edge with respect to the rest of the population in the town (29). Ursulita is astute about the town, the mayor is 'un pícaro' (29) and the old priest is 'un bruto' (27) while the young priest she sees as a serious young man, emphasising that he is from 'la ca-pi-tal'. These disingenuous compliments reflect the internal value system of Colombian society in which people are judged according to the knowledge that comes with letras. As Anacarsis remarks in admiration at the manner in which his godfather speaks: 'Caramba [...] es lo que yo digo, mi padrino habla como un periódico!' (146). Thus literacy is an advantage for the minority who possess it and a limitation for the majority who do not. That difference in literacy levels leads to a sharply divided society in which 'Los gamonales no tenían caridad [...] ni sensibilidad social' and the peasants are 'los miserables [...] bestias de carga' (54), there simply to dig the soil.

The old priest as a 'letrado' figure, also plays a fundamental ideological role in the novel. At one point, sounding like a politician, he observes that: 'años hubo en que no pudimos poner ni un solo voto, no teníamos en la administración pública ni un guardia municipal [...] ni un secretario de juzgado, ni un solo celador de rentas, ni un concejal ni nada' (122). The old priest, who was replaced by the young priest, is identified with the 'pueblo de arriba' and he gives his direct opinion as to who is the appropriate man to succeed don Roque, thus hinting that he is part of the local network. The old priest recommends that it should be the notary because he is 'inteligente, astuto, desconfiado y tiene un santo odio por los liberales', and particularly because he possesses an important skill that sets him apart: the notary 'habla muy bien [...] es un Demóstenes' (122) pointing to the importance of rhetoric and oratory, which will be extendedly analysed in Chapter Five. The old priest also argues that 'los liberales son ateos, los ateos masones, los masones tienen deseos de asesinar al papa, el cual es el padre de todos los conservadores del mundo y alienta una especial predilección por los conservadores del pueblo' (123). *El Cristo de espaldas* expresses the ideology of bipartisanism through rivalry between the old priest, who represents the old conservative regime, and the young priest who represents a new generation and in that sense a more liberal stance. But this more liberal stance loses out when the letter from the archbishop arrives ordering the young priest to leave the town and go back to the city, which shows how effective the complaints made by the town's 'notables' were about his annoying interference in politics: 'me costó [...] creer a los miembros del Directorio Conservador cuando se presentaron en masa a poner una queja contra ti' (159). Evincing the importance of being a let-rado the bishop suggests that, indeed, there is something more (though it is not explicitly mentioned) than 'letras' that is required to serve in these towns. The bishop mentions that 'para servir un curato de aldea no sólo se requieren luces y letras [...] sino otras condiciones de que posiblemente careces' (160). Clearly the bishop refers to the importance of abiding by the rules maintained by the social network in the town which in turn follows the central government in power. This is why the notary's complaints reached the bishop's ear so quickly: 'recibí una carta del notario del pueblo, que me pareció hombre sensato aunque ampuloso y un tanto perturbado por la pasión política' (160–161). The notary had argued, for example, that 'los curas de pueblo no deben ocuparse de política, pero que si lo hacen debe ser por lo alto, es decir, con los buenos y no con los malos, "no con los liberales sino con los conservadores"' (162). The sergeant had accused the young priest of intervening in 'la acción pacificadora que desarrollan las autoridades en la provincia' (161), with which the bishop agreed: 'tengo que concederle más importancia que a tu opinión a la de un sargento en quien ha depositado su confianza el gobierno' (161). The young priest is revealed, in the end, to be a 'letrado' though without the required political tactfulness to be successful in a small town so as to join the network and its political system. In that sense the young priest is a 'letrado' who comes to a small town representing change, even though he was told to avoid involvement in politics (23). Politics was one of the temptations along with 'oratory' and 'rhetoric': 'Entre las tentaciones más difíciles de vencer y que asaltan el corazón de los predicadores, figura la de ceder a la cadencia de la palabra y al encanto indefinible de la retórica' (36). The young priest is attracted to rhetoric via his love for scripture: 'el joven sacerdote tenía talento para la oratoria sagrada y una feliz disposición para las letras divinas' (22). It was a talent that would be wasted if kept in a small village: 'Hundirlo en un pueblo sería perderlo para los destinos más altos de la ciudad, donde tanta falta hace un clero docto' (22). He is sent to the 'seminario menor' to teach 'gramática y ortografía' (160–163).

Up to this point we have seen that the conflict narrated in the story encompasses both liberal and conservative parties, how their networks are maintained, the profits yielded by power politics and the economic benefits accrued as a result. This division between the 'pueblo de arriba' and the 'pueblo de abajo' becomes the backdrop against which the emergence of a rebel movement whose leader is the liberal Pío Quinto Flechas is silhouetted. The rebels in *El Cristo de espaldas* are different from the potential activists found later in novels such as *La mala hora*, *Años de fuga* and *Bulevar de los héroes*, as we shall see later. The rebel movement described in *El Cristo de espaldas* is still supported by the liberal party and hints at the so-called liberal guerrilla discussed in Chapter One. The rationale for this assertion, however, is a) the fact that only two parties are depicted in the novel, b) that the above-mentioned characters Flechas and Piragua are recognised as 'gamonales', liberal and conservative, respectively (54), and c) that, as stressed by the notary, the period depicted is 'una era política de alianzas, que los gobiernos llaman de concentración nacional' (55).

It is in this light that I shall turn to the two predominant ideologies portrayed in the novel and analyse the purpose they serve in the society depicted in *El Cristo de espaldas*. It is important, though, to mention the issue of 'estado de sitio' which emerges in the plot as a measure taken in the 'pueblo de arriba' after the confrontation in which the acolyte lost his life. As I have noted in Chapter One, the 'estado de sitio' refers to a constitutional procedure established as a state security measure whipped up by anti-communist threats; it was applied as a 'doctrina de seguridad nacional' engendered by the Cold War.[11] Although the suggestion of rebellion is only depicted as a liberal problem in *El Cristo de espaldas* it becomes clear as election time is getting closer; the conservatives state that there are only 'tres o cuatro' liberals around in town because 'los otros se encamaron en Llano Redondo con los bandidos' (47). This comment needs to be contextualised with references to the liberal Pío Quinto Flechas and his standing as a rebel (47, 132) ensconced in the mountains with other bandits. The theme of banditry goes beyond the reach of this study, but suffice it to add that banditry in Colombia, as mentioned in Chapter One, was a type of social rebellion which arose in the 1950s and produced individuals generally of liberal affiliation who operated *à la* Robin Hood and had backing from the peasants of the area of Llanos. This clarification is important in this analysis because of the distinctive characterisation of the rebel gradually developing within the Colombian novel of this period as a character of opposition.[12] In *El Cristo de espaldas* this opposition is channelled against the conservative party, but in novels such as *La mala hora* the characterisation of the rebel emerges as an ideological force opposing the very regime of bipartisanism itself; the same as in *Años de fuga* and *Bulevar de los héroes*. As we have seen, in *El Cristo de espaldas* the political division is fuelled by two dominant ideologies only, whose aim is to maintain a grip on power and dominance. That is what explains in principle the political network maintained by the town's henchmen who are linked to the central government and thereby maintain control of the regime. But it is also this systematic procedure which creates rupture within rural society and, instead of producing cohesion, promotes divided loyalties fuelled

11   On the issues related to the 'estado de sitio' see Apolinar Díaz-Callejas, 'Estado de sitio ante la Constituyente Colombiana', in *Nueva Sociedad*, 112, March-April 1991, 66–72. Also available at <www.nuso.org> [Accessed 25 March 2009]

12   Aspects of banditry are detailed in Gonzalo Sánchez and Donny Meertens, *Bandoleros, gamonales y campesinos* (Bogotá: El Ancora, 1985).

by the networks, and even more, fosters a local administrative chaos. An interpretation that offers a suitable fit with the particular political scenario portrayed in *El Cristo de espaldas* is based on the theory which explains the dominance of ideologies in early capitalist societies. As suggested by Eagleton, according to *The Dominant Ideology Thesis*, in 'early capitalist societies the mechanisms for transmitting ideologies to the masses were notably weak'.[13] The reason for this was the lack of 'communications media or institutions of popular education' and indeed, that 'many of the people were illiterate'. The channels of transmission, such as they existed, offered no kind of seamless unity for the masses to internalise their own ideology, on the one hand, and, on the other, 'the culture of dominated groups and classes' retained a 'good deal of autonomy'.[14] Thus the system survived 'on account of social divisions between the various groups' it exploited since this brought more effective strategies of control to the powerful.[15] As we can see, this theory about how ideology operates in early capitalist societies offers an appropriate model for interpreting the functioning of ideological structures in *El Cristo de espaldas*.

El Cristo de espaldas articulates the dismemberment of the democratic system, the point at which power, following the two-party system, should revert from the conservative party (epitomised by don Roque) to the liberal party (symbolised by Anacleto, don Roque's son). That this is a 'legitimate' transfer of power is suggested by the fact that Anacleto – unlike Anacarsis, don Roque's favoured though illegitimate son – is the legitimate heir. The novel thus focuses on the point at which the two-party democratic system breaks down, and is short-circuited by the murder of don Roque by a conservative henchman, the acolyte, who prefers to kill don Roque rather than let the liberals come to power. The intriguing part of *El Cristo de espaldas* is that its pro-liberal ideology (in that Anacleto is portrayed as the undeserving victim of the conservative party's violence) is inserted into

13   See Nicholas Abercrombie, Stephen Hill and Brian S. Turner, *The Dominant Ideology Thesis* (London: George Allen & Unwin, 1980), p. 124. See Eagleton, *Ideology*, p. 35.

14   Eagleton, *Ideology*, pp. 35–36.

15   Eagleton, *Ideology*, pp. 35–36.

a pro-conservative casing (the rhetoric of the novel is couched in religious terms, the murder is described as if it occurred during Holy week from a Thursday to a Monday, the town is like a place of purgatory on which Christ turns his back), which makes of the novel a prototypical hybrid, that is a liberal-conservative, two-party-system novel. The configuration of these ideological elements – liberal party ideology – is also present in the next novel, *Siervo sin tierra*, but, as we shall see, the ideological mix produces a different artistic formulation.

Landownership and False Ideological Cohesion: *Siervo Sin Tierra*[16]

Central to *Siervo Sin Tierra*'s plot and themes is its source, the hacienda, around which the central character of the story and the many others who surround him revolve. The hacienda is the space within which the story is narrated and what it represents to the protagonist, together with the local rural area in which the hacienda is located. The place is 'La Vega del Chicamocha', between the Boyacá and Santander departments, and the district of Capitanejo within which small towns such as Soatá are located. It is worthwhile bearing in mind some other issues central to Eduardo Caballero Calderón's writing which I have already introduced above in the analysis of *El Cristo de espaldas*. Although Caballero Calderón was a letrado himself, he dedicated his life to politics, as a member of the Colombian liberal party. He belonged to the ruling class and held, for example, a few diplomatic postings in Spain, France and Argentina. One of his bureaucratic positions in Colombia was as 'registrador del estado civil', that is, director of the official national civil registry, an institution in charge of the identity

---

16   Eduardo Caballero Calderón, *Siervo sin tierra* (Medellín: Bedout, 1978). Further references to this novel are taken from this edition and given only the page number after quotations in the text.

registry, population statistics and electoral matters.[17] A crucial issue related to Caballero Calderón as the author of a novel such as *Siervo sin tierra* is that of landownership in Colombia during the 1950s. Caballero Calderón, as a member of the upper and ruling classes, was heir to a hacienda in the interior highlands of Colombia, in the area of Boyacá.[18] Politically, as suggested by Caballero Calderón, the locality is a liberal core sitting in the middle of a territory surrounded by conservatives, as indicated in the author's writings.[19] Caballero Calderón is, thus, a prime source about issues such as landownership, bureaucracy and liberal ideas in Colombia, as well as power and liberal ideology since he himself championed them.[20]

Some of the factual aspects of the tobacco production and market and production relations, thus found in *Siervo sin tierra*, are grounded in the author's own experience. Likewise the description in this novel of the conditions peasants suffer under the hacienda as 'arrendatarios', i.e. their struggle for utilities such as water are also rooted in the author's life experience in Boyacá. The novel also draws on Caballero Calderón's knowledge of bipartisan relationships in Colombia in the period 1930s-1950s.

The novel tells the story of a peasant called Siervo Joya, a man whose dream to own a small farm-like plot of land never comes true. After serving in the army Siervo Joya heads back to the 'rancho' where he was born and where his mother used to live.[21] On his way back home Siervo finds Tránsito and brings her and her baby to the 'rancho'. As time progresses

17   See Palacios, *Entre la legitimidad*, p. 203.

18   Caballero Calderón's hacienda Tipacoque in Boyacá department was converted into a municipality in 1968 with the author himself as its first mayor. In this respect see 'Ordenanza No. 17' of 28 November 1968.

19   References in this sense are found in autobiographical books such as Eduardo Caballero Calderón, *Tipacoque: estampas de provincia* (Córdoba: Club del libro, 1940) and *Diario de Tipacoque* (Bogotá: Oveja Negra, 1983) (first publ. in 1950).

20   Important notes pointing these articulations are found in Ricardo Silva Romero, 'De ayer a hoy: año Caballero Calderón 1910–2010', document, 23 April 2010. Available at <http://www.bibliotecanacional.gov.co/recursos_user/documentos_bnc/catalo-caballeroe.pdf> [Accessed 23 April 2011]

21   The meaning of 'rancho' in this context refers to a poorly built house used as a dwelling by peasants in rural areas, and without a water supply.

Siervo and Tránsito grow as a family abiding by the rules and customs of life in the hacienda. Attached to haciendas by 'arrendamiento' worker peasants are under the administrators' orders and brought to a small town to support a liberal political social event carried out on a Saturday – the market day when people stop and gather to have a drink and catch up (92). Disrupted by someone falling on him while asleep Siervo retaliates and kills his assailant who happened to be a conservative (102). Subsequently Siervo is accused of being the head of a gang of bandits and reported to the president of the Republic as the liberal boss (104). Siervo is jailed and stays there until 9 April 1948 when the news about Gaitán's murder breaks and the news spreads that a 'revolución liberal o comunista' is happening in Bogotá (130). Shouting '¡Que viva la revolución!' prisoners escape (133) and Siervo heads home, as all he wants is to take his land back (135). Once in the hacienda, the news is that the country and the capital are calmed and a democratic coalition, conservative and liberal, has reshaped the government. The town, though, is sent a military mayor from the central government. With everything now back to normal Siervo seeks a loan at Caja Agraria to buy his plot of land, to no avail. By this time Siervo's eldest teenage son joins the 'revolution' and becomes a conservative hit-man; Siervo's daughter dies in the troubles. Rigged elections bring conservatives to power and local disputes lead to legal arguments which become political rows (160). The 'arrendatarios' leave, either to go to urban areas or to a new job in the new industries, while others head either to the mountains or 'el llano' to form guerrillas (170–173); the 'patrones' go abroad, 'al extranjero' (172). Reluctantly Siervo leaves the 'rancho' to work for the railway company in Paz del Río (178) until a general takes power and 'guerrilleros' surrender their arms (178). Once he is back in the hacienda Siervo uses his savings to broker an agreement with the administrator Ramírez to buy his plot of land, including three days of water taken from don Floro's spring for which he pays a deposit of one hundred and fifty pesos. Tragically, while walking to the 'rancho' Siervo dies. The following day Tránsito goes back to the administrator to cancel the agreement as she does not have money to cover Siervo's funeral expenses, only to hear Ramírez say '¡Ah vida esta, mana Tránsito! ¡Conque se quedó en fin de cuentas mano Siervo sin tierra!'

The Politics of the Agrarian Capitalism

Whereas the novel *El Cristo de espaldas* by Caballero Calderón informs us specifically about the political practices operating in rural areas, *Siervo sin tierra* focuses on the issue of landownership and particularly the political connections by which it was conditioned. As with *El Cristo de espaldas*, thereof, to understand the relationship between politics and ideology in *Siervo sin tierra* some aspects of Eagleton's discussion of Abercrombie, Hill and Turner's view are equally appropriate for the analysis. Accordingly, Abercrombie et al's *The Dominant Ideology Thesis* takes into account that in early capitalist societies 'ideological transmission was hardly well developed';[22] the limited or nonexistent communications media and institutions of popular education led to illiteracy.[23] The everyday discourses of the subaltern class were formed 'largely outside the control of the ruling class', and incorporated significant beliefs and values at odds with it, therefore cohesion did not exist. Thus the consent of the dominated to their masters was achieved by economic means. In this case, strategies such as 'reformism' implying rather the 'ability of a capitalist system to yield tangible benefits to [...] its underlings' brought more effective strategies of control to the powerful and their system which was maintained by 'social divisions between the various groups it exploit[ed]'.[24] Drawing on this view I argue here that, in the hacienda system portrayed in the novel *Siervo sin tierra*, we see the consent of the dominated classes to their masters. With this argumentation I also draw on Macherey's view that, behind the entire narrative structure, there is an elusive space of meaning that the novel does not explicitly express.[25] Behind the visible political plot there lies a much more decisive factor expressed by what land possession represents to the

---

22 See Eagleton, *Ideology*, p. 35–36. See Abercrombie, Hill and Turner, *The Dominant Ideology Thesis*, p. 124.

23 Eagleton, *Ideology*, p. 35.

24 Eagleton, *Ideology*, pp. 35–36

25 For further discussion of Macherey's ideas see *A Theory of Literary Production* (London: Routledge, 2006), pp. 92–95.

landless. Land possession provides an apparent political cohesion that is articulated as an unconscious consent of the dominated classes towards their political masters, which is achieved by an economic pressure which, in turn, is veiled by a local political discourse. While portraying property and production networks the novel *Siervo sin tierra* articulates the pressures the landless experience in labour as in political and ideological commitments. The novel alludes to actual events which took place on 9 April 1948, particularly the bipartisan feuds among the rural population: the story takes place in a rural society in which the old hacienda system of production is locked into an ideologically rigged large-scale ownership, as shall be seen.

Relying on Terry Eagleton's paradigm and also his interpretation of ideology and power relations I analyse *Siervo sin tierra* in the context of the following ideas: a) the hacienda as an economic system, b) the hacienda as a political apparatus and provider of a false ideological cohesion and c) 'Revolution' as a signifier for the liberation of land.

a) *The hacienda as an economic system.* I have mentioned essentially how the hacienda system was politically connected to power reproduction in Chapter One. However, the hacienda system is complex as suggested by Siervo's story. The hacienda is essentially a production machine based on landownership which is sustained, firstly, by a system of 'arriendo' and, secondly, by agricultural exploitation. Within this system landowners are at the same time landlords, 'arrendadores' to the tenants, 'arrendatarios' who are compelled to pay their tenancy with part of their salary ('jornal'), while part of the produce is reserved for the sustenance of the peasant workers. The hacienda produces mainly tobacco, but also sugar cane and sugar as a by-product, and the farming produce is what generates wealth, including 'arriendos'. Reflecting this production system the novel shows the relationship existing between 'arrendadores' and 'arrendatarios' in which the former are never called by their proper names and are only known by the anonymous term 'patrones'; finally they are represented by the 'administrador' Ramírez and the 'mayordomo', Roso, to which Siervo and don Floro are accountable. Subsequently, there is a rank dividing 'arrendatarios' from top to bottom; so there is a small 'arrendatario' such as Siervo and a medium 'arrendatario' such as don Floro, which makes the latter a 'medianero'.

The difference between Siervo as a small 'arrendatario' and don Floro in his position of 'medianero' is that Siervo is only allowed to grow maize to contribute to the sustenance for the 'peones', but not tobacco which is sold to the external buyer, the trading 'company', through the hacienda. An important signifier within this system is 'home' (or attachment to 'home') which inevitably binds together the 'arrendatarios', the 'administrador', the 'mayordomo' and workers such as the cooks, as it is the case of Tránsito, all of whom are tied to the landowners or 'patrones', as portrayed in the novel. This attachment to the hacienda inevitably entails political allegiance as needed by the 'patrones', as shall be demonstrated.

Landownership is articulated from the very beginning of the novel via the protagonist Siervo Joya. Siervo describes the huge extension of the land possessed by his 'patrones' as 'la vega' (10), where he was born, which is the area close to another town called Capitanejo between the 'páramo' and 'Valle del Chicamocha'. The area includes part of a mountain which has cold weather along with part of the north of the country which has hot weather; all of which belongs to 'los patrones de la casa de teja'. 'La casa de teja' is the big house where the 'patrones' and their family stay when not in the city, whereas Siervo leaves in a 'rancho', or hut. Siervo says at one point that 'los patrones son gente rica [...] mucha peonada tienen, mucha [...] y tierra, tierra, más tierra' (8). The bosses' wealth, compared with his own, is obviously enormous because Siervo effectively owns nothing: 'y uno sin un terrón donde sembrar dos palitos de maíz' (8). But Siervo's life and circumstances are attached to the 'rancho' where he was born and where his mother lived all her life. Located in the hacienda Siervo's 'rancho' sits on a plot rented first by his mother where they lived as 'arrendatarios' and where he comes to live with Tránsito under the same terms. But Siervo's plot is circumscribed within don Floro Dueñas's larger 'arrendamiento' whose 'rancho' is fitted out with a 'trapiche' (an industrial sugar cane mill for sugar production) and 'acequia', the irrigation ditch which provides the water supply. Siervo is entitled to use the irrigation ditch for three days a week for his produce. These relationships are to the advantage of the landowner and reflect the hacienda's trade-off of economic advantage for political gain, which entails the inevitable and hidden allegiance to the hacienda proprietors. The 'arrendatarios' owe the 'patrones' their loyalty which derives from political affiliation from which, in turn, the 'patrones' benefit as a result of the bipartisan system of power-sharing, as shall be demonstrated in the following section.

b) *The hacienda as a political apparatus and provider of a false ideological cohesion.* The imposed hacienda system is based on a duplicitous relationship of obligation and allegiance. The obligation is suggested by the nature of 'arriendo' itself. Allegiance is, however, always mediated by a deceptive distance. This is determined by the very antithetical condition of their economic, social and cultural rank. In reality Siervo rarely sees his 'patrones'; they are almost a ghostly entity even though they are powerful since they are wealthy (8). However close he may be, they are extremely distant: 'aunque Siervo se hallaba a dos dedos del patrón, tenía la impresión de encontrarse a muchas leguas de distancia' (59). That distance is determined also through the opposition between the letrado and the illiterate individual. Siervo, for example, is an illiterate man never valued beyond his condition: 'el patrón reía de su manera de hablar, de su pronunciación defectuosa, de su torpeza natural, de su planta rústica y pintoresca' (59). Secondly in 'la casa' the 'patrones' are high and mighty 'encumbrados señores' who live in a world apart while doing nothing, 'nada' (45) contemplated by their servants and, like politicians, they are addressed as 'doctores' (92). The 'letrado' class in this novel is represented by 'doctores', politicians and by unnamed priests. The characterisation of the culture of the 'letrado' which prevailed and evolved in Colombia across the twentieth century will be analysed in depth in Chapter Five. In *Siervo sin tierra* we have a politician who shows rhetorical prowess, loudly pledging reforms such as 'revolución agraria, reforma tributaria [...] legitimidad, cedulación, redención del pueblo, antialcoholismo, plan vial, proletariado, etc' (93). A priest, for his part, plays the 'letrado' role from the pulpit telling off the liberals for being 'ateos, masones librepensadores, protestantes, volterianos', all of which equated to a 'sin' for which they will receive 'condenación eterna' (98).

Nonetheless Siervo and Tránsito, who represent the illiterate class, are aware of 'doctores' and distrust them: 'Mire mano Siervo [...] no me venga con doctores' (49). Tránsito depicts 'doctores' as men with 'conversa muy fina' (48), who are elegantly dressed and read newspapers (49). Tránsito warns Siervo about their position within that social environment, noting that they '[doctores] son de los mismos [...] y nosotros somos de los otros' (49). Siervo and Tránsito, i.e. the others, are the mute subaltern. For example, Siervo is heard by 'patrones' 'como quien oye llover' (45), or disdained, 'después hablaremos de tu asunto Siervo' (61). Likewise Tránsito's feelings lead her to tell Siervo: 'a quien le creerá más el alcalde, al agente o a nosotros' (49) and Siervo declares, for example, that 'ellos apenas si me miran como a un perro cuando me ven por la calle' (104). Siervo feels that this difference and distance is made from something that 'doctores' possess, that is, property, 'casa de teja y tierra' (23). Siervo's distrust towards 'doctores' is, nevertheless, justified since when he is in trouble he is presented to the authorities as the head of a gang, 'el cabecilla de una cuadrilla de bandidos' (104), reported to the president of the Republic as a liberal boss (104). To top it all, he is forgotten in jail without proper judicial process. Conversely the top politician who created the troubles in the first place in which Siervo got involved, wrote to declare himself as not responsible at all for the disturbance as other personalities could attest (104); but rather duplicitously, he also reassures Siervo: 'Eres una víctima de la causa [...] yo me encargaré de tu defensa [...] te defenderé de balde por lo que eres liberal' (104–105). That perceived duplicity persuades Siervo to say what he thinks about 'doctores': 'Los jefes [...] se lavan las manos y nos vuelven la espalda' (105). Other members of the hacienda such as don Floro, for example, approach things differently. Don Floro who does not know how to read pays for his son's education so that he can be a 'doctor' (162) and pursue 'letrado' status; hopefully he may reach positions such as 'alcalde y diputado' (162).

Deception and manipulation are shown in the novel to be driven by the middlemen of the 'patrones', that is, the 'administrador', Ramírez, and the 'mayordomo', Roso, through whom Siervo must negotiate his virtual closeness to the 'patrones'. For example, it is the 'administrador' who orders the hacienda's workers around; he orders them to attend the political gathering in which Siervo gets in trouble: 'don Ramírez nos ordenó desde hace ocho días que nos presentaramos hoy todos en la plaza' (92). It is only in town where Siervo is able to see 'los notables' among whom are the 'administrador' and the 'mayordomo' along with the VIPs such as the mayor, the attorney, the council's president and even members of the unions (92). As

I have shown in Chapter One alliances between unions and parties were part of customary political practice. It is also the 'administrador' who keeps the 'cédulas' of the workers 'guardadas en el escritorio' (154) to avoid liberal IDs to be decommissioned by conservatives in election times. These cunning schemes are, however, solved among the ruling class by the policy of 'unión nacional' (120–121) or power 'coalition' between liberals and conservatives (141). In effect, there are agreements between 'letrados' because, as the narrator expresses it, there was no difference between them, 'todos eran cortados por una misma tijera' (101).[26] Likewise the state apparatus run by the hacienda brings a political candidate who has been hand-picked by the 'gobernador del departamento y el directorio liberal de la provincia' (91) and Siervo is forced to attend a prepared special political meeting that brings false cohesion through food and drinks paid for by 'patrones' even though the latter do not show up (94).

Reflecting the impact of proposed liberal reforms of the 1930s, as described in Chapter One, *Siervo sin tierra* shows the convoluted bipartisan strategies used to maintain power whilst exposing also a class struggle at the core of the hacienda system. Siervo mentions that the candidate speaks 'mucha palabra bonita' (94), which refers to the language of reforms spelt out by the candidate: '"constitución, revolución agararia, reforma tributaria, reacción cavernaria, legitimidad, cedulación, redención del pueblo, antialcoholismo, plan vial, proletariado, etc"' (93). Siervo's illiteracy does not prevent him, however, from understanding what the meaning of land possession is, as it is his ambition 'tener un terrón de tierra para sembrar maíz' and to grow some tobacco he can trade (8, 146); thus the word 'revolución' means for him, at least, the obvious route to realising his dream. Siervo is, indeed, not a disingenuous peasant either as he has served in the army and gained valuable experience as a result. He is a person who takes things at face value as, for instance, the idea that land is going to be distributed: 'andan diciendo por ahí que el gobierno liberal va a repartir las tierras de los patrones' (95). To dispel any doubt, he questions his interlocutor directly: '¿de manera que el doctor dijo que van a repartir las tierras?' and

---

26   Local idiom that translates into English as 'they were all cut out of the same cloth'.

he is told affirmatively by Roso that land is going to be distributed 'a los que trabajen, a nosotros los pobres' (95). It is this promise that explains his political affiliation; as the 'mayordomo', Roso's exclamation accentuates: '¡para eso somos liberales!' (95). Siervo knows in reality that what everybody says about 'jefes' is true, namely, that 'A don Ramírez, al alcalde, al personero y a los concejales sólo les interesa manejar la platica del pueblo, y seguir mandando y haciendo contratos con el municipio' (96), that is, power and the wealth that comes as a result of that power. After the disturbances led to the conservatives winning rigged elections, Tránsito nags at him, '¿a mano Siervo qué le va ni qué le viene con que suban los unos y se caigan los otros?' (156) and reminds him that the only thing liberals gave to him was 'tres añitos de cárcel' (156). Thus, although Siervo is a liberal 'porque así me criaron sumercé' (166), disenchantment and distrust about politics is evinced when he dismisses his liberal neighbour, 'yo le tengo tanta desconfianza a don Floro como a los godos' (158). Political cohesion based on bipartisan values is shown in this novel to be based on a false consciousness since it simply mimics the interests of the ruling class; as spelt out by Tránsito who tells Siervo 'yo no quiero políticas' (93). Tránsito's advice is in all acknowledged by Siervo: '[Tránsito] siempre tiene la razón' (105).

c) *'Revolution' as a signifier for the liberation of land.* Reflecting the events of 9 April 1948 the novel expresses the ideas of revolution and land reform vividly. When news breaks in the prison (where Siervo was serving a sentence for murder) that 'habían asesinado un caudillo popular' in the capital, the prisoners were told that it was either a 'revolución liberal' or 'comunista' (130) happening in Bogotá. Whether liberal or communist, the inmates greet the news with the words: '¡Que viva la revolución!' (133). Despite the confusion everybody agreed it was a 'revolution' and Siervo was among these who greeted the news enthusiastically. Once free Siervo immediately set off for home in order to re-claim his land, 'ya que estamos en revolución lo único que deseo es ponerle la mano a mi parchecito de tierra en la Vega del Chicamocha'. He wanted to go ahead with his plan, to open an outlet from the reservoir controlled by don Floro Dueñas so he would be able to grow 'tabaco' (135).

The revolution is connected in Siervo's mind with the idea of growing tobacco, which he had not been allowed to do before. That is why for

Siervo landowning also means freedom to grow profit-making produce, while knowing the extra value of producing and selling tobacco to the trading 'company'. As shown in Chapter One, in the 1930s a government whose motto was 'la Revolución en Marcha' proposed 'el uso de la tierra en función social'. Set in a period of more than two decades running between the 1930s and the 1950s *Siervo sin tierra* expresses what that language signified to a transitional peasant population. Siervo was told previously, as we have seen above, that the distribution of 'tierra' was a plan proposed by the government, which meant to Siervo that there was a revolution in the making. As Siervo suggests, 'en las revoluciones las tierras son de quien las coja primero' (135); in his view land has to be distributed (p. 138). In the hacienda a 'jefe' tells Siervo that 'en la capital de la república los godos asesinaron a Gaitán y los liberales queremos tumbar al gobierno: eso es todo' (138). Although told that 'Gaitán era el amigo de los pobres y por eso no lo querían ni los conservadores ni los ricos' (138), such a predicament makes little or no political sense to Siervo because he replies: 'Así será. Pero [...] en la revolución lo primero que se hace es repartir las tierras de los ricos' (138). Even the simple idea that 'la revolución consiste en tumbar a los godos y poner otra vez en el mando a los liberales' (139) is received sceptically by Siervo who suggests that revolution means going beyond the two-party system: '¡yo creí que la revolución era otra cosa!' (139). Certainly the revolution awaited by Siervo does not develop because, after waiting for two days in the house of the 'patrones', the news presenter announces that the country is 'otra vez en calma'. A democratic mixed government, based on a bipartisan agreement, has taken place in the capital and everything has returned to normal (141).

As we have seen up to this point, within these three specific traits, the novel *Siervo sin tierra* brings to the fore the issue of political power and local political discourse as masking a false ideological bipartisan cohesion which is attached to landowning, and which is undermined by an emerging class struggle and an interest in the liberation of land linked to the idea of revolution. For one thing, as suggested by Abercrombie et al's *The Dominant Ideology Thesis*, what *Siervo sin tierra* depicts is an early capitalist society whose mechanism for transmitting ideologies to people is notably weak given the weakness of communications media or institutions of popular education, since Siervo is illiterate. Even so the people are incorporated into the world-view of their political masters which operates via a capitalist system – in particular, the 'arriendo' and tobacco economy. The novel's representation of capitalism shows changes in land management and those resulted from a generational change based on the emergence of new pressures deriving from the birth of new social forces. In terms of land the 'parcelación de las haciendas' refers to a gradual land plot redistribution in which 'arrendamiento' plots were sold to peasants partly by means of Caja Agraria loans (122), a facility denied to Siervo. A rapidly changing environment resulting from infrastructural changes in the transport system led to the transition to a 'new life' characterised by the 'aparición del chofer' (119). Whereas the 'chofer' is seen by the narrator as a 'libertador' but also 'corruptor' of the peasants (119), Siervo instead sees him as part of 'progreso' in that the new generation are studying to be drivers, 'estudiando para choferes'; indeed the 'máquinas y camiones' are bringing commerce to Colombia in the form of 'tiendas, asistencias, posadas, guaraperías' and even 'mujeres malas', bad girls (121). The trend of new factories and imports from Europe suggests that other economic activities which are 'más productivas' than the local production are attracting the population and changing their world-view (120). Siervo's one hundred and fifty pesos deposit with which he agreed the purchase of his piece of land just before he died was in fact earned while working for the railway company in a small town known as the steel producer (178).

Siervo sin tierra suggests that the dominated classes were beginning to gain a good deal of autonomy during this period and, thus, everyday discourses of the subaltern classes were being formed largely outside the control of the ruling class, and embodied significant beliefs and values at odds with it, as epitomised by Siervo for whom the revolution means obtaining his own plot of land. Echoing Macherey's notion of the 'unspoken' we have seen that the nature of politics attached to a system of power secured by landownership is hidden beneath a set of conditions determined by economic obligation, submission and political allegiance. The ideological cohesion thereby created is false and, as the novel shows, the consent of the dominated to their masters is achieved much more by the utilitarian effect that land represents rather than by adherence to an abstract notion of bipartisanism.

Repression, State Absence and Clandestine Resistance:
La mala hora[27]

Within this group of novels produced by historical contingency *La mala hora* stands out for being part of a larger oeuvre of the most important and representative author of Colombian literature. Throughout his writing career Gabriel García Márquez consistently modelled his works on politics, ideology and power patterns, as we shall see. In his creative work such as novels, short stories and chronicles or as a columnist, García Márquez often linked literature with politics. In a crucial piece of writing García Márquez recorded his views about novel production in Colombia in the 1950s and set the ideological tone for his novels.[28] Addressing the pressures for writers to write 'libros políticos' at the time, in the article 'Dos o tres cosas sobre "la novela de la violencia"' (1959) García Márquez hinted significantly at what the real meaning of the novel should be. Arguing that the pressures involved in taking advantage of 'la violencia con todas sus posibilidades literarias y con todas sus implicaciones políticas' was leading writers to solve their 'preocupaciones políticas' while writing 'malas novelas'.[29] García Márquez argued that the lack of 'experiencia necesaria' in writers who either witnessed or only attempted to write about that violence wasted their testimonies by fitting them into their 'formulas políticas'. Therefore novel writing needed to start from the beginning as there was neither a tradition to be continued, in terms of a technical training, nor a professional writer 'que haya sido testigo de la violencia'. He believed the novel was not 'en los muertos sino en los vivos', that is, that the latter had it 'dentro de ellos mismos' and the former simply needed 'la justificación documental'.

27   Gabriel García Márquez, *La mala hora* (Barcelona: Bruguera, 1984). Further references to this novel are taken from this edition and only the page number is provided after quotations in the text.

28   See Gabriel García Márquez, 'Dos o tres cosas sobre "la novela de la violencia"', in *Eco* vol. 34/1, 205, Bogotá (November 1978), 103–108 (first publ. in *la Calle*, 9 October 1959).

29   'Dos o tres cosas' (1978).

García Márquez thus advised writers to take their time to learn how to write that novel whose content would be inevitably political at any time.[30] With that statement García Márquez set the template for his own novels and made clear that the issue was to 'contar lo que nuestra posición política nos indica aunque tengamos que inventarlo'. Gabriel García Márquez's ideologico-political convictions led him to bond with the left wing after his literary success in 1967 with the publication of *Cien años de soledad*. The novel *Cien años de soledad*, apart from being regarded as a major work of magical realism and earning García Márquez the Nobel Prize in 1982, has also been hinted at as being a political novel.[31] Magical realism is not discussed here for it is beyond the scope of this study though it suffices to state that the 'political ideologies' of that work are a predominant interest of the author.[32] The political has been proposed as a common factor operating in García Márquez's works.[33] Given the importance of the elements of politics and ideology in García Márquez's work I trace some aspects of his political trajectory. Although it is unclear when in the 1970s García Márquez joined the communist party in Colombia his support for the left wing cause is known to exist particularly since that decade.[34] He donated to the Venezuelan socialist party Movimiento Al Socialismo (MAS) the

30   García Márquez, 'Dos o tres cosas', 1978.

31   See George R. McMurray, *Gabriel García Márquez* (New York: Ungar, 1977), p. 68. McMurray's original and extensive work approaching magical realism notes that 'religion and political ideologies' are part of the complexity of magical realism, which find affinity with García Márquez's works.

32   McMurray, *García Márquez*, p. 68.

33   Important views for political links between *Cien años de soledad* and *La mala hora* together as a reading from the perspective of the national political allegory is Juan Pablo Dabove, 'Los pasquines como alegoría de la disolución de la ciudadanía en "La mala hora" de Gabriel García Márquez', in *Revista de Crítica Literaria Latinoamericana*, vol. 26, 52 (2000), 269–287. Available at <http://www.jstor.org/stable/4531133> [Accessed 26 November 2008] and also Stephen M. Hart, *Gabriel García Márquez* (London: Reaktion Books, 2010), pp. 67, 75, 83.

34   García Márquez recognised his 'variables' and 'a veces conflictivas' relationship with the communist party though as he puts it 'ni en las peores circunstancias he hecho yo nunca declaraciones contra ellos'. See Plinio A. Mendoza, *El olor de la guayaba* (Barcelona: Mondadori, 1994), p. 124.

prize money obtained for the Rómulo Gallegos award in 1973.[35] In 1974 he took part in the foundation and funding of the Colombian leftist weekly magazine *Alternativa*, and also participated in the Second Russell Tribunal for human rights.[36] García Márquez's growing popularity in the 1970s made him friends with members of the Colombian upper class and very powerful individuals regardless of their political affiliation.[37] Worldwide, Bill Clinton the former president of the USA and the Cuban leader Fidel Castro number among his friendships.[38] García Márquez's political commitment might be summarised in his own words: 'quiero que el mundo sea socialista y creo que tarde o temprano lo será'.[39]

After the Cuban revolution García Márquez worked with the Cuban news agency Prensa Latina and, in 1962, his novel *La mala hora* earned him the then Colombian Esso novel prize. García Márquez's extraordinary literary life demonstrated how his novels were built around the essential core of politics in his work as well as the role letras played in his development as a writer, a theme reflected in *La mala hora*. It is not a coincidence that the aspects of 'letrados' and poetry are connected to politics in García Márquez's work, as he himself confirms when alluding to Pablo Neruda and his 'callejones difíciles' that is, Neruda's 'poesía política'.[40] It was through poetry as well as through another letrado tradition that he found the path of his novels. That other tradition was the law career that García Márquez

35   *El Tiempo*, 6 August 1972, p. 5.
36   Gerald Martin, *Gabriel García Márquez: A Life* (London: Bloomsbury, 2008), p. 378.
37   García Márquez divides his friends between before and after celebrity. However, the late Father Camilo Torres, an important figure in the Colombian political process, as shown in Chapter One, was García Márquez's friend before celebrity; they were university comrades. See Castro Caycedo Germán, interview with García Márquez, '"Gabo" cuenta la novela de su vida' (2), *El Espectador*, 17 March 1977, p. 5-A. On celebrity see Mendoza, *Olor*, pp. 153–156.
38   Plinio A. Mendoza, lecture in London Metropolitan University on 8 December 2008, commented on García Márquez's attraction to the idea of power and powerful men. See also Mendoza, *Olor*, pp. 153–163. A revealing reportage about García Márquez's intimacies and power is that of John Lee Anderson, 'El poder de Gabo', in *Semana*, 'Documento', 909 (4–11 October 1999), 46–54.
39   Mendoza, *Olor*, p. 76.
40   Mendoza, *Olor*, p. 65.

began at the law faculty in the National University of Bogotá, and which he then abandoned for fiction writing. As he says: 'dejé todo, inclusive mi carrera de Derecho, y me dediqué solamente a leer novelas y escribir'.[41]

In the 1950s, after the publication of his first novel, *La hojarasca*, he was criticised by his friends because that was 'una novela que no denuncia, que no desenmascara nada'.[42] The pressures created by those comments forced García Márquez to re-evaluate his relationship with Colombia. In his words: 'aquel momento me llevó a pensar que yo debía ocuparme de la realidad inmediata del país'.[43] It was from that sense of a new commitment that *La mala hora* was conceived and written.[44] It is inspired by the 'realidad política y social de mi país' and therefore it is a work of 'estructura racionalista determinada por la naturaleza del tema [...] constituye un tipo de literatura premeditada'.[45] Confirming this idea García Márquez asserted that 'en mis opciones políticas personales soy un hombre políticamente comprometido'. A close reading of García Márquez's thoughts in the 1950s sheds more light on the ideological value of the novel that he was writing at the time. He expressed, for example, some reservations about what was called committed literature:

> tengo muchas reservas sobre lo que entre nosotros se dio en llamar literatura com-
> prometida [...] porque me parece que su visión limitada del mundo y de la vida no
> ha servido, políticamente hablando, de nada. Lejos de apresurar un proceso de toma
> de conciencia, lo demora.[46]

The political intention suggested here by García Márquez is also an expression within which he inserted the many constituent elements combined within *La mala hora*. These elements are implied in what the characters themselves say along with the 'pasquines', and 'hojas clandestinas'. 'Pasquines' typically convey an open criticism or accusation of the actions of a particular

---

41   Ibid., p. 65.
42   Ibid., p. 75.
43   Ibid.
44   Ibid., pp. 75–76.
45   Ibid., p. 75.
46   Mendoza, *Olor*, p. 76.

sometimes named individual, and may be broadsheets slipped under the front door or stuck on it, or they may be drawn on a wall, and are always anonymous and left by a non-identifiable source.[47] Furthermore 'clandestinity' in oral and handwritten form was a de rigueur channel of communication for political groups developing in the 1960s and 1970s. Whereas 'pasquines' sought to reveal the hypocrisy of the upper class, the 'hojas clandestinas' by contrast convey surreptitious written messages whose significance is only known to their reader, which in Vargas Llosa's interpretation means they convey a 'revolución silenciosa' targeting the hypocrisy of the regime.[48] As the very denomination suggests, 'hojas clandestinas' bring to light a furtive plan which is being 'cooked up', in other words, a conspiracy. It is, indeed, conspiracy that is at the heart of *La mala hora* and vividly emerges in the novel's plot. Interestingly, conspiracy is considered to be an important trait in García Márquez's own life. García Márquez is often seen as a conspirator and he seems to acknowledge it. Anderson has stated that 'a Gabo le encanta conspirar, hacer las cosas clandestinamente [...] él mismo dice que es un "gran conspirador"'.[49] This connection between power and secrecy is found in García Márquez's own life as he recounts, for instance, that Omar Torrijos used to say that his [García Márquez] work was that of 'diplomacia secreta'.[50]

The Politics Behind the Pasquinades

The events narrated in *La mala hora* develop in a town with no name. It is a town living in an inertia caused by stagnation, poverty and utter boredom. The town is suddenly plagued with 'pasquines' telling infamous

---

47   'Pasquines' have been considered as a form of private/public communication accusation in Colombia. For more discussion on 'la crítica abierta' represented by 'pasquines' see Orlando Fals Borda, *Historia doble de la costa: Mompox y Loba*, vol. 1 (Bogotá: Carlos Valencia Editores, 1979), p. 156B.

48   Mario Vargas Llosa, *García Márquez: historia de un deicidio* (Barcelona: Barral, 1971), p. 421.

49   Anderson, 'El poder', 46–66 (p. 52).

50   Mendoza, *Olor*, p. 132.

things about individuals of the upper class and particularly their personal
relationships such as bedroom secrets, abortions, adultery or unclear kinship, but they are devoid of political content. The 'pasquines' reveal nothing that is not already common knowledge in the 'pueblo' (81) but they do
affect a small sector of the population and furthermore, they give people
something to talk about. The 'pasquines' are very important since it is their
content which triggers the action when a man, César Montero, kills Pastor,
a trumpeter musician, for allegedly being involved in a love affair with his
wife. That hypothesis will be a matter of speculation among some of the
characters in the story. That initial event brings about a series of events
which involved the town's priest, the mayor who is a lieutenant, the judge,
the barber, the doctor and the dentist. In a narrative action that develops
over 18 days from Tuesday 4 to Friday 21 October the story shows the
townspeople's concern about who might be responsible for the 'pasquines'.
As the story progresses in its search for the identity of the author of the
'pasquines' various daily things, such as the cinema censorship routines or
the arrival of a circus in town, among other things, happen. Meanwhile the
mayor suffers from toothache and we find more about his relations with
members of the community until finally a curfew is imposed in order to
discover the individual responsible for the 'pasquines'. A young man, Pepe
Amador, is arrested for distributing 'hojas clandestinas' in the cockfighting
pit (173). The clandestine propaganda printed in mimeograph persuades
the mayor to ask the arrested man to reveal who is the mastermind behind
it all (173–174). As the town carries on with its curfew and gossip about
Pepe Amador's arrest news about guerrilla groups plotting against the
government (178) is heard. Later the town learns that Pepe Amador has
been killed. At that point the mayor orders the guards to bury the body
and later in his office he is confronted by Father Angel and Dr. Giraldo,
and he tells them that Pepe has in fact fled (213). At last people forget
about the 'pasquines' but the search for the clandestine papers carried
out by the government reveals a hidden arsenal under the barber's floor-
ing and members of the community then hear that men are leaving for
the mountains to form guerrilla groups, though life in the town seems to
carry on as usual.

The Ideology of Prohibition

Criticism on García Márquez's work is varied as well as inexhaustible. Criticism points to a coded message as a common denominator of García Márquez's work. For example, in addressing the distinctiveness of García Márquez's work, Benedetti made a key point about its cryptic message: 'García Márquez no es un escritor de obvio mensaje político', and hinted at a coded political message to be deciphered.[51] A productive way to follow this cryptic code is Maturo's view which suggests that *La mala hora* is all about 'mensaje',[52] along with critics such as Rama who observed that García Márquez's work operates 'sobre un juego de implicancias políticas'.[53] The importance of the hidden message together with the political implication conveyed by certain clues within the story may be illustrated with some specific cases. For instance, *La mala hora* contains a 'telegrafista' who reads the novels of Victor Hugo; a doctor who discusses literary genres with his wife and frequently sends messages; a notice which reads 'prohibido hablar de política' in the barber's shop; the ciphered messages with the dialogues between the judge and the secretary; a priest who repeats the message of a song and writes letters; 'pasquines' and 'hojas clandestinas' messages, among others. The meaning of these messages becomes clearer if linked with 'pasquines', the prototype for the coded message in the novel. The 'pasquines' are defined as verbalisations,

51   See Mario Benedetti, 'Gabriel García Márquez o la vigilia dentro del sueño', in *9 Asedios a García Márquez* (Santiago de Chile: Editorial Universitaria, 1969), pp. 11–21 (pp. 13–14).

52   Graciela Maturo, *Claves simbólicas de Gabriel García Márquez* (Buenos Aires: García Cambeiro, 1972). See particularly the chapter about 'El juego de los enigmas', in which Maturo provides very important clues regarding the painstaking detail with which García Márquez constructs his work.

53   See Angel Rama, 'Un novelista de la violencia americana', in *9 Asedios a García Márquez* (Santiago de Chile: Editorial Universitaria, 1969), pp. 106–125 (p. 106).

speech or texts that publicly satirise or ridicule people.[54] In *La mala hora* the 'pasquines' generally say things that are already 'de dominio público' (81) and denigrate infidelity and people's moral conduct. An example of this is when Roberto Asís tells his mother that a 'pasquín' states that Rebeca Isabel is not his daughter (39) and in the same conversation they comment that 'todo el mundo sabe que Rosario de Montero se acostaba con Pastor [...] su última canción era para ella' (40). As Roberto Asís's mother clarifies, 'todo el mundo lo decía, pero nadie lo supo a ciencia cierta' (40). The truth according to 'la viuda de Asís' was that 'ahora se sabe que la canción era para Margot Ramírez. Se iban a casar y sólo ellos y la madre de Pastor lo sabían' (40). The conversation reveals, then, that the killing of Pastor was caused by jealousy provoked by the public revelation in a 'pasquín'. The 'pasquines' in *La mala hora* are relevant to its ideology. 'Pasquines' in the work are not of a political character but the social tension caused by them, when they are revealed, makes them the fulcrum of the ideological problems haunting the town, i.e. political animosity and conspiracy.

My aim is to analyse how in this novel politics and ideology are intertwined. I follow Terry Eagleton's theory, first, on the relation to the concealed structure of values underlying factual statements that connect with power structure and power relations of the society reflected in the novel.[55] Second, on his definition of the structure of politics as the 'machine' that accompanies the 'technical management' to which ideology adheres with the 'content' that comes with 'preaching or indoctrination'.[56]

A key ideological reference in *La mala hora* appears in the visible sign in the barber's shop which reads: 'prohibido hablar de política' (57). That prohibition, though, is seen paradoxically as an invitation and the barber's shop becomes a space in which people's varied views about politics in the town and the country are aired. The barber's customers discuss state

---

54   The word 'pasquín' translates as 'pasquinade', see Oxford English Dictionary at <http://www.oed.com.libproxy.ucl.ac.uk/search?searchType=dictionary&q=pasq uinade&searchBtn=Search> [Accessed 26 November 2008]
55   Terry Eagleton, *Literary Theory: An Introduction* (Oxford: Blackwell, 1996), p. 13.
56   Eagleton, *Ideology*, p. 38.

management, the way politics manifests itself throughout the government's administration in the 'town' and in the 'country', they comment on the official media opinion, the absence of the state, landownership, if there is a conspiracy in the town and who is involved in it. It is the outspoken barber, for example, who throws light on the media and the matter of land possession in the town. It is also he who takes a position against the 'official' opinion given by the 'periódicos' by rejecting them and therefore papers are banned in the barber's shop: 'no entran en este establecimiento mientras yo esté vivo' (55). It is also the barber who hints at the matter of landownership. The large estates owned by very few wealthy people like the Montiel widow who owns land 'que no se atraviesan en cinco días a caballo [...] dueña como de diez municipios' (55) – the same issue of landowning previously addressed in *Siervo sin tierra*. It is at the barber's shop that issues revealing the people's attitudes and feelings about politics are discussed. For instance, Carmichael suggests that people dwell in the past, 'ustedes todavía con odios políticos' (56), but this also shows his own acquiescent attitude towards the rich he works for since he would rather not talk about politics. Others wryly gossip that Carmichael does in politics what needs to be done, that is, calculate (he is an accountant) with closed eyes, 'con los ojos cerrados' according to 'los sirios' (the immigrants). 'El sirio' Moisés, for example, thinks that politics is a matter of bad luck because his countryman Elías has been 'tan de malas que el hijo le salió político'; politically Moisés believes that it is better not to get involved (58).

But it is also in the barber's shop where the repressive power of the state is exerted and 'democracy' is alluded to through synonyms while it is noted that the only agency allowed to 'prohibir' is the government (126). Thus the mayor, who takes the 'prohibido hablar de política' sign off the wall, accuses the barber's shop of being a 'nido de conspiradores' (127), while making clear that it is the government that exerts power. In the barber's shop the middle-class lack of commitment is epitomised by Judge Arcadio, who is neither with the military nor the government, nor the opposition; he fades away in the end and his departure is announced by the barber (187), as we shall see later. Judge Arcadio thinks that the conspirator's nest is no more than a place in which people talk but do nothing, 'hablan, pero de ahí no pasan' (127).

The Encoding of Politics and Ideology

Conspiracy though, derives from a combination of ideas and actions. Conspiracy comes through 'pasquines' and 'hojas clandestinas'. Whereas 'pasquines' conspire directly against the upper class, 'hojas clandestinas' conspire against the government regime, which shows that these messages are a contest for power. The 'hojas clandestinas' express concealed ideas in papers that are circulated clandestinely: 'le dio una hoja doblada. – léela y hazla circular' (133). Thus coded messages emerge from a telegrapher who reads *Los miserables* by Victor Hugo (108) or Dr. Giraldo who reads Dickens and discusses the interpretation of one of the English writer's stories. At this point it is helpful to refer back to Maturo's argument about García Márquez's use of a 'lenguaje cifrado'.[57] Maturo refers to the allusion to '*Los miserables* de Víctor Hugo como novela que el telegrafista *transmite en su código*' which discloses the 'lenguaje cifrado'. In this sense the novel reveals the code word 'freedom' through an intertextual message within which poverty is addressed by a significant name such as Victor Hugo and also throughout Charles Dickens's name, as an author that also sympathises with the poor and helpless.[58] These ciphered messages become clearer by the end of the story when the real state of the political power is revealed, as we shall see shortly. Nevertheless this conspiracy is latent and this idea is voiced by the mayor. The mayor mentions regularly that there is a 'confabulación' (67), a 'conspiración nacional' and openly accuses the dentist: 'usted sigue pensando como un conspirador [...] su actitud perjudica al pueblo' (74–75). An important observation about 'el pueblo' in *La mala hora* is made by Vargas Llosa when he points out that 'el pueblo como colectividad no es escenario sino protagonista'.[59] From the beginning to the end of the novel 'el pueblo' is characterised by a collective discontent which shapes the way politics develops in the town. Politics develops in the

---

57   Maturo, *Claves simbólicas*, p. 94.
58   Victor Hugo's ideas, together with many other socialist French writers and thinkers, were highly influential particularly in the leftist groups that developed along the first decades of the twentieth century in Colombia.
59   Vargas Llosa, *Historia de un deicidio* (Barcelona: Barral, 1971), p. 421.

town in that 'el pueblo' fights control. Control over 'el pueblo' is exerted by the local authority which is anchored in turn to the greater authority from the 'country' (177), and opposition is a force which grows from within the collective unit of 'el pueblo'.

Control is embodied in both Father Angel and the mayor who represent authority in the town via the related notion of 'morals' and 'order'. Father Angel controls entertainment, as evidenced in the bell ringing system at the cinema, and maintains the conservative structure of power so that the town is the 'más observante de la prefectura apostólica' (49), while 'moral familiar', in his view, has been 'mantenido intacta' after crossing a 'momento político difícil' (50). The mayor is also obsessed by control: 'al que me desordene el pueblo lo meto a la guandoca' (19), though it is known that the lieutenant arrived in the town with the mission to subdue it 'a cualquier precio' carrying a letter addressed to an obscure government 'partidario' (171) which offers a clue to the matter of partisanism and elections. Both the priest and the mayor make the decision to bring the curfew about (139, 151).

Opposition against the ecclesiastical power on the other hand is reflected in a character such as Dr. Giraldo whose scepticism about religion is made clear when he argues that the priest put 'esparadrapos a la moral' (196); besides there is also a deeper conviction that 'el país entero está remendado con telaraña' (177), that 'todo sigue lo mismo que antes' (178) and 'son los mismos con las mismas' (84) since the 'funcionarios' continue to be the same (178).

Contrary to what Vargas Llosa suggests I argue that the town certainly functions as an 'escenario' besides being a 'pueblo como colectividad' and that both 'escenario' and 'colectividad' stand politically for a 'democracy'.[60] The town as 'escenario' is encapsulated within a larger space which is the

---

60   A comparison between García Márquez's use of code messages and Daniel Pécaut's socio-historical analysis sheds light on where *La mala hora*'s real politics lie: 'Colombia es uno de los pocos países de América Latina en los que el régimen político ha conservado casi permanentemente el carácter de democracia civil en el transcurso del siglo', see Daniel Pécaut, *Orden y violencia: Colombia 1930–1954*, vol. 1 (Bogotá: Siglo XXI, 1987), p. 15.

'country' (177), from which 'el rol político del "letrado nacional"', to use Dabove's argument, derives.[61] Dabove's reading of the political role of 'letrado nacional' provides a different view from other interpretations such as those by R.L. Williams and Arango with respect to this novel, in that he argues that La mala hora indicates the 'fracaso de la Novela de la violencia'.[62] Asserting that in La mala hora 'la violencia *no se da a la lectura*', Dabove opens up the possibility of the ideologico-political significance of La mala hora.

Although the town has a military authority it functions politically and ideologically within a larger entity, namely the 'country' (177) from which the ideological notion of 'democracy' predicated by the mayor is provided, according to the polity it represents; i.e. the state of the 'letrado nacional'. García Márquez's novel shows the structure of politics as the 'machine' that comes with the 'technical management' as maintained by Eagleton. Some characters in the novel represent the 'letrado nacional' that champions the latent meaning of democracy within the story, which, as suggested by Eagleton, constitutes the 'preaching or indoctrination' maintained by the regime. These characters are the virtual 'registrador del estado civil' (78) who represents the civil authority, as do the 'personero' (80) and the judge. These characters attend to administrative issues to be solved: 'cuando salgamos de la vaina de las inundaciones resolvemos la vaina del personero' (the attorney) (80). 'La vaina del personero' brings about a dialogue between the judge and his secretary which reveals the deeper code behind the conspiracy: there is a 'régimen del estado de sitio' (79) that is, the state may adopt emergency

61   Dabove, 'Los pasquines', p. 273.
62   R.L. Williams and Arango, as I have shown in the Introduction, both maintain the reading of La mala hora within the context of violence, see R.L. Williams, *The Colombian Novel*, p. 49; and Manuel Antonio Arango, *García Márquez y la novela de la violencia en Colombia* (México: Fondo de Cultura Económica, 1985), p. 50. In contrast Dabove asserts that in La mala hora 'la violencia *no se da a la lectura*', masking his interpretation as different from those of R.L. Williams and Arango. See Dabove, 'Los pasquines', pp. 274–275.

measures when public order is disrupted.[63] The revelation of the 'estado de sitio' becomes an important political factor since it refers to state security and social control, as implied by Eagleton's 'technical management'.[64] This 'technical management' involves the structure of justice and human rights in that it is the juridical instrument that allows the system to take exceptional measures to protect national security and in relation to oppositional ideologies such as that of communism. In *La mala hora* the idea of 'estado de sitio' becomes a crucial code that throws light on why there is a military man in power in the town and why the mayor – advised by a 'letrado', the priest (139), 'el letrado por excelencia'[65] – imposes a curfew (151). The curfew is directly linked to the macro-power coded under the idea of 'los partidos', the 'registrador civil' and other civil authorities such as the 'personero' and the very judge (who in the end leaves the town), the ideology of democracy and the right to vote (38). Thus the judge and his secretary, who are representatives of bureaucracy and the 'letrado' culture as important pieces of the government machinery, discuss state functionalism, which is their speciality: 'el personero era nombrado por el concejo municipal – explicó el juez Arcadio. Como ahora no hay concejo, el régimen del estado de sitio lo autoriza a usted para nombrarlo' (79). As Judge Arcadio confirms, the appointment of a 'personero' is a 'procedimiento de emergencia bajo un régimen de emergencia' (79). That emergency is

---

63   We have seen previously the mention of 'estado de sitio' (state of siege) in *El Cristo de espaldas* by Caballero Calderón, as well as in Chapter One as a law enacted in Colombia after the 9 April 1948 events and kept for many years by the Colombian bipartisan democracy, as an anti-communist statute; in this sense compare Pécaut, *Orden*, p. 481; and Christopher Abel, *Política, iglesia y partidos* (Bogotá: FAES/ Universidad Nacional de Colombia, 1987), p. 156. An important concept to understand the contradiction posited by the idea of democracy and the military in town is Díaz-Callejas who maintains that Colombia is the country with the longest record of 'estado de sitio' in history for which 'el autoritarismo se hizo componente del sistema social y político Colombiano' and 'se profundizó la concepción militarista en el interior del estado', in *Nueva Sociedad*, 112 (March-April, 1991), 66–72. Available at <http://www.nuso.org> [25 March 2009]

64   Eagleton, *Ideology*, p. 38.

65   Dabove, 'Los pasquines', p. 278.

announced in 'hojas clandestinas' which read: 'dos años de discursos [...]
y todavía el mismo estado de sitio, la misma censura de prensa, los mismos
funcionarios' (188), the same words used by Toto Visbal (177–178). The
expressions 'son los mismos con las mismas' (84) and 'los funcionarios siguen
siendo los mismos' (178) refer not only to the town but to the 'country'
which symbolically mirrors the antics of democracy in Colombia in this
period, as seen in Chapter One.

The regular mention of words such as democracy, government and
elections reflects how 'el pueblo' collectively and as a class perceives the
government. Democracy, parties, government and elections are the super-
structural constituent parts of an entire society managed by a government
whose bureaucracy is in the town representing the central regime. Symbols
of that democracy are visible in the government offices and through 'propaganda del régimen' (86). For example, both in the judge's office (32) and
the mayor's office (65), a picture of the president carrying a golden sash
across his chest reading 'paz y justicia' is de rigueur. This representative
image is also accompanied by the mayor's repeated refrain that they are
living within a democracy: 'Estamos en una democracia' (44, 126), the
radio news reports containing extracts from the president's speech and a
list of prohibited import commodities (59), in sum, the 'propaganda del
régimen' (86). That particular democracy is built on two things: parties and
elections. However the elections are corrupted by the government's shady
methods used to keep itself in power, that is, the confiscation and destruction of the opposition party's people's IDs (78); as a result the majority of
the town's population do not have an identification document with which
to vote, though people still do vote. 'Cada día estoy mejor para votar' (38)
as 'la viuda de Asís', a member of the upper class, says.

The upper-class support of a military government in the town becomes
apparent even though they keep a hypocritical distance from that regime:
'una cosa es cuidar el pellejo y otra es saber guardar las distancias' (184).[66]

---

66   This distance between the upper class and the military regime suggests that, though
     not named, is the Rojas Pinilla government. The Rojas Pinilla government came
     to 'restablecer la hegemonía burguesa temporalmente quebrada', thus a political

The upper class is shown to be close to power as they are protected by the authorities, 'los Asís están en el pueblo [...] pase lo que pase, no se metan con él' (173); alternatively they are far away from the country – Montiel's widow's daughters live in Paris (102). Elections (91) and the need to appoint members of the cabinet such as 'registrador del estado civil' (78) and the 'personero' (80) exhibit the government's instrumentalist use of politics through its bureaucrats. It preaches democracy particularly by mentioning the need for a 'registrador del estado civil', the authority which governs the polls, the 'cédulas', IDs, as mentioned above. The need to appoint important members of the cabinet suggests a need for 'honesty' (79) and also simultaneously discloses the unreliability of the civil servants such as the judge and his secretary, pointing to the incompetence of the system's bureaucracy and the need for reforms in the town as voiced by the barber. The judge, for example, hypocritically suggests that 'el alcalde quiere que la oficina funcione' (32) though he took office eleven months after being appointed (31–33) and we are told that his mental clarity is enhanced after drinking half a dozen beers in a working day (32–34) while the office's secretary plucks chickens for the cook of the hotel next door (31, 34). As for the 'registrador', we soon learn that he has not arrived in the town despite having been appointed a year ago (78). Things are, indeed, revealed through 'small episodes of daily life' (185), according to the narrator. The need for judicial reform, for instance, is suggested by the outspoken barber who welcomes the judge to his shop with the words: 'La justicia cojea pero llega' (185). The pun is a direct criticism of a justice system which is physically unwell – it limps. Most importantly it shows the dishonest and fraudulent methods used by the mayor and the new rich to cash in on their position. As Vargas Llosa notes the wealthy people do not give their political opinion but 'sabemos que al menos dos de ellos deben su fortuna al régimen'.[67] Don Sabas, for instance, steals the cattle of the 'viuda de Montiel' and marks

---

bipartisan strategy to keep power in the 1950s. See Laura Restrepo, 'Niveles de realidad en la literatura de la "violencia" en Colombia', in *Once ensayos sobre la violencia* (Bogotá: CEREC, 1985), pp. 117–169 (p. 118).

67   Vargas Llosa, *Deicidio*, p. 432.

it with his own branding, while the mayor who knows he is committing 'abigeato' – the crime category for stealing cattle – simply makes him pay extra tax for each head of cattle (192). It is also known that the mayor commits crimes on behalf of the regime and the 'democracy' he represents: 'había orden de asesinarte en una emboscada y de confiscar tus reses para que el gobierno tuviera como atender a los enormes gastos de las elecciones en todo el departamento' (91).

In contrast with the upper class characterised by 'la buena vida' (182) there is the lower class which is characterised by extreme poverty. That extreme poverty is due, according to the barber, to 'abandono' and 'persecución' which is another way of 'darnos palo', to bully people (56). The 'abandono' which is reflected in the mayor's words when referring to the town's infrastructural problems: 'la vaina de las inundaciones' (80) disclose the issue of the absence of state, which fails to provide health services or housing for the people (64). Thus the barber becomes the spokesman for reason in the madness that the country has become:

> lindo negocio: mi partido está en el poder, la policía amenaza de muerte a mis adversarios políticos, y yo les compro tierras y ganados al precio que yo mismo ponga [...] cuando pasan las elecciones soy dueño de tres municipios, no tengo competidores, y de paso con la sartén por el mango aunque cambia el gobierno. (55–56)

Not surprisingly, the barber's conclusion is that politics is better business than printing counterfeit notes (56).

As a result of this palpable injustice, the lower class feels hatred towards the government embodied by the mayor. As Vargas Llosa points out: 'las clases populares alientan resentimiento y deseo de venganza contra la autoridad'.[68] That resentment is not hidden: the 'pobres' talk about 'pasquines' with a 'saludable alegría' (113) and remark ironically: 'quiera Dios que se le indigeste' (83), and 'hasta que nos resuciten los muertos que nos mataron' (84). On the other hand, there is a middle class that might be called 'letrada', following Dabove's meaning of 'liberales e ilustradas', though,

---

68   Vargas Llosa, *Deicidio*, p. 432.

like the lower classes, it shares the 'abandono' identified by the barber.[69] Vargas Llosa has noted two important points in this respect: one is the matter of middle-class organised opposition to the regime: 'la oposición organizada se recluta en la clase media, el dentista, el médico, el peluquero' in what Vargas Llosa calls the 'enemigos conscientes del gobierno'.[70] The second is the definition of 'el pueblo' which in *La mala hora* is articulated with its ambivalent Spanish meaning: 'el pueblo' referring both to the town and the population. It is the population, the 'colectividad', as mentioned above, that rejects everything that comes from the government, namely, 'estado de sitio'. These 'enemigos conscientes' are within the 'colectividad', 'todo el pueblo y nadie' (160) and produce the political response, that is, 'hojas clandestinas'. 'Hojas clandestinas' represent at one and the same time the new forces which are opposed to the old political regime, not only 'el pueblo' but also the struggling middle-class professional intellectuals who are fighting the fossilised political system which is incapable of change. It is in this way that a social consciousness produces a 'revolución silenciosa' haunting the town and attempting to dislodge the ruling class that governs in collusion with the consenting upper class and the central government. The 'revolución silenciosa' shows thus a class struggle waged by 'el pueblo', 'en la conciencia de todos' (151) combined with the 'enemigos conscientes del gobierno', the disenchanted middle class, as identified by Vargas Llosa whose next stage occurs with men forming guerrillas (217) and whose destiny is not known in *La mala hora*.[71] That process of social consciousness-raising and political repositioning is next analysed in the novel *Años de fuga*.

69   Dabove, 'Los pasquines', p. 273.
70   Vargas Llosa, *Deicidio*, p. 432.
71   Vargas Llosa, *Deicidio*, p. 432.

CHAPTER FOUR

The Politics and Ideology of Contradiction and Memory

Two novels that share historical contingencies relating to bipartisanism, although they have two opposite protagonists, a liberal and a conservative, are *Años de fuga* and *Una y muchas guerras*. The first belongs to the bogotano upper class and the second to the rural middle class though, at some point, he makes his way to Bogotá city. These two different destinies belong to one and the same environment of the bipartisanism viewed through the memorialisation of the events of 9 April 1948. In these two narratives the model of 'letrado' evolves and his world-view changes as time progresses. To some extent these novels articulate a post-memory of 9 April 1948, given their year of publication: 1979 and 1985, respectively.

Both novels are marked by contradiction. In *Años de fuga* contradiction is seen through the eyes of a liberal intellectual that swims between two riverbanks: one, the liberal side that flirts with the left wing through the trend of revolution suggested by the Movimiento Revolucionario Liberal, MRL, which was in essence a dissident flank of the liberal party, as seen in Chapter One. The evolution of the MRL was influenced by the Cuban revolution which began in 1959, and increased in intensity in the 1960s, when the Colombian guerrilla itself gathered momentum. *Años de fuga* portrays an intellectual who does not commit to the first nor to the second, while enjoying a life of voluntary exile masked by a bohemian life in Paris, as shall be seen.

As for *Una y muchas guerras* politics and ideology are seen through the conservative lens of post-memory. A conservative rural middle class bureaucrat rooted in the old tradition of bipartisanism, dating back to the 1940s and 1950s, is forced to travel to Bogotá and change his way of life to follow his politics, as time progresses, because he is unemployed and needs to feed his family. He is a character who is at once a penpusher and a bureaucrat who experiences the challenges that bipartisan agency offers in the capital city.

The protagonists in these two novels are different from the characters in the previous set of novels. The first are generally characters of the upper class, looking from a position of power and privilege. The second are middle class characters and their relation to politics is essentially marked by party agency. The historical contingencies related to power, social, economic and institutional, as well as cultural issues are present in *Años de fuga* and the class struggle is seen as part of the social process whereby change is brought about through revolution. In *Una y muchas guerras* the need for reform is seen from inside the bipartisan system, which, is shown to be wearing out from the inside, as it were.

Political Contradictions and Voluntary Exile: *Años de fuga*[1]

The novel *Años de fuga*, is the major creative literary work by Plinio A. Mendoza, which was published after it was entered into the Plaza & Janés Colombian literary competition in 1979; it won the award. It is important to see a few aspects of the author's life before I concentrate on his novel, since they offer key insights into the contradictory character of his work. Plinio A. Mendoza, born in 1932 in Tunja (Boyacá), is typical of the Colombian writerly tradition in that his career encompasses both writing and politics. As a writer Mendoza dedicated his life to journalism, short stories and novels; his short stories have been compiled in a volume entitled *El desertor* (1974) which was followed by the novel *Años de fuga* (1979). More other fictional as well as non-fictional works came afterwards, but without doubt his weightiest and best known work is *El olor de la guayaba*, a lengthy interview with Gabriel García Márquez, with

---

1   Plinio A. Mendoza, *Años de fuga* (Bogotá: Plaza & Janés, 1980). Further references to this novel are taken from this edition and given only the page number after quotations in the text.

whom Mendoza maintained a long friendship.[2] Mendoza's close relationship with García Márquez allowed him to be an exceptional and valuable witness to Colombia's most successful writer and, more importantly, his affinity to power and socialism. That affinity to power and politics is also evident in Plinio A. Mendoza's own life and work. Mendoza, for one thing, on a number of occasions, was appointed ambassador by the Colombian government to represent his country in several European countries. For another his political opinions were often controversial and won him general antipathy, especially since the 1990s when his strong views on the unsuitability of socialism and the benefits of capitalism have been perceived as reactionary by his readers, though I will not dwell on his political views since this is beyond the aims of this book.[3]

Notwithstanding his reputation as a writer and journalist in his own right research shows that he belongs to a Colombian upper middle class family, a circumstance that makes Mendoza's an important work of the period covered by this book, since his ideological views offer sharp contrast to that of other Colombian writers. With reference to Mendoza's family, his father, Plinio Mendoza Neira, was a lawyer and a liberal politician who played an important part in the presidential cabinet during the 1950s and, apart from being an outstanding figure in politics, he personally witnessed the events of 9 April 1948, given his close friendship with J.E. Gaitán. As it happened Mendoza's father was one of the two friends walking along with the politician J.E. Gaitán at the moment he was shot to death – a fact that gave the writer immediate access to this crucial historical event.[4] Plinio A.

2 See Plinio Apuleyo Mendoza, *El olor de la guayaba* (Barcelona: Mondadori, 1994).

3 See in this respect Plinio A. Mendoza, Juan Carlos Montaner and Alvaro Vargas Llosa, *Manual del perfecto idiota Latinoamericano* (Barcelona: Plaza & Janés, 1996), a well-known essay in which the author discusses the inconveniences of Latin American left-wing trends and favours liberal capitalism and North American influences on the continent.

4 In an interview on Spanish television Mendoza recalls that on 9 April 1948 as a boy he witnessed the last minutes of Gaitán's life after the shots and before the politician was taken to the hospital. Further details on this testimony may be seen in Víctor Gago interview, *Contemporáneos*, Libertad Digital TV, 28 March 2008, available at <http://www.youtube.com/watch?v=E_pY7pmqRy4> [Accessed 17 February 2009]

Mendoza thus shared with members of his generation significant memories of the events of 9 April 1948 and, more importantly, first-hand experiences concerning pivotal developments of the Colombian political process in the decades that followed. Clearly these historical events were crucial to the author's work and raise questions as to the extent to which they become ideological reflections in Mendoza's work. The question is pertinent since the occurrences narrated in this novel were basically inspired by events developing in an empiric political process. As in the previous novels there is reference in *Años de fuga* to the old political common-places but there is also a sensitivity to the ideological-cum-political Colombian process as it was evolving during those years.

The novel recounts the events of 9 April 1948 when Jorge Eliécer Gaitán was killed and caused *El Bogotazo*. But *Años de fuga* also had additional elements which gave the novel a new dynamic. There were aspects not depicted at all in previous works and only barely touched on García Márquez's work which suggest that novel writing in Colombia was stepping into new territory even though it was keeping the common denominator of politics at its core. The new element in *Años de fuga* was the guerrilla factor featuring 'insider' details about its development in Colombia together with information on its ideological influences. An analysis of the novel compared with historical accounts shows that the novel depicts the growth of guerrilla groups in Colombia during the 1960s and the 1970s, and the direct influence and participation of the revolutionary Cuban regime in this process. The guerrilla group Ejército de Liberación Nacional (ELN) was certainly born in the 1960s and created after the Movimiento Obrero Estudiantil Campesino (MOEC) that brought workers, students and peasants together, and enlisted the support of Cuban leaders. ELN was known for receiving training from Cuba, which adds a new component concerning ideology in the development of the Colombian novel of this period.[5] As for the author, Plinio A. Mendoza, he, like his contemporary García Márquez, belongs to a generation which was intellectually and politically influenced by both the

---

5   The political character of these groups and development within the political process has been addressed in Chapter One.

internal process of Colombian bipartisanism and those external European ideologies that influenced Colombian political life through the first half of the twentieth century.[6] As I have mentioned above Mendoza's father belonged to the liberal ruling class and Mendoza was naturally influenced by the culturally ingrained liberal and conservative bipartisanism and its power conflicts.[7]

The influence of liberalism is crucial to an understanding of the mixed messages transmitted by the novel, though. Culturally, liberalism in Colombia throughout the twentieth century saw itself as being close to socialist thought, which brought about the frequent alliances with factions of leftist unionism, as seen in Chapter One.[8] This, together with the influential ideological trends of Marxism, Leninism and Maoism derived from the world of the 1940s, 1950s and 1960s and also the Cold War imposed by the USA and right-wing governments, and even the Latin American political process, e.g. Chile, need to be taken into account in an analysis of Mendoza's work.[9] Mendoza's text echoes ideas of revolution whose living heroes were Fidel Castro, Ernesto Che Guevara and Régis Debray and, very importantly, the Colombian priest, Camilo Torres, of whom he was a personal friend.[10] It is true that the Cuban revolution led by Fidel Castro and Che Guevara in 1959 significantly influenced

6   In this respect see Mendoza, *El olor*, p. 123.

7   According to Mendoza's words 'en Colombia nacemos liberales o conservadores'; see Víctor Gago interview with Plinio A. Mendoza, in *Contemporáneos*, Libertad Digital TV, 28 March 2008, available at <http://www.youtube.com/watch?v=E_pY7p-mqRy4> [Accessed 17 February 2009]

8   This tendency is clearly seen in three specific examples. First, the liberal reforms pledged though not accomplished by López Pumarejo in the 1930s; second, the liberal J.E. Gaitán wrote a thesis on 'Las ideas socialistas en Colombia' and thirdly, the liberal party affiliated to European socialist liberalism in the 1990s.

9   His literary testimonies such as *La llama y el hielo* or *Aquellos tiempos con Gabo* and even the very *Olor de la guayaba* bring shared experiences with García Márquez, such as the case of Prensa Latina and worldwide journalism, in countries such as Venezuela, France and Spain.

10   Plinio A. Mendoza not only shared generational interests with García Márquez but experiences with him; they both were Camilo Torres's friends since their university years. In this respect see *Olor*, pp. 127–128.

the left wing not only in Colombia but across Latin America.[11] It is also true that the Argentinian Ernesto Che Guevara together with the French intellectual, Régis Debray, became important intellectual figures in Latin America for their revolutionary participation as well as their works on the ideological significance of the revolutionary ethos. As for Camilo Torres, he was a deeply religious man who became a priest, trained intellectually at the University of Louvain (Belgium), founded the Christian movement 'Frente Unido' and carried out important social action to feed the poor and create among them a revolutionary conscience. Camilo Torres eventually joined the Ejército de Liberación Nacional (ELN) but he was killed in his first engagement with government troops – Camilo has been a revolutionary icon in Colombia ever since. Thus Mendoza's sources in many cases come from actual historical figures, among them Camilo Torres, Fidel Castro, Che Guevara, Régis Debray and the Vázquez Castaño brothers, Fabio and Manuel, as well as the Movimiento Revolucionario Liberal (MRL) and the guerrilla organisation ELN, as we shall see below.

The Memorialisation of Politics

Años de Fuga depicts a Colombian man recounting his political acts through his memories while living a voluntary and relaxed exile in Paris. The story develops in three days, over a weekend, in which the central character, Ernesto Melo, is relaxing at a party in Paris with some Latin American 'exiled' friends. Although the story develops in the present

---

11   The influence marked those years because it was intended to make a 'revolución en la revolución'. Detailed minutiae about the influence of the 'Ministerio de la Revolución' and the Cuban Revolution on the Latin American revolutionary movements is found in Jorge G. Castañeda, *La utopía desarmada* (Bogotá: Tercer Mundo, 1994), pp. 63–106 (p. 82). See also Carlos Uribe Celis, *La mentalidad del colombiano. Cultura y sociedad en el siglo XX* (Bogotá: Alborada, 1992), pp. 102, 168–175; See also Gonzalo Cataño, *Educación y estructura social* (Bogotá: Plaza & Janés, 1989), pp. 191–197.

time it narrates a complex account of past events which happened to the protagonist mainly in Colombia, but also in Chile. Insight into more than forty years of events is provided in a continuous retrospection which narrates how Ernesto experienced the events of 9 April 1948 as well as his political involvement with the Latin American revolutionary trends of the 1960s and the direction that such tendencies took in Colombia afterwards. Focusing in particular on the *bogotano* middle-class 'intellectual' who assumed a political leftist stance in his youth, Ernesto's memories also reflect a life of personal conflicts related to the day-to-day demands of his middle age spent in the 1980s in Paris. Important in this narration is the portrayal of how leftist groups developed as new political forces in order to claw back the power denied them by traditional Colombian bipartisanism. Time, thus, is divided in the novel between a) the present in which Ernesto is a 45 year-old man enjoying life with friends while letting b) the past emerge via an extended narration covering over forty years. This past subsequently develops in three different moments: (i) the recent past: Ernesto's exile and third period of residence in Paris; (ii) an intermediate past: Ernesto's voluntary 'fuga' from Colombia and his second period in Paris, and (iii) a remote past: Ernesto's vague memories of his childhood and adolescence in, and then flight from, Paris as a young student. These three periods of time overlap with each other in a convoluted sequence. A productive way to follow this progression is to divide the narration time into three moments as follows: remote past, intermediate past, and recent past, linking them to the present since it is crucial to this analysis to unfold the narrated events in such a way that it maintains a sense of their historical evolution.

In the remote past Ernesto provides insight into his childhood, life with his family as a teenage student, his classmates and the witnessing of Gaitán's assassination on 9 April 1948 (329). Ernesto gives an account of family events such as the early loss of his parents, his closeness with his uncle and his teenage friends with whom he has his first political experiences (p. 263). In the intermediate past Ernesto recalls days spent back in Bogotá after his studies, the philosophical trends of his generation and the guerrilla movement which began in the 1960s. In the recent past which links to the present, Ernesto, now 37 years old, leaves the country, voluntarily, escaping to Paris where he meets María and they go to live in Deyá (Mallorca) and then Paris. Separated from María, frustrated and not very clear about what to do with his own life, Ernesto then travels to Chile invited by Allende's supporters; he stays there briefly up until Allende is overthrown and killed in a coup d'etat. This is how Ernesto, along with a few of his surviving friends, manages to obtain exile in the French embassy and get back to Paris for the third time to find himself at the party with which the story began.

Plinio A. Mendoza's novel *Años de fuga* presents a particular case of ideology in terms of its liberal-conservative disenchantment. This disenchantment is created by a duplicitous position between 'class consciousness' and belonging to the upper class (including its cultural inheritance of bipartisanism) as mirrored by Ernesto, the protagonist. R.L. Williams briefly comments that *Años de fuga* is a novel of adventures that gives 'an account of the protagonist's experiences in Paris',[12] while Wolfgang A. Luchting's view is that Mendoza's novel is 'infinitely entertaining, though self-indulgent and exemplarily facile'.[13] Luchting suggests that the novel's characteristic bohemian ethos is 'leavened', however, 'by memories of the protagonist's childhood, adolescence and early manhood [...] and by political memoir about Camilo Torres'.[14] Narrated throughout by an informant living in voluntary exile, the story articulates the need for personal redemption that persuades Ernesto to confess to the ideological influences that youngsters of his generation received and which drove them to political action. Nevertheless there is something false about the class consciousness which emerges in the novel. Ernesto's contradictions become apparent through his reflections on 'conciencia social' and his own social class, temperament and world-view, as I shall show below.

---

12   Raymond Leslie Williams, *The Colombian Novel 1844–1987* (Austin: University of Texas Press, 1991), p. 196.

13   Wolfgang A. Luchting, Untitled Review, in *World Literature Today*, 54, 3, University of Oklahoma (1980), p. 409. Also available at <http://www.jstor.org/stable/40135088> [Accessed 9 November 2009]

14   Luchting, Untitled Review, p. 409.

The Politics of Populism's Reminiscence

These contradictions are echoed in the novel through three important ideological themes, which are the figure of the 'revolutionary', the meaning of the 'revolution' during the period 1960s–1980s, and the issue of the upper-class 'intellectual'. *Años de fuga* exhibits the contradictions of a worn-out bipartisan hegemony that led to an opposition based on the armed movement. Reading *Años de fuga* on the basis of Eagleton's view in which ideology is regarded also as a 'set of beliefs which coheres and inspires a specific group or class in the pursuit of political interests judged to be desirable', I argue that this story expresses both politics and ideology by modelling the story on historical references and names while revealing a 'class struggle' in which class and cultural contradictions are brought to light.[15]

Ernesto's autobiographical story first describes the upper class worldview that characterises his childhood which will be transformed later on during his teenage years, as we shall see. Ernesto's early link to a world of politics and privilege comes via his father, who is portrayed as a professional, a lawyer (127) recognised also as a journalist of *El Tiempo* (122–123) and a politician (178); a liberal 'líder' who was 'presidente de la Cámara', a liberal 'líder' of the 1930s (64) expected, if he were still alive, to be 'en la presidencia' (178); all of these details offer a picture of a tightly ideological network.[16] Hence high social connections and friendships with highly ranked politicians including J.E. Gaitán seemed natural (183) to Ernesto's family, 'tu papá era muy amigo de Gaitán' (183). Ernesto's father is depicted as a disciplined journalist and a lawyer whose legal performances

15   Terry Eagleton, *Ideology: An Introduction* (London: Verso, 1991), p. 44.
16   *El Tiempo* has historically backed the liberal party; between 1938–1942 Eduardo Santos Montejo, its owner, became president of Colombia and other members of the family have also been in power in recent years: during the writing of this research Francisco Santos Calderón, for instance, was vice-president between 2002 to 2010; his cousin, Juan Manuel Santos Calderón, was a member of the same government's cabinet and later elected president for the following period 2010–2014, and successively re-elected for 2014–2018.

are broadcast on the radio: 'que tal jefe. Estuvo magnífico anoche. Lo oí
por la radio'.[17] As someone who is well known Ernesto's father is recognised by the public: 'cuando el auto se detiene [...] reconocen a papá, se
quitan la gorra, salud, jefe [...] vamos encontrando gentes que saludan a
papá quitándose el sombrero' (123). The characteristics of the upper class
are also suggested by the area where Ernesto's family live (123) and the
fine music they listen to (125). Although Ernesto lost his parents early on
in his childhood, he then lives with his aunties and they also had servants, 'las sirvientas' (126) and he studies at a Catholic boarding school
(128). Ernesto's uncle Eduardo, 'diplomático y hombre de mundo' (64),
married to a wealthy Colombian woman, works in the United States as a
representative of the Colombian government; in general his comments
are not exempt from the political sarcasm that typified the members
of the parties: 'aquí le traigo padre, este hijo de un liberal comecuras,
dice sonriendo' (128) or 'Espero que los curitas no vayan a volverte godo'
(182). Likewise Ernesto's mother's brief reference to politics is nevethe-
less explicit, stressing social privilege: 'una luchadora. Siempre al lado de
los pobres [...] cuando triunfó al fin el partido liberal [...] Olaya Herrera
la citó en un discurso' (183–184).

This power and privilege is contrasted with the poverty, manners
and habits of people from poor areas of the city visited by Ernesto and his
friends, in other words, Gaitán's followers, with whom remarkable ideological differences are highlighted too. They are generally perceived as rabble
('chusma'). Ernesto sees them as a 'compacta marejada de caras mestizas, de
ropas mugrientas, de olores agrios, la habitual muchedumbre de los barrios
del sur [...] de la plaza de Mercado [...] repitiendo el estribillo: Gaitán sí,
otro no!' (263). 'Chusma', as the middle and upper classes refer to poorer
people, hints at the class barrier which separates Ernesto from the 'mob'

17   Political and legal trials were broadcast by radio stations and were extensively popular
      and passionately followed by listeners. These aspects are connected to rhetoric and
      oratory and are analysed in greater depth in Chapter Five.

from poor areas such as 'barrios del sur', when visited by Ernesto and his friends when they were teenagers.[18]

It is during this period until his coming of age that Ernesto's worldview starts to change, particularly as a result of his experiences with Gaitán's followers. They see people living on menial jobs who often go hungry; hunger was an issue raised by Camilo Torres, 'en Bogotá, enteramente entregado a oscuros apostolados de barrio [...] distribu[yendo] tazas de chocolate entre los indigentes de los barrios del sur' (66). But Ernesto is positioned at the opposite end of the scale; there are very few people who are at his social level (264). A similar contrast is seen in the way Gaitán was called by the upper class who linked him to his followers and the lower class: 'el indio, el negro, así lo llaman'. Gaitán is shown as getting ideologically close to his followers when he is depicted as an active politician on the Colombian stage addressing his people: 'Gaitán es un modesto hijo del pueblo [...] el poder es una hacienda [...] el poder es un privilegio de clase [...] coto de caza de la oligarquía!' (263–264). The 'oligarquía' fought by Gaitán emerges in *Años de fuga* even in informal conversations held between Ernesto and his two closest friends in which class difference is clearly highlighted: Camilo is a 'niño bien' who is imbued with the 'oligarca' attitude but who later becomes a priest and 'guerrillero'. Strikingly the mention of the riots provoked by Gaitán's assassination in the novel mirrors the deep class division, political affinities and antipathies prevalent in Colombian society at the time. For instance, Vidales's mother supports the conservative party which is in power at the time and she thinks that all Gaitán did was to upset the crowd, the poorest of the poor who are not only drunk but also 'comunistas' (334). In contrast the youngsters Ernesto and Vidales interpret the situation as a 'revolution' in the making and expect also that 'la fórmula es junta revolucionaria de

---

18   The language, expressing deprecation towards the lower class, concurs with the analysis by Sharpless in relation to the manner with which the upper class referred to Gaitán's followers particularly, and generally as the 'deprived'. See Richard Sharpless, *Gaitán of Colombia: A Political Biography* (Pittsburgh: Pittsburgh University Press, 1978), p. 124.

gobierno' (333); soon they hear on the radio that an agreement has been made between the president Ospina Pérez and members of the liberal party, at which point Ernesto and Vidales conclude that everything has been a farce: 'Qué farsa! Liberales y conservadores se ponen de acuerdo por arriba, mientras al pueblo lo masacran en las calles. La burguesía se une' (338). The unexpected coalition makes the two young upper-class men think more deeply about their decisions on their careers and future. Ernesto and Camilo need to decide between 'foreseeable destinies', or rather pursue more 'meaningful lives'. Ernesto, Camilo and their friends, for example, can afford to plan their future though they need to choose between either the safe side or to commit to a social cause.

Upper Class, Privilege and Life Options

The 'destinos previsibles' meant for them to pick and choose a conventional career, which was generally being a lawyer, 'seguir una carrera, ganar dinero, casarse, reproducirse, envejecer y morirse' (65). A good example of this life-option was their friend Vidales, who later became a lawyer involved in traditional liberal-conservative politics. Though a member of the privileged class Ernesto Melo is tempted to become a rebel in his own right and join the 'revolution'. Camilo, for instance, thought that people in poverty 'suffered', and that such a condition should be changed. Ernesto for his part chose to join 'JUCO', Juventud Comunista, but also chose to go and pursue his studies in Paris.[19] Ernesto and Camilo Torres thought that life should be challenging and fulfilling, which could be achieved through social commitment to the suffering poor. Camilo subsequently followed his spiritual calling and became a priest in order to make his life meaningful (65) and, as it happened, Ernesto met him years later in Paris at a time when Camilo was already ordained and dressed

---

19   'JUCO', as it was commonly called in informal parlance, was in the 1960s and 1970s the youth branch of the Colombian communist party (Juventud Comunista, from the initials in Spanish).

in his sacerdotal attire, 'con sotana, en París, tres años después. [Camilo] Iba para Lovaina' (66).[20]

With regard to the depiction of social and political change, the most significant episode is the change of gear in the country's political process, which galvanised various guerrilla groups during the 1960s. *Años de fuga* refers to how a generation saw the need to create a fair society and the ideal of communism as a means to achieve this. It was not only the anger of the social destitution witnessed by members of Ernesto's generation but also encouragement coming from the Cuban revolution which made the ideal of a revolution in Colombia a distinct possibility. In other words, the young generation that witnessed not only the events of 9 April 1948 but were appalled by poverty and political repression thought that 'la única solución para la miseria de todos los explotados de Colombia, no podía ser otra que una revolución como la que Fidel Castro estaba haciendo en Cuba' (66). After the events of 9 April 1948 there was widespread frustration at the agreements achieved by party members and the inclusion of liberals in the conservative cabinet. We see this disenchantment in the novel in the dialogues between Vidales and Ernesto in which they reject the coalition as a farce and argue that 'La burguesía está unida' and that the liberals and conservatives have joined forces in order to 'massacre' the people in the streets (338). The perception of politics as 'a farce' leads them later on to join the communist party. Ernesto was impressed by Camilo Torres's devotion to the poor. It was the vocation of the young Camilo Torres that drove him to reflect on the need for change and reform; he firmly believed that a large proportion of his society was poor and suffered as a result. Camilo's convictions were put into practice when, according to Ernesto's recollection, he combined his catholic faith with social action: his 'vocación' drove him to support and feed the poor, to blend with them in the poorest areas. His friends saw him as: 'entregado a apostolados de barrio' (66). At the beginning of the 1960s, the political affiliation evolved towards

---

20   Important observations on his faith and convictions are found in Camilo Torres, *Cristianismo y Revolución* (México: Era, 1970); and also in Walter Broderick, *Camilo el cura guerrillero* (Bogotá: El Labrador, 1987).

the liberal party, and Ernesto and his old classmate Rodrigo Vidales, both joined a political liberal group called Movimiento Revolucionario Liberal (MRL); they were thinking of setting up an organisation with 'orientación Castrista' that would take up arms and thereby create enough pressure to change political life in Colombia.[21] The conviction that a revolution, like that led in Cuba by Fidel Castro, would bring the end to the misery of the exploited population in Colombia (66) encouraged Ernesto and his friend Vidales to initiate a clandestine organisation. Ernesto reflects on the way his generation thought, 'así pensaban entonces' (66) and, thus, the only solution to solve the problem of all 'explotados de Colombia' would be a Cuban-style Revolution:

> Mientras Camilo reunía sus juntas de acción communal en los barrios [...] sus amigos [...] viajaban a Cuba. Cuba amenazada; los discursos de Fidel; la fraternidad tumul-tuosa [...] plazas hirvientes de banderas y consignas; los milicianos, tan jóvenes, acechando desde el malecón o en las terrazas del Vedado [...] temiendo una invasión norteamericana [...] aquello los había marcado profundamente [...] Se interesaban por primera vez en problemas de organización militar, en los manuales guerrilleros del propio Che. (66–67)

These recollections suggest that the Cuban process, the atmosphere of revolution, the anti-American climate and the fear of a North American invasion 'marked them thoroughly', although they saw that a Revolution in Colombia looked like an almost impossible project. Ernesto's memories recall in some detail the process that followed: hosting meetings with university friends, 'dirigentes universitarios' and colleagues affiliated to the MRL, some of them with clear political ideas and some without; they

---

21 As mentioned in Chapter One MRL was a liberal dissident group led by former president López Pumarejo's son Alfonso López Michelsen, considered by the young generation at the time as a radical wing of the liberal party. Later in time MRL was dismantled and López Michelsen became a liberal president for the period 1974–1978, after the last presidency of Frente Nacional. Further information about the influence of this political group on this generation is found in Alvaro Tirado Mejía, 'El MRL y la cultura', in *Credencial Historia*, 3, March 1990. Available at <http://www.ban-repcultural.org/blaavirtual/revistas/credencial/marzo1990/marzo2.htm> [Accessed 21 March 2009]

were students belonging to different social layers, novices and completely unskilled in handling weapons, all of them were poor (many had been born in little villages) wearing worn-out clothes and shoes and being hungry most of the time, but nevertheless they were enthusiastic followers of Marxist ideas and 'Castrismo' (67–68). Such ideas were part of an inevitable trend happening not only in their continent but even in other parts of the world: 'Toda la América Latina respiraba el mismo aire de agitación [...] surgían muchos grupos armados en muchos países: Venezuela, Perú, Guatemala y aun Argentina' and beyond; in Algeria, for example, Algerians had their Frente de Liberación Nacional (FLN) (71–75). Then it seemed to become more real when Ernesto's friend, Rodrigo Vidales, went to Havana to talk to Fidel Castro and Che Guevara. Fidel Castro who in his time had witnessed personally what had happened on 9 April 1948 in Bogotá gave them some advice: 'él había visto durante El Bogotazo el pueblo anarquizado, desbordado, su insurrección liquidada por falta de organización' (76). Castro also told Vidales that it would not be easy:

> la agitación de masas, el trabajo legal, todo eso tenía su importancia, pero no había que hacerse ilusiones, chico, la lucha armada en Colombia, como en todas partes donde el imperialismo y las oligarquías se sintieran realmente amenazadas sería inevitable [...] había que formar cuadros, entrenarlos, ir constituyendo ya un dispositivo de lucha [...] el asunto iba en serio, Fidel ofrecía entrenarles gente en Cuba. (76)

Accordingly, the idea of a revolution was no longer a 'quimera' nor a simple students' game or a slogan written on a red flag, it had become an urgent enterprise that required planning and determination. And the project grew gradually, not just in the city but also across the country particularly in areas where workers were concentrated through union membership, in places where a 'conciencia revolucionaria' was developing, which meant they could be trained in Cuba (76–77). Tactics and strategy were provided by the Cuban leaders. Hints on how to select individuals and instruction on the theory and practice of revolution as imparted by Che Guevara and Régis Debray are also narrated by Ernesto (78–79). Ernesto's account suggests how the men selected were instructed in techniques such as communication systems 'prepared by the Soviets', and also encouraged with ideological principles such as Che Guevara's motto: 'el primer deber de un revolucionario es hacer la revolución' (80). Ideological resilience was also reinforced as a result of Régis Debray's analysis of how to use ideas in order to unleash a 'proceso revolucionario' (79–80). Ernesto draws attention to their determination in pursuing the revolution, such that postponing or compromising the 'lucha guerrillera' would be simply 'oportunismo, [o] electorerismo' (80). As a job needs to be done, '[la] lucha guerrillera' should go ahead while proceeding on two levels: 'uno legal de agitación, electoral inclusive [...] y otro clandestino' (76–77), to avoid being simply agitators without political impact.

The thought that Colombia lacked the conditions to carry out a revolution was counterpoised by the idea that 'la coyuntura insurreccional podía crearse', reinforced by Che's suggestion that the 'actividad agitacional y electoral era transitoria' (73–80). Electoral campaigning with the MRL was used to introduce 'adoctrinación ideológica' to 'obreros de la Texas', and many of their leaders later took up weapons rather than believing in elections any more (74). They believed that their duty was to create a 'conciencia revolucionaria' along with 'agitación social' (75) via popular marches chanting 'Cuba sí Yankis No' or 'revolución, revolución, revolución'. They wanted to exert pressure on the traditional political leaders and thereby create the 'coyuntura apropiada para otras formas de lucha' (75); it was the Latin American trend at the time.

The Politics of Mutation

Nevertheless the ideals of Ernesto's generation later on turned to disenchantment with the revolutionary methods and procedures of his comrades. He distanced himself from the revolutionary process and left for exile in Paris. In his reflections Ernesto is in no doubt that they had been betrayed by the Revolution. Among the dead was his classmate, Camilo Torres (66–77). As his disappointment mounted, Ernesto thought that 'Camilo', the 'revolución' and all those illusions had died once and for all (17), and that he and his friends had no idea 'de quién o quienes habían sido en realidad instrumento' (67). Many of his revolutionary friends were dispersed throughout the country 'libres de toda cucaracha revolucionaria' and became 'abogados, funcionarios, diplomáticos; Vidales, senador', or even began their own private businesses. Finally, in his present circumstances, in Europe, Ernesto comes to the realisation that everything was no more than an illusion; 'podía ver toda la ilusión lírica que había en aquellas previsiones' (69). Ernesto's friend Vidales became an 'abogado pobre, defensor de presos políticos', first as a 'comunista' and later as a 'liberal de izquierda' (70). As for Ernesto – a thinly veiled allegorisation of Plinio Apuleyo Mendoza himself – he is revealed to be caught halfway between the 'lyric illusion' of his younger years when his liberalism blended into communism, and his later years when his liberalism blended into conservatism. The novel is valuable in that it demonstrates the resilience of the liberal-conservative alliance within a section of the Colombian middle class, even when exposed to other more illiberal strains of thought such as communism. As a reflection of the 'letrado' tradition and specifically through its authorial ideology this novel shows the ideological sinuosities that inspired a specific group or class 'in the pursuit of political interests judged to be desirable', as theory suggests.[22]

Partisan Agency and Disenchantment: *Una y muchas guerras*[23]

Among the scant critical reviews on *Una y muchas guerras* is R.L. Williams's view that sees Aristizábal as a 'writer that pursued fundamentally a modern fiction'.[24] Writers pursuing modern fiction in Colombia,

22 Eagleton, *Ideology*, p. 44.
23 Alonso Aristizábal, *Una y muchas guerras* (Bogotá: Planeta, 1985). Further references to this novel are taken from this edition and given only the page number after quotations in the text.
24 See R.L. Williams, *The Colombian Novel*, p. 195.

accordingly, tend to exhibit 'their social agenda more explicitly by portraying an identifiable Colombian empirical reality'.[25] It is thus that the
novel *Una y muchas guerras* might be seen as one of those works identified by R.L. Williams as heterogeneous in the sense that it reproduces a
narrative of marginal and repressed discourses that surfaced in the 1980s
in Colombia. The novel, published in 1985, has not been widely studied
apart from brief lines dedicated to it by Pineda Botero, for example, who
in few lines dispatches it under the easy label of 'la Violencia'.[26] Aristizábal
is an author of short stories which have received some attention but critical work on this novel is practically non-existent.[27] Though published
in the 1980s, *Una y muchas guerras* belongs to a traditional set of novels
that at first seem to deal with issues related to conflicts between liberals
and conservatives during the first half of the twentieth century.[28] If, as
it is said, this novel is autobiographical, Aristizábal's novel sets its story
in a period which stretches approximately from the 1930s to the 1940s
in Pensilvania, the author's town of birth located in the department of
Caldas. Like *Años de fuga* Alonso Aristizábal's novel uses memory as its
main structuring device. Seen in this way the novel reproduces images
of political bipartisan struggles characteristic of the 1950s; hanging onto
power becomes the main priority for politicians and civil servants, since
office brings with it permanent employment. Another aspect disclosed
in this novel is nepotism via job inheritance, when employment is passed
to family members. *Una y muchas guerras* shares with *Años de fuga* the
common denominator of 9 April 1948 though in *Una y muchas guerras* the *Bogotazo* is referred to tangentially, and exists as a backdrop.
Nevertheless, in common with the previous novels there is the inclusion

25   Ibid., p. 187.
26   Alvaro Pineda Botero, *Del mito a la posmodernidad* (Bogotá: Tercer Mundo, 1990),
      pp. 89–90.
27   Brief notes on Aristizábal's short stories are found in Isaías Peña Gutiérrez, 'De la
      niebla a los muros', in *Boletín Cultural y Bibliográfico*, 21, 2 (Bogotá: Colcultura, 1984).
      Available at <http://www.banrepcultural.org/blaavirtual/publicacionesbanrep/
      boletin/boleti3/bol2/niebla.htm> [Accessed 10 April 2010]
28   Ibid., p. 141.

of the 'letrado' figure embodied by the narrator who writes the memoirs as an amanuensis who assists the protagonist; he is the incarnation of the conservative party in the small town called Pensilvania, and, true to 'letrado' type, he writes.

From Bureaucracy to Unemployment

The narration tells the story of the life of a man called Rubelio and his family while living in Pensilvania, a provincial town, and subsequently in Bogotá. Rubelio is a bureaucrat who works at the municipal 'concejo' (the council), while supporting the conservative party, but he also writes for the local newspaper, *La Patria*. Characteristically a troublemaker, Rubelio is stubborn, and a jealous and bullying father; he likes fighting and his passion for the conservative party fills his entire life to an extent that makes his family miserable. The men in the town are either liberal or conservative and, at the beginning of the novel, the town witnesses continuous political clashes instigated by local politicians. Rubelio's life revolves around his wife Sola and his family. Sola is a woman who is more than a simple believer, she is a 'sufferer' for Catholicism. Sola is devoted to her husband and children, and she struggles to keep her husband's political passion under control. Sola's 'wars' are in general her struggles to keep her family united amidst the troubles caused by her husband initially and later by her sons too; but her sufferings principally derive from the family's lack of money as they are not a well-off family. As a numerous family, they struggle on a daily basis to get the shopping for dinner, often having to resort to asking for credit in the local shop. One day Rubelio is given the sack for being a liability in his job (63) and, although he is promised another job as the town's attorney, this never arrives; instead they offer his son Rubelito an appointment in the telegraph office. Unemployed Rubelio starts working as a penpusher (63), but the money he earns is not sufficient for the whole family. To make things worse their son, employed at the telegraph office, does not help out as expected because this 'Rubelito' becomes an alcoholic, a gambler, a womaniser, though he carries on living at his parents's house (91). Eventually Rubelio and his wife leave for Bogotá following their oldest daughter, Carmen, who gives them hope that things may get better in the big city (111). There Rubelio begins his job hunt through his political conservative connections but he is unsuccessful and becomes disillusioned. While economically dependent on his daughter Rubelio goes daily to meet up with friends (124) until he is finally offered a bureaucratic job provided that he is presented as a liberal (128), which Rubelio refuses because that for him would be 'voltearse', as he is a die-hard conservative (129). Once Rubelio's wife makes him realise that the job is more important than politics (125) since all they need is a job to make ends meet, he starts working as a notary's legal clerk and also starts attending Gaitán's political meetings, although he still feels his allegiance to the conservatives. The day Gaitán is assassinated Rubelio manages to get home early. Older, tired and ill, Rubelio goes back to Pensilvania to live though he is overwhelmed by his troubled sons (190). Finally Virgilio, the writer son, goes back to live in Bogotá and closes the notebooks where he has recorded the story.

In *Una y muchas guerras* Alonso Aristizábal offers a story of disillusionment based on the discovery that political bipartisanism is no more than an illusion that destroys family lives in a world where livelihood is the imperative. This disenchantment has been articulated in novels such as *El día del odio* in characters such as Olmos who, although a supporter of Gaitán, distrusts politicians. But if *El día del odio* mirrors the nascent urban life and its precarious political organisation which destroys the rural culture of characters such as Tránsito, in *Una y muchas guerras* we see how the bureaucratic machine created by bipartisanism makes belonging to a political party indispensable for a job. The job is what keeps Rubelio, his wife and family going as a small urban middle-class family.

Rubelio's job is in the municipal council, which is a representative political institution in which members of the two parties can sit once they are elected, and it employs people based on their political affiliation. Rubelio is a conservative whose membership card gives him a sense of entitlement that brings him into conflict with liberals. The political festive event shows a top politician, Gilberto Alzate Avendaño (63) – the real name of a far right-wing conservative politician of the 1950s known for his rhetorical dexterity – visiting the town to take part in a parade in which 'encendidos vivas al partido conservador' and 'vivas al partido liberal' are in competition (39), stimulated by alcohol (51). Rubelio's over-zealous political passion makes him a liability and in turn he gets the sack and both his breadwinning and recognition in the town come to an end. In this way Rubelio's real life in *Una y muchas guerras* addresses two specific dilemmas of a society at large. These two dilemmas are a) the beginning of the end of a period of strong rural bipartisanism and b) the transition to a new urban capitalist way of life in which that bipartisan ideology is deconstructed. The novel evokes Colombia at the crossroads between the two ways of life, rural bipartisanism on the one hand and urban capitalism on the other.

The first part of the novel depicts the way of life in rural towns during the years before the assassination of Gaitán in Bogotá. It is through a character like Rubelio that we see how political power is 'reproduced' and 'maintained' within the bipartisan system he inhabits, to use Eagleton's terms. It is through Rubelio that the 'largely concealed structure of values which informs and underlies' the ideology of bipartisanism is articulated, particularly via the ways in which people connect with the power structure and power relations of that society. These particularities, as we will see, are embodied in the protagonist and those who surround him with 'modes of feeling, valuing, perceiving and believing' and in relation to his grip on political power.[29]

Rubelio is a bureaucrat and as such he epitomises the functions of the bipartisan system in Colombia during the 1940s and 1950s. Though he exists as a short-hand for a number of real people of the time, he is fictional. Rather like the Spanish writer Benito Pérez Galdós, Aristizábal also includes in his novel real people who managed town politics at the time such as the far-right wing conservative Gilberto Alzate Avendaño. Gilberto Alzate Avendaño is an empirical individual who exerted a strong influence on right-wing conservative followers in the 1940s as a result of his oratorical skills, together with Laureano Gómez. Thus the 'discursive justification' is maintained through the 'viva' to parties, as 'viva el partido

---

29　Terry Eagleton, *Literary Theory: An Introduction* (Oxford: Blackwell, 1996), p. 13.

conservador' and 'viva el partido liberal' (39, 51), suggesting how ideology
is conveyed directly through political speeches and public meetings as
well as via a bureaucratic machinery run by parties as public institutions,
e.g. the council.[30] Jobs are supplied through 'clientelismo' which makes of
political parties and the bureaucracy an institutional machinery sustained
and maintained by two parties in power. Yet, when Rubelio was sacked
from the council politicians offered him a job that then never arrives (63),
and this fact expresses the twist and turns of bipartisanism. It points out
the typical moment when the former bureaucrat struggles to survive as a
result of falling out with a powerful ally from the political network and
finds himself without friends to put him back in his job. He later has
to migrate to the capital, Bogotá. It is at that moment when important
aspects of both job creation in that political environment and the real
needs of people in rural towns are revealed. As a bureaucrat and journalist
Rubelio is a middle-class man who necessarily depends on his salary and
the meagre salary paid to him for his reporting by the newspaper. As we
have seen above, the family struggled on a daily basis to get the dinner on
the table, 'viviendo casi de la caridad' (64, 111). Someone who looked like
a man of power fades in the day-to-day tragedy of life, as there are days
without breakfast, resorting to local credit in the neighbourhood shops to
make ends meet for the household (64). His failure is, in effect, the failure
of the bipartisan system.

Transition: Bipartisanism and Agency at the City's Open Market

Rubelio's impecunious situation throws into relief the twilight of the
rural conservative 'letrado'. Rubelio is the archetypal 'letrado' character,
first, because his job is about writing as a secretary and, second, because
he wrote simultaneously for the town's newspaper *La Patria*. *La Patria* is
a conservative-oriented newspaper, which is still published in Colombia.
But, more significantly, as a 'letrado' we see Rubelio when he loses his job

---

30   On 'discursive justification', see Eagleton, *Ideology*, p. 37.

in the municipal council and has to work only as a casual writer for the
paper, as well as working as a penpusher, which means as a quasi-lawyer or
writer of all sorts of documents – a character similar to Olmos in *El día
del odio*, or the notary in *Siervo sin tierra*, or the judge and señor Benjamín
in *La mala hora*. By writing 'memoriales' and legal documents, 'Rubelio
trabajaba en su oficinita para hacer memoriales y tinterillar' (63) and this
will also be his job later on in Bogotá. Bogotá then becomes the only way
out for this character and his family who now struggle for survival. The
crucial turning point is represented by the road to Bogotá where they
place their hopes because there 'hay de todo para hacer' (111); their relatives are in the sales business (110) and they are optimistic: 'ya verá que
salimos adelante' (117). The city also shows Rubelio and his wife an open
world, for instance, in which the young are interested in reading and reading groups, '[los] muchachos se encuentran para leer no sé que clase de
libros' (71), but there are also the pressures of increased rent, 'la plata ya
no me alcanza para nada y la vida sube cada día' (129–131); also the need
for their children to be educated, 'Cuándo será que trabajo en algo para
ver si entra a estudiar su bachillerato completo' (129) and clothes so he
can impress in the city (131). Eventually his job search is worked out via
political 'amiguismo' (120). This sort of legwork has to be done in 'cafés'
and political meeting places until he, paradoxically, meets the people he
passionately dislikes: liberals. But approaching his 'copartidarios' fails as
they simply dismiss Rubelio rather than help him: '¿Es usted el recomen-
dado de [...]? los liberales están mandando' (124). When a liberal friend
offers Rubelio a job he feels disillusioned, since his own friends are not
ready to help him despite his political passion. The most humiliating part
for Rubelio is the fact that he has to be presented as a liberal in order to
get a job: 'Yo le consigo puesto si deja que lo presente como liberal' (128).
That is the only way to be in the bureaucracy's employ. Throughout the
novel Rubelio's feelings of loyalty towards a party within the old bipartisan system is apparent. Rubelio is the last heir of that generation of rural
old-fashioned men forged in the old guard of bipartisanism, and that is
why he feels offended when offered a job by the liberals: 'hoy me dijeron
que me volteara a liberal y me conseguían puesto' (129). At first there
is no question about 'voltearse', but they live in the hour of need and

money is the imperative: '[si] recibiera siquiera algo de corresponsalías, pero no mandé más porque no me publican ya [...] ¡Lo que nos servían esos chequecitos! (125). That imperative implies also that there is no difference between liberals and conservatives – both are 'de los mismos', as suggested in Siervo's words in *Siervo sin tierra*, or 'los mismos con las mismas', as in *La mala hora*. The whole situation, which in the end despite his political objections makes Rubelio understand that getting a job and working for a living is more important than fighting for a political cause, points to the pressures exerted by capitalist ideology: liberal and conservative ideas are revealed to be one and the same and in the last analysis less important than urban capitalism.

This new situation presented to Rubelio signals that the two parties compete with each other to stay in power, even while adapting to the spirit of capitalism. Once Rubelio takes the job in the notary office his home finances improve and this makes Rubelio feel better off; in the urban capitalist world, the novel suggests, everything is exchangeable, even ideology. In fact Rubelio demonstrates this when attending Gaitán's political meetings with his liberal friends even though he still feels his allegiance to the conservative party. Gaitán meetings were carried out in the 'teatro municipal' and were called 'viernes culturales'. These meetings are important since they are articulated to the role of entertainment played by these politicians and also to rhetoric and oratory, as analysed in the next chapter. Rubelio finds also that his sons Héctor and Virgilio are attending Gaitán's meetings at the 'teatro municipal'.[31] Thus Rubelio's life in the city (joining Gaitán's movement, working with liberals) reveals that the idea that in Colombia (where the novel's space is situated), people are born either liberal or conservative is false.[32] It also suggests that the old way of ruling the country

31   It is worth noticing that the 'teatro municipal' in Bogotá was re-named 'Teatro Jorge Eliécer Gaitán' on 8 March 1973. See at <http://www.teatrojorgeeliecer.gov.co/index.php?option=comcontent&view=article&id=127&Itemid=107> [Accessed 19 September 2009]

32   According to Santa and Mendoza's theory. See also the declaration by Plinio A. Mendoza to Víctor Gago: 'en Colombia nacemos liberales o conservadores', in an interview in *Contemporáneos*, in Libertad Digital TV, 28 March 2008. Also available

held the country back, blinding it with its rhetoric of a two-party system which, deep down, was based on non-participation.

In *Una y muchas guerras* the author uses the archive of memory and thereby creates a political memoir inspired by the times he 'acaso conoció de niño y por referencias de sus familiares'.[33] The novel reveals the manipulation of power at different levels caused by a misleading bipartisanism as well as the real stress families and society were put through in their material struggle to survive. It also expresses the ideological shift in Colombian society from an old system of reliance on a non-participative bipartisanism towards a new system in which employment is driven by a modern, urban-based capitalist system.

at <http://www.youtube.com/watch?v=E_pY7pmqRy4> [Accessed 17 February 2009]

33   See Pedro Gómez Valderrama's presentation of *Una y muchas guerras* (Bogotá: Planeta, 1985).

CHAPTER FIVE

The Politics and Ideology of 'Letrados' and Utopia

The key term linking culture to politics as articulated in the Colombian novels of the period 1951–1987 is that of 'letrados' as seen in the works I have been discussing. This presence makes the notion of 'letrados' a key issue that is important to define and introduce in the study of these novels. In what follows I formulate an alternative view of the novels of this period, by focusing on the subject of 'letrados'-politicians in their role as intellectuals and power reproducers. First I explore the ideological and cultural factors propagated in fictional works with particular reference to twentieth-century Colombia, which will allow us to understand the connection between the novel and politics in the cultural context in which the novels were published. Second I study the novel *Bulevar de los héroes* by Eduardo García Aguilar, the last of the nine works selected in this book, with especial attention to the role of the 'letrado' in Colombia, together with the political and ideological aspects previously studied.

I continue following Eagleton's notion of ideology on which I have based this study, with reference to beliefs that connect with the power structure, as proposed from the outset.[1] Instrumental is also Eagleton's 'The Rise of English', which I follow as a model.[2] The study of the development of literary creativity in England offers important considerations on how multiple articulations become visible through the ideology of discourse and the process of 'maintenance and social power

---

1   Further discussion on Eagleton's theoretical views is found in Terry Eagleton, *Literary Theory: An Introduction* (Oxford: Blackwell, 1996), pp. 15–46. See also *Ideology: An Introduction* (London: Verso, 1991).
2   Eagleton, *Literary Theory*, pp. 15–46.

reproduction'.[3] That perspective is applied, particularly in that the convergence of culture and literature provides insight into literary creativity as well as the relevance of the discursive dialectic enunciated through the process of capitalism.

The notion of the 'letrado' expressed in these novels is particularly complex. Hence Rama's broad interpretative dimension lends sound elements of analysis and articulation to understand the Colombian 'letrado' with his distinctive traits, which are specific to the society in which he developed.[4] This is because the 'letrado' illustrates a multifaceted intellectual of strong ideological significance directly associated to his role in the socio-political process.

In order to understand the particular permutation of the ways in which politics and literature were interwoven in the Colombian novel of 1951–1987 it is important to trace the pre-existing backdrop against which this relationship was articulated. For Colombia, even before the 1950s, was a country in which politics and literature were tightly connected. The premises underlying that connection are analysed in the following pages.

Turning from the process of making politics to the cultural influence politics exerted on the societal world-view that then contributed in giving shape to the novels, I begin by showing that men of politics were also men of letters, and vice versa, which subsequently made of the practice of 'letras' a reproduction of social power. This combination exerted a direct cultural influence on writing as related to politics as well as the shaping of the social structure as a result of the creation of a category of writers known

---

3   Eagleton, *Literary Theory*, p. 13.
4   See Angel Rama, *La ciudad letrada* (Hanover: Ediciones del Norte, 1984). The notion of 'letrado' in Latin America has elicited some scholarly attention in recent years. See, for example, Patricia D'Allemand, *José María Samper: Nación y Cultura en el Siglo XIX Colombiano* (Bern: Peter Lang, 2012); see also Juan Pablo Dabove, *Nightmares of the Lettered City: Banditry and Literature in Latin America 1816–1929* (Pittburgh: University of Pittsburgh Press, 2007), particularly focused in banditry; and with particular important views on José Martí's intellectual influence on this matter is, Julio Ramos, *Divergent Modernities: Culture and Politics in Nineteenth Century Latin America* (London: Duke University Press, 2001).

as 'letrados'.[5] 'Letrados' in Colombia have been men dedicated to the cultivation of language in all its possible dimensions and their role has led to
the maintenance and reproduction of social power. Angel Rama on this
matter argues that in Latin America the very exercise of 'letras' produced
the 'letrados': men who since the past exercised a 'poetic function' which
was 'versificadora'. Versifying was the common asset of all 'letrados', whose
defining aspect was 'el ejercicio de la letra', an exercise within which anything could fit from 'una escritura de compra-venta' to 'una oda religiosa
o patriótica'.[6] With this concept Rama defines the 'ejercicio de la letra' in
its broadest sense, that is, as the profession of writing any kind of writing
be it a poem, a hymn whether religious or patriotic, or even a public document such as a property deed.

The notion of 'letrados' and the varied aspects articulated within it
raise important questions, particularly those related to the political process,
and specifically those ideological influences underlying the historical contingencies studied in the novels. How did literature in Colombia become
politically committed? What are the main components that nurtured that
ideology? In addressing these questions we turn to the issue of how other
structural aspects of ideology beyond the purely political gave rise to novels
of historical contingencies and their elucidation may open a conceptual
space occupied by these categories to address ideology, particularly in mid-
twentieth-century Colombia.

Although the time span runs from the 1950s to the 1980s when these
novels were published, some reference to previous years and even to the
nineteenth century must be made. This is because such references point

5   In his original notes Pedro Henríquez Ureña refers to 'hombre de letras', 'el poeta, el
      escritor', 'las artes y las letras', in Hispanic America, referring to the complex problem
      of expression in the language received from Spain. See 'Seis ensayos en busca de
      nuestra expresión', in *Obra crítica* (México: Fondo de Cultura Económica, 1960),
      pp. 239–270 (pp. 245–253).
6   See Rama, *La ciudad*, p. 29. Rama has shown the important significance and impli-
      cations of 'letras' and 'letrados' as a Spanish feature which together with political
      institutions and society grew culturally to develop as well a 'ciudad escrituraria', a
      'ciudad modernizada' and 'ciudad política'.

to foundational elements that prevailed throughout the twentieth century in Colombian society, and particularly its culture. The epitome of it is the national constitution of 1886, already mentioned in Chapter One, which despite numerous amendments and reforms, was not definitively changed until 1991. The national constitution of 1886 was an exclusive ideological product of the liberal and the conservative parties, written by one of its presidents, Rafael Núñez, a man who combined the distinctive activity of politics with that of 'letras'.[7] The activity that combined letras with political ideas created an internal dynamic that was maintained throughout the twentieth century, as we shall see.

Ideology, 'Letras' and Political Power

The merging of 'letras' with political practice is the link which produces what is known in Colombia as 'presidentes gramáticos'.[8] I will return to a discussion of this essential link after I clarify the term 'gramático' in this context. The term 'gramático' here is understood beyond the meaning of 'basic grammar'. In a broader sense it works rather as a descriptive epithet applied to individuals who number among their accoutrements the knowledge of language and literature and who also happen to be politicians.[9] In twentieth-century Colombia this dynamic may be exemplified by reference to individuals. Rafael Uribe Uribe and Marco Fidel Suárez, for example, devoted their lives to both 'letras' and active politics. Uribe Uribe was not only a politician but also a writer of journals, a lecturer on topics such as socialism, a diplomat and even a writer of children's tales.[10] Such versatility, common in politicians as well as 'letrados', included the capacity to translate

---

7   Malcolm Deas, *Del poder y la gramática* (Bogotá: Tercer Mundo, 1993), pp. 329.
8   Deas, *Del poder*, pp. 25–60.
9   Rama, *La ciudad*, p. 29.
10   Deas, *Del poder*, p. 25.

or adapt texts as a part of their activities. Uribe Uribe, indeed, translated a work by Herbert Spencer to prepare a defence of himself, and even wrote a dictionary: the *Diccionario Abreviado de Galicismos, Provincialismos y Correcciones de Lenguaje*.[11] The thorough knowledge of language and the practice of 'letras' gave 'letrados' the advantage of having access to a rhetorical virtuosity which aided them in their political rows, because 'el conocimiento de galicismos, provincialismos y correcciones era, sin duda, una ayuda en el ataque y en la defensa'.[12] The second important example of the 'letrado' was the president Marco Fidel Suárez. Suárez belonged to the conservative party and wrote about both politics and grammar, thereby epitomising what is meant by the 'presidente gramático'.[13]

The writing exercise of the 'letrados' that prevailed after Independence was a product that flourished, combined with politics, throughout the twentieth century.[14] It is within these categories that the literary roots of ideology are found in Colombia if we apply Eagleton's equation that suggests that 'literature is ideology', in the sense that it is the literary which reveals 'the most intimate relations of social power'.[15] This particular connection is suggested by Deas, who finds that, throughout the years, when the republic was formed, 'la política colombiana ha contenido desde un principio un vigoroso elemento ideológico y pedagógico'.[16] Men of 'letras' knew that education and ideas, once merged, would be the essential categories to support and maintain the bureaucratic republican state.[17] Thus

11　Deas, *Del poder*, p. 25

12　Deas, *Del poder*, p. 26.

13　Marco Fidel Suárez held the presidency between 1918 and 1921 and wrote *Sueños de Luciano Pulgar* and *Estudios gramaticales*.

14　See Raymond Leslie Williams, *The Colombian Novel 1844–1987* (Austin: University of Texas Press, 1991), p. 21. R.L. Williams underlines that in the twentieth century later presidents such as Alfonso López Michelsen (term 1974–1978) and Belisario Betancur (term 1982–1986) pursued literary careers. López Michelsen author of the novel *Los elegidos* (1953) and Betancur author of the volume of poetry *Poemas del caminante* (2005) are the recent representatives of letrados.

15　Eagleton, *Literary Theory*, pp. 19–20.

16　Deas, *Del poder*, p. 28.

17　R.L. Williams, *The Colombian Novel*, p. 21.

the combination of 'letras' and politics became the mechanism that demonstrates the motives of those writers whose real ambition was to achieve
power through political practice. To become a political leader, and even a
president, the condition of being a writer was a *sine qua non*.[18] That tradition institutionalised a 'letrado' elite that together with a type of 'cultura
académica en la política colombiana' led to the reproduction of social
power.[19] In addition, 'cultura académica' was the rule for social acceptance
established since Spanish rule, when the 'non-noble sector of Spanish society that could gain aristocratic status was the university-educated letrado'.[20]
It was, indeed, the command of language, 'dominio del idioma', which
became a factor of 'poder político' in Colombia.[21] Writing in Colombia as
R.L. Williams argues has always been 'intimately associated with politics',
in essence a political activity 'often subversive in nature'.[22]

Linguistic skills were the quality needed for acceptance by the elite.[23]
Deas suggests that this value pursued the preservation of grammar and the
correct use of language, a tendency maintained in the former colonies, and

18   See R.L. Williams, *The Colombian Novel*, pp. 34, 63.
19   Deas, *Del poder*, p. 27.
20   See R.L. Williams, *The Colombian Novel*, pp. 20–21. In this respect see also Deas,
     Del poder, p. 42. Deas affirms that 'para los letrados, para los burócratas, el idioma
     correcto es parte significativa del gobierno. La burocracia imperial española fue una
     de las más imponentes que el mundo haya jamás visto y no es sorprendente que los
     descendientes de esos burócratas no lo olvidaran; por eso, para ellos lenguaje y poder
     deberían permanecer inseparables' (p. 42).
21   Deas, *Del poder*, p. 45.
22   R.L. Williams, *The Colombian Novel*, p. ix, p. 20.
23   Deas, *Del poder*, pp. 30, 42, 46. On that particular Colombian upper-class ability to
     keep power Deas sustains that 'estas familias estaban acostumbradísimas al poder,
     sin poseer grandes tierras ni riqueza comercial'. In reference to Miguel Antonio
     Caro: '[Caro] es representante de una clase que tiene su existencia en el gobierno,
     no en ningún sector o faceta particular de la economía. Es heredero de la antigua
     burocracia del imperio español'. The best example among these characters in the
     1920s was Marco Fidel Suárez, the president known for his essays about language,
     and his personal economic antics even whilst in power. See also R.L. Williams, *The
     Colombian Novel*, pp. 21, 36.

entailed the enterprise of maintenance of social power.[24] It was by means of the correct use of language that they wrote partisan manifestos and the national constitution, but, by the same token, it was with linguistic skills that since the past, they wrote in other literary genres, bringing ideology with it.[25]

By writing political manifestos they propagated ideas of freedom and social reforms as suggested by Europeans thinkers such as the Destutt de Tracy, Lamartine, Sismondi, Fourier, Saint Simon, Proudhon and Victor Hugo, among others, and the English utilitarian, Jeremy Bentham.[26] Those combined ideas that in the nineteenth century informed Colombian 'letrados' thought underpinned their desire to build a modern state and its institutional organization, as well as maintain the urban-agrarian capitalist system, and turned out to be the legacy to their peers and the population of the twentieth century. Liberals, for instance, were supposed to promote advanced ideas and even socialist tendencies in order to implement social reforms, and 'pluriclasismo', to encourage people to follow these notions of freedom and participation.[27] In part 'pluriclasismo' possessed the flexibility which allowed for the existence of ideological dissidence between and within the two parties, of which Gaitán was the best example.[28] For their part the conservatives originally advocated a republicanism mixed

---

24　See Deas, *Del poder*, p. 27. Prominent examples of grammatical works are *Apuntaciones Criticas sobre el lenguaje Bogotano* (1872) by Rufino José Cuervo — a work of 'erudición', and *Tratado de Ortología y Ortografía Castellana* (1858), by Jose Manuel Marroquín, popularly known as the 'gramatica en verso', with which many generations learnt vocabulary spelling through rhyme.

25　This double role assumed by Colombian 'letrados' as their preoccupations to build the nation and create the culture in the nineteenth century is studied in Patricia D'Allemand, *José María Samper: nación y cultura en el siglo XIX Colombiano* (Bern: Peter Lang, 2012).

26　See Jaime Jaramillo Uribe, 'Tres etapas de la historia intelectual de Colombia', in *La personalidad histórica de Colombia y otros ensayos* (Bogotá: Instituto Colombiano de Cultura, 1977), pp. 105–130; 183–191. Also, Jaime Jaramillo Uribe, *El pensamiento colombiano en el siglo XIX* (Bogotá: Temis, 1974), pp. 341–345.

27　Tirado, 'Colombia: siglo y medio', p. 105.

28　Tirado, 'Colombia: siglo y medio', p. 105.

with Catholicism and even 'monarchism', as inspired by the French coun-
terrevolutionary Charles Maurras. By the 1950s the conservatives were supporting Franco and Mussolini's doctrines as well as being North America's
friend during the Second World War and the Cold War.[29]

These were the ideas of the 'letrados', that fuelled the 'political machine',
up until the mid-twentieth century. This interrelation of 'letrado' and
politician emerges from the 'political machine', and provides pointers to
the ways in which that 'machine' operates in the novels analysed thus far.
The political machine functions through social fabric, social institutions,
values and practices conditioned in a significant sense by the general cultural
context within which they dwell. Thus, conveyed through speech, ideas
are 'essentially a matter of meaning' that makes sense in a cultural core that
pervades individuals' lives and social fabric, and play an important role in
the life of the individual and in group behaviour.[30]

The ideological meaning of the 'letrado' legacy may be gauged from
a reference to the 'discursive formation' as identified by Eagleton in his
analysis of England's discursive period. The 'discursive formation' of the
nation corresponded to the demarcation of discourses that occurred in
England in the nineteenth century.[31] When applied to the Colombian
case this 'discursive formation' can be seen in the political manifestos,
i.e. ideological substantiations within which the new demarcation of discourses as well as the radical reorganisation of the spirit of the romantic
period took place, thereby allowing literature to become synonymous
with the 'imaginative'. In this way 'letras' came to represent something
intrinsic to the society they lived in. Thus the definition of the 'formative period' may well contribute to reveal the basis on which 'letras' and
discourse brought by the 'letrados' founded and maintained the country:
that is, on the basis of 'imagination', through the imitation of European
romanticism and idealism.[32]

---

29   Tirado, 'Colombia: siglo y medio', p. 105.
30   Eagleton, *Ideology*, p. 37.
31   Eagleton, *Ideology*, p. 16.
32   Eagleton, *Ideology*, pp. 16–17.

America's revolutions gave an extra fillip to the idealism of Romanticism with the 'tragic contradictions' posed by the new bourgeois regimes of Europe that included the ideology of Utilitarianism.[33] In utilitarian terms, institutional instruments such as the Colombian constitution (1886–1991) became an intellectual apparatus directly derived from the rule of 'letras' and 'letrados' since it literally represented their symbolic language and their power. As Rama suggests 'los lenguajes simbólicos [...] no sólo sirven a un poder sino también son dueños del poder'.[34] That symbolic language of power signified 'a triumph' not only for the 'centralization [of the] nation's political and cultural power' but also for the 'hegemonic culture of the neoclassical humanists'.[35] The tradition based on language, literature and rhetoric was promoted by a writing culture centred around Bogotá, the core of power, or even in Spain, where the National Front agreement was signed in 1956 and 1957, as seen in Chapter One. The ideological imagination of the liberal conservative bipartisanism brought into being José María Samper's dream of a 'liberalismo conservador' and a 'conservatismo liberal', one hundred years later, whose development gained ground throughout the first half of the twentieth century and beyond.[36] The power that in the twentieth century coalesced around the cities that embraced wealth and culture was the natural headquarters of 'las autoridades, los ricos, los *doctores*'.[37]

This is the world portrayed in *El 9 de abril*, by Gómez Corena, that is, the conservative idealised country identified as the Athens of South America, with witty *bogotanos* attending lavish soirées with the high society of the international community, as seen in Chapter Two.[38]

---

33 Eagleton, *Ideology*, p. 17.
34 Rama, *La ciudad*, p. 31.
35 *The Colombian Novel*, p. 63.
36 D'Allemand, *Samper*, p. 67.
37 Marco Palacios, *Entre la legitimidad y la violencia: Colombia 1875–1994* (Bogotá: Norma, 1995), pp. 144–186.
38 For an analysis of the general ambience promoted by the upper classes see R.L. Williams, *The Colombian Novel*, p. 63.

The legacy of the 'letrados' in Colombia has had a long shadow and it also relates to the way that trend reproduced itself through education. This legacy may be seen from the way education was pursued by the elites since the past. Safford, in questioning the Colombian educational tradition, remarks that although the upper classes considered education important for economic growth, they concentrated on 'institutions of higher education to serve only the elite, neglecting in that way the primary education', particularly that of the lower classes. He also adds that this tradition indicates the 'elite's greater concern with secondary school, which trained the sons of the upper class and provided them with their ideological furnishing'.[39] That, certainly, was not the case for 'public primary schools, whose pupils had little to do with the potential exercise of power'.[40] The inference that logically follows is that economic growth, education and power, together with the progress and welfare those assets provide, seemed to favour the upper classes only.

Nonetheless, recently discovered documents show that during the 1930s and 1940s the politicians and 'liberal intellectuals' represented a new stream, whose purpose was to transform the country so that 'people were counted as part of that [social] process'.[41] The education of the masses, Silva argues, had been an important part of the ideological preoccupations of the liberals. That suggestion chimes with Rama's emphasis in that during the process of modernisation concessions were made by the upper class, one of them being the education plan applied primarily to the urban population, which offered opportunities for social mobility.[42] According to Silva, during the 1930s and 1940s, when the liberals were in power, the

---

39   See Frank Safford, *The Ideal of the Practical* (Austin: University of Texas Press, 1976), p. 49.

40   Safford, *The Ideal*, p. 50.

41   See Renán Silva, *República liberal, intelectuales y cultura popular* (Medellín: La Carreta, 2005), pp. 65–66. These Colombian archives show official documents and testimonies from local libraries, communities and schools in small towns, and correspondence from communities asking for series of 'national authors' published and distributed by the National Library.

42   Rama, *La ciudad*, p. 94.

notion of culture was taking a new definition in the sense that it was given a popular 'social character' which was in tune with the idea of 'social function' as proposed for land property reform.[43]

These changes allowed a degree of social mobility for the masses and the plans, consequently, encouraged social projects such as reading. During the 1930s and 1940s cabinet members of López Pumarejo's government were 'men of letters', among them Luis López de Mesa and J.E. Gaitán, who encouraged the growth of 'national book fairs with surprising sales records' when minister of education.[44] It is well known that Gaitán himself came from a modest middle-class family and that he was also a role model to his contemporaries. Gaitán belonged to a generation of divided opinions conveyed by the waves of change arriving in Colombia. These are part of the 'structure of feeling'[45] discussed above in *El día del odio* and *La mala hora*, as they are important symbols of a society that was dramatically changing during the 1950s in Colombia.

Since the early decades of the century the challenge to 'letrado' culture had been growing not only with influences such as the Córdoba (Argentina) students' movement that gave momentum to the interest in university reform, but also Marxist ideas which had been influencing the growing population since the early 1920s. Marxism encouraged ideas of social change after the Partido Socialista Revolucionario and 'sociedades obreras' came to prominence. Various sectors of the population, particularly the workers, were being attracted by more 'informal' ways of learning ideas. From peasant movements to the urban working population, together with the growth of reformist liberalism, socialism and communism, all played an important ideological role during the first half of the twentieth century.[46]

---

43   Silva, *República liberal*, p. 66.
44   Silva, *República liberal*, pp. 33, 38.
45   See Raymond Williams, *The Long Revolution* (London: Hogarth Press, 1992), pp. 48–49.
46   See Richard E. Sharpless, *Gaitán of Colombia: A Political Biography* (Pittsburg: Pittsburg, 1978), pp. 24–25. Groups of literary and political character such as Los Nuevos and Los Leopardos were part of this trend.

As a liberal minister in the 1930s reported: 'el socialismo está enseñando a leer a todos los analfabetos en la biblia de Marx y Lenin'.[47]

While the upper class championed Italian fascism, German Nazism and post-war anti-communism as championed by the United States, opposition forces echoed the ideas of the Soviet socialist revolution.[48] The opposition grew as a result of that social division which was chiefly reinforced by economic hardship. According to Safford and Palacios this division split opinion and also led to anti-Americanism.[49] North American interventionism in the Colombian economy began to be criticised and anti-American sentiment increased after the loss of Panama.[50] In addition, ideological waves conveyed by similar movements taking place within Latin America had an impact in the country. Examples of these influences are the Mexican Revolution and later the 1940s Peruvian reformist movement 'Aprismo'. In the 1940s oppositional ideas grew exponentially in those sections of society assembled by Gaitán's populism and embodied by 'workers, shopkeepers, professionals and employees, whose interests were backed in part by the National Federation of Commerce'.[51] As we have seen previously Gaitán was a professional lawyer, a detail that becomes crucial in *El 9 de abril* by Gómez Corena and *El día del odio* by Osorio Lizarazo.

This advent of new ideas in Colombian society characterised by bipartisan manoeuvring led to the creation of unavoidable contradictions by the 1950s. By the 1950s Colombian society was the product of a legalised

47   Luis López de Mesa in *El Tiempo*, 28 January 1930. Cited by Carlos Uribe Celis, *Los años veinte en Colombia: ideología y cultura* (Bogotá: Aurora, 1985), p. 90.

48   See Uribe Celis, *Los años*, pp. 12–13. Compare Christopher Abel, *Política, iglesia y partidos en Colombia* (Bogotá: FAES/Universidad Nacional de Colombia, 1987), p. 50. Abel does not believe in these influences; in his opinion 'la revolución rusa no causó más que un leve escozor en Colombia; no logró nada del impacto de la revolución Cubana de 1959 cuando Colombia se hallaba más integrada al concierto internacional'.

49   Frank Safford and Marco Palacios, *Colombia: Fragmented Land, Divided Society* (Oxford: Oxford University Press, 2002), pp. 266–267.

50   Safford and Palacios, *Fragmented Land*, pp. 278–280.

51   See *Grandes potencias, el 9 de abril y la violencia*, ed. by Gonzalo Sánchez (Planeta, 2000), p. 161.

idealism imposed by the ruling class, the state was supported by this structure of legality, and the ideology implemented by virtue of the bipartisan mechanisms remained unchallenged. By the end of that decade new forces were not only opposing bipartisanism as an ideology but they were also challenging its power at the ballot box. The Latin American 'dissidence' symbolised by the Cuban Revolution not only inspired subsequent ideological movements but also provided ideological and practical training for them. A student faction broke away to become a guerrilla movement in Colombia, gathering peasants, students and workers together in the Movimiento Obrero Estudiantil Campesino, MOEC, and as mentioned in Chapter One, many other groups stood for elections for the sections of society they represented and the masses.[52]

We have seen this 'structure of feeling' fictionalised in the novel *Años de fuga*, which describes a liberal intellectual who is committed to his social class and living an existentialist youth until he opts for a leftist adventure that reveals him to be more liberal than leftist. The socio-political scene that gathered momentum in the student movement is also depicted in the story of a cosmopolitan Colombian intellectual in the novel *Bulevar de los héroes*, as shall be seen in the next section of this chapter. This moment of transition mirrors a specific historical contingency in which the student movement plays a pivotal role in the process of social change.

Research by Celis and Cataño suggests that the student movement was the crucial transitional link between the previous bipartisan system and left-wing ideology in Colombia.[53] This changed ideological horizon led to new demands for social reform and democratic participation, which had been the exclusive remit of the ruling class, first under the tradition of

---

52   For further information about the role played by the Cuban 'Ministerio de la Revolución' in the ideological and instrumental training offered to the Latin American guerrilla movements see Jorge G. Castañeda, *La utopia desarmada* (Bogotá: Tercer Mundo, 1994), pp. 63–106.

53   See Carlos Uribe Celis, *La mentalidad del colombiano: cultura y sociedad en el siglo XX* (Bogotá: Alborada, 1992), pp. 102, 168–175; See also Gonzalo Cataño, *Educación y estructura social* (Bogotá: Plaza y Janés, 1989), pp. 191–197.

bipartisanism and then under the National Front umbrella, as suggested in Chapter One.

I have analysed some aspects of the role played by the Colombian 'letrado' within bipartisanism and the ideological instruments used to exercise political power in the mid-twentieth century and beyond, and pointed to how this character-type is portrayed in a number of Colombian novels. In that process, other important ideological instruments such as the media were exploited politically by 'letrados' and intellectuals alike, as well as mirrored in the novels.

Ideology, Media, Rhetoric and Oratory

We have seen that in the majority of the novels studied in previous chapters the media is portrayed as a powerful instrument that has deep repercussions within society. As Eagleton argues: 'communications media are [...] a potent means by which a dominant ideology is disseminated'.[54] The media in Colombia, indeed, pervaded social groups in a profound way. Studies by Jaramillo, Fals and Cataño show that this was possible because in the cities, and more particularly in the capital, Bogotá, the middle class was growing and creating diverse groups with a differentiated economic status.[55] Sectors of middle-class employees, workers such as 'artesanos' or small merchants sought inclusion in urban life, in the realm of employment, housing, social security and education. This growing population transformed the social map of Colombia's cities towards the mid-century, particularly in Bogotá.[56] That new social map reflected not only people's

---

54   *Ideology*, pp. 34–35.
55   See Jaramillo, 'Tres etapas', p. 123; also compare Orlando Fals Borda, *Las Revoluciones inconclusas en América Latina 1869–1968* (México: Siglo XXI, 1981), pp. 40–41. Fals explains that 'Democratic societies' in the nineteenth century started as 'cultural societies' or 'cultural groups' (p. 40). See Gonzalo Cataño, *Educación*, pp. 189–225.
56   See Uribe Celis, *La mentalidad*, p. 81.

behaviour but those new ways of thinking which were prompted by the media. The development of the media in Colombia occurred early on and did so for political reasons, as we shall see.

Abel points out, for example, that 'La aridez de la política colombiana a comienzos de los años cuarenta se reflejaba en la prensa y el debate ideológico'.[57] On the bipartisan side liberal opinion was expressed chiefly via *El Tiempo* and *El Espectador*, which were the main national newspapers in the twentieth century. Eduardo Santos, who became president in 1942, had owned *El Tiempo* since 1913, and he, like the newspaper, was of a liberal persuasion.[58] *El Espectador* reflected generally the same opinion although, occasionally, it adopted a more radical stance in opposition to the privileges of the Church.[59] This detail shows in principle that at least one of the two most influential newspapers was owned by the ruling class, while pointing at the same time to the media power of the 'letrado'.[60] *El Tiempo* transmitted a syncretistic ideology in a simple and straightforward language in order to reach a bigger audience. Liberty, constitution and continuity with the past were its key concepts, while identifying itself with western European democratic regimes and the United States, as well as demanding alliances with international progressive movements.[61] The liberal party's own publication was *Acción Liberal*, a newspaper designed to propagate advanced political ideas; sometimes it expressed support for Marxist ideas, in opposition to *El Tiempo*. Conservative ideology was expressed in the newspapers, *El Colombiano* from Medellín and *El Siglo* from Bogotá. The latter – Gómez's paper – strongly opposed *El Tiempo*: while *El Siglo* welcomed General Francisco Franco's seizing of power in Spain, which was

57 Abel, *Política*, p. 212.
58 Abel describes Santos as a 'baron' of the liberal press of Francophile tradition that used *El Tiempo* to project democratic language, style and techniques in the manner of the French radical party. See *Política*, p. 129.
59 Abel, *Política*, p. 202.
60 Recent years show media-cum-politics: Francisco Santos vice-president, 2002–2010, and Juan Manuel Santos president during two consecutive terms 2010–2014 and 2014–2018.
61 Abel, *Política*, pp. 205–206.

envisaged as a new epoch for conservatism in Latin America, *El Tiempo* praised the 'resistencia republicana' and presented the nationalist triumphs as a source of encouragement for liberals.[62] The press, indeed, became a challenge in the 1930s to the Church's ideological control as a result of its broad social reach: there were 44 weeklies; 60 monthlies and 13 fortnightlies.[63] The Church gave momentum to anti-communism in the 1930s and it derived support for this in the publication *Acción Católica*. Censorship was also used by the ruling classes to combat the growth of populism.[64] This censorship eventually caused a state of affairs in which much information circulated in clandestine publications. An example of this trend is the book *Mordaza: diario secreto de un escritor público* (n. d.) by Fernando Gómez Martínez, a journalist who worked for the newspaper, *El Colombiano*, whose ideas, which had been censored by the government, were published in order to denounce the ruling elite's policy against freedom of speech. Newspapers developed into significant commercial enterprises in the course of the twentieth century and journalism became recognised as a profession more and more as the century progressed. Some publications, though of little commercial value, were of high ideological value.[65] This is why the press as a medium contributed greatly to the dissemination of alternative ideologies in a rapidly changing social environment. Of the writers included in this study, for instance, only one did not write for the newspapers. Print media is perceived to be of decisive importance for the development of a generation's literary groups. I have shown in Chapter One that a number of social groups joined trade union organisations which eventually took on a political character. These organisations assimilated influences derived from overseas revolutions and particularly their utopian political ideologies.

As seen already, the novel *Años de fuga* demonstrates that external ideologies contributed greatly to the creation of clandestine political organisations. Similarly, *Bulevar de los héroes* invokes a comparable 'structure of

---

62   Abel, *Política*, pp. 209–210.

63   See Abel, *Política*, p. 207. Based on the Ministerio de Educación Nacional report 'La Iglesia y el Estado en la educación pública' (Bogotá, 1935).

64   See Abel, *Política*, pp. 50, 199, 215.

65   See Abel, *Política*, p. 50.

feeling', although in a different way, as shall be shown in a moment. These organisations were often vehicles for the ideas of the young intelligentsia of the middle class, workers and traders, and became radicalised in the 1950s.[66] During these years trade union groups shared the fundmentals of modernisation including, in Rama's concept, 'la política de los campos que fue vista desde la misma perspectiva urbana con que la evaluaron positivamente los intelectuales'.[67]

It is important to clarify that up until the 1950s the bedrock of clandestine political organisations was 'artesanal'; 'artesanos' was the traditional term for workers who formed 80% of the unions.[68] Marxist ideas of change influenced by the Partido Socialista Revolucionario and 'sociedades obreras' were propagated by means of newsletters and local newspapers published in villages and towns.[69] Hand-copied documents or low-budget printed papers, characterised by a plethora of idealism, circulated among the popular classes: 'hojas mimeografiadas o manuscritas y con deficiente ortografía circularon'.[70] J.A. Osorio Lizarazo, a journalist and the author of *El día del odio*, suggests in one of his journalistic chronicles that clandestine newspapers conveying communist ideas were printed cheaply in family

---

66 Jaramillo, 'Tres etapas', p. 209.

67 Rama, *La ciudad*, p. 95.

68 See Sánchez, 'Los bolcheviques del Líbano', in *Ensayos de historia social y política del siglo XX* (Bogotá: El Ancora, 1985), pp. 11–108 (p. 22).

69 As noted by Sánchez, Marxist theory had permeated parts of Colombian society since the early decades of the century and as such it gave momentum to strikes and popular mobilisation. It was on this basis that socialist leaders such as Raúl Mahecha, Ignacio Torres Giraldo and María Cano organised the Revolutionary Socialist Party and communicated with its supporters in a paper called *El Luchador*. María Cano had been called 'oráculo de los revolucionarios' and 'la virgen roja del proletariado Colombiano' by *El Tiempo*, the paper owned by the liberal president Eduardo Santos, and in Líbano village local leaders had called her a 'propagandista genial, que a pesar de su delicada condición de mujer arrostra toda clase de fatigas y sacrificios por llevar de uno a otro confín el mensaje sagrado de la liberación proletaria'. As quoted by Sánchez from Juzgado 20 Penal Municipal del Líbano. Radicación 1608, folio 22, 23 February 1929. See further details in Sánchez, 'Los bolcheviques', p. 55.

70 See Sánchez, 'Los bolcheviques', pp. 18–26.

houses because other outlets were not available.[71] Print media played a crucial role in the development of left-wing ideology during this period. Sánchez notes that the liberal party redefined its political project so that it appeared as a popular alternative to the conservatives. Such a tendency encouraged other groups to enter the political scene and declare themselves as political parties.[72] It is in this way that socialist ideology flourished among groups that thrived in small villages of the hinterland, epitomised by the revolutionary, self-proclaimed group 'Bolcheviques del Líbano'. Thus, the 'proletarian emancipation' that involved workers, 'artesanos', peasants and the urban middle-class was born.[73] The ideological vehicle for these movements within the provinces were their 'periódicos artesanales' such as *El Obrero* (*The Worker*), *El Camarada* (*The Comrade*) and *El Comunista* (*The Communist*), which had evolved since the 1920s alongside the socialist party of Social-Democrat and Social-Christian inspiration that also published *El Socialista*.[74] Many of these papers had an important impact on *La Voz Proletaria*, the main publication of the communist party and the communist youth, Juventud Comunista (JUCO), that informed ideas and opinions of the leftist generations during the second half of the twentieth century.

The growth of the press during this period encouraged 'tertulias' and literary, philosophical and political discussion. 'Tertulias' are gatherings of groups of people sharing the same interests, generally literary, never short of a poet, and rarely missing politics. Examples of these gatherings were the 'Gruta Simbólica', established at the beginning of twentieth century and 'El grupo de Barranquilla', by mid century. Bushnell refers to these groups as 'forms of cultural activity' which reflected the intellectual scene, and from where '[m]en of letters produced, learned essays and clever conversation

---

71   J.A. Osorio Lizarazo, 'El hombre que durante 40 años publicó un periódico del que era el único lector', *El Tiempo*, 26 March 1939. A tongue-in-cheek chronicle by J.A. Osorio Lizarazo about the idealism and scant resources with which these papers and specifically the paper *La Libertad* was printed at the time.

72   Sánchez, 'Los bolcheviques', pp. 18–19.

73   Sánchez, 'Los bolcheviques', p. 19.

74   See Sánchez, 'Los bolcheviques', p. 22. Only in that region many papers were published: *El Moscovita, El Centinela, Avance*, among others.

on almost any subject, except the deprivations suffered by the Colombian masses, and they excelled above all in the writing and recitation of poetry on every conceivable occasion.'[75] The leftist movement made its presence felt in these 'socialist discussion groups', and also in the 'appearance of ephemeral radical publications'.[76] In a mutual way 'tertulias' were connected to the press since they reached the public and took place in cafés, educational venues, such as universities, where conversation could become an influential channel for ideology.[77] The role of these 'tertulias' has been evidenced in Pedro Gómez Corena's *El 9 de abril* and J.A. Osorio Lizarazo's *El día del odio*, and they are symbolised in a distinctive manner in Eduardo García Aguilar's *Bulevar de los héroes*. J.A. Osorio Lizarazo and some of his work colleagues used to attend 'tertulias' with a Russian called Silvestre Savitsky who lived in Bogotá and who attempted to indoctrinate intellectuals.[78] In their meetings 'leían con entusiasmo a Marx' and often, while drinking beer, 'instalaban cátedra de comunismo' to workers who were present and who wanted to hear them. That this was a common experience is confirmed by the comment quoted above that socialists were teaching the illiterate how to read the bible according to Marx and Lenin.

By the same token it is clear that bipartisanism exploited the media commercially, politically and ideologically, as suggested by the fact that newspapers such as *El Tiempo* and *El Siglo* were owned by politicians who went on to presidential office, which hints at how the role of 'letrado' evolved in this process of power-mongering. Politicians either from the capital or the provinces invested strategically in this valuable vehicle of

75 David Bushnell, *The Making of Modern Colombia: A Nation in Spite of Itself* (London: University of California Press, 1993), p. 163.

76 Bushnell, *A Nation in Spite of Itself*, p. 163.

77 R.L. Williams, *The Colombian Novel*, p. 36. See also Alvaro Tirado Mejía, 'El MRL y La cultura', in *Credencial*, 3, March 1990. Available at <http://www.banrepcultural. org/blaavirtual/revistas/credencial/marzo1990/marzo2.htm> [Accessed 21 March 2009]

78 See *Novelas y crónicas: J.A. Osorio Lizarazo*, selection and introduction by Santiago Mutis Durán (Bogotá: Instituto Colombiano de Cultura, 1978), p. xxxiv. See also Diego Montaña Cuéllar, *País formal, país real* (Buenos Aires: Platina, 1963), p. 131.

ideological diffusion. As the century progressed new infrastructures for communication were built. Radio stations had proved to be decisive in Colombian life since their introduction in 1925.[79] The president Alfonso López Pumarejo bought a 'radio-periódico' called *La República Liberal* and in order to counteract this development, the conservative Laureano Gómez bought the radio station *La Voz de Colombia*.[80] Furthermore, in line with a trend occurring in the majority of Latin American and Caribbean countries, radio adopted the North American system of programming as financed by advertising; from its marginal role radio jumped suddenly to a new level from the 1930s onwards: 'la radio se convirtió en un medio indispensable de movilización'.[81]

Radio stations not only contributed to the propagation of ideas but also encouraged their listeners to perceive enmity between parties when, in reality, it was part of one and the same relationship maintained by the partisan leaders.[82] In the uprising of 9 April 1948, for instance, the radio played an important role in encouraging the mob to attack the government headquarters. Not surprisingly, therefore, media and radio transmission are repeatedly alluded to in the novel *El 9 de abril* by Gómez Corena, in which there is a scene in which a poet uses the radio in order to harangue the people for specific political ends. The role played by radio and newspapers is also clearly evident in *El Cristo de espaldas* and *Siervo sin tierra* as well as *Años de fuga*. Likewise newspapers are seen as central to the ideological expression of bipartisanism in the novels *Una y muchas guerras*

---

79 The first radio broadcasting in Colombia was 10 June 1925; about general aspects on the development of the Colombian communication infrastructure during 1920s see Uribe Celis, *Los años*, p. 13. For critical views on the marked contrast between the Colombian culture and its modern systems of communication see Jean Franco, *La cultura moderna en América Latina*, trans. Sergio Pitol (México: Grijalbo, 1983), p. 279.

80 Palacios, *Entre la legitimidad*, pp. 144–145.

81 Palacios, *Entre la legitimidad*, pp. 144–145.

82 Shrewd views on the deluding bipartisan relationship are that of Jorge Child, 'Correspondencia: la comedia de las contradicciones liberales', in *Mito 1955–1962: Selección de textos*, ed. by Juan Gustavo Cobo Borda (Bogotá: Instituto Colombiano de Cultura, 1975), pp. 301–315.

and *Bulevar de los héroes*. Although *La mala hora* is much more cryptic in its portrayal of the role played by the media, communication is illustrated via the pasquinades, the above-mentioned 'tertulia' and clandestine flyers. The media played an active role not only in galvanising a bipartisan public opinion but also in creating a credible opposition; during this period the meaning of 'el pueblo' gathered momentum as an ideological concept.

The political meaning of 'el pueblo', which came via romanticism, needed many years to mature in Colombia. The political flank of romanticism in its early years had proclaimed the redemption of those socially forgotten classes: orphans, convicts, beggars, exploited women: 'yo he rehabilitado el bufón, el histrión [...] los condenados, las prostitutas.'[83] Victor Hugo's social idealism ran parallel with the romantic interpretation of Christianity as a religion of the oppressed and the figure of Christ as the redeemer of the dispossessed. The romantic ethos in Colombia expressed a message of 'forbearance and tragedy', where there is no 'rebelliousness against society' and this idea complemented the notion of Christianity as a popular religion for the oppressed. It was a 'structure of feeling'[84] which still held sway in Colombia in the 1950s. In the novels here studied, 'el pueblo', in line with this tendency, is romanticised and depicted as in need of 'redemption', as we have already seen in novels such as *El día del odio*, *La mala hora* and *Siervo sin tierra*.

A number of historical texts allow us to piece together what is meant by 'el pueblo' in this period. Based on official files Palacios reproduces a view of 'el pueblo' as part of a homogeneous underworld of 'servitude', 'resignation', 'indolence' and 'ignorance'; that is, the reflection of people seen as 'a formal subject of a political society unknown to itself'.[85] 'El pueblo' was subject to a romantic interpretation that became a powerful political signifier because it went beyond the simple meaning of the word. To

---

83　The verse corresponds to Victor Hugo, *Las contemplaciones*, quoted by Jaramillo, 'Tres etapas', p. 126.

84　See Williams, *The Long Revolution*, pp. 48–49.

85　For comments and notes on Colombian idiosyncrasies from British diplomatic missions' Public Record Office in the early decades of the twentieth century, see Marco Palacios, *Estado y clases sociales en Colombia* (Bogotá: Procultura, 1986), pp. 13–24.

appreciate this political resonance it is important to clarify at this point the meaning of the term 'el pueblo'. 'Pueblo' means typically a little village, but translated into Spanish from the French 'le peuple: ensemble humain réuni par l'appartenance à une société' (according to the *Dictionnaire de la Langue Française*), it became for political discourse 'el pueblo', the human group, the crowd.[86] Thus it came to be identified within the political populism that I have referred to in Chapter One in such a way that, by the 1940s, it became so robust as to end up in populist slogans such as: 'yo no soy un hombre, soy un pueblo'.[87] This phrase that may be translated into English as 'I am not only a man, I am the people' was one among other ideologically laden significances that gained ground and brought the term 'el pueblo' into the socio-cultural atmosphere of those years. The term 'el pueblo' taken from Victor Hugo and passed on by 'artesanos' in the early decades of the twentieth century was alive and well in the oratory of politics practitioners in the 1940s, 1950s and beyond. García Márquez's *La mala hora* is a case in point, as we have seen, as it shows a character reading *Los miserables* and others engaged in the discussion of stories by Charles Dickens. 'El pueblo', the people, to which Abel refers, became the 'motor and dynamo' of that machine that politics was fuelled by the ideas of their leaders.[88] The term 'el pueblo' reached a strong social momentum, particularly via skilled orators such as Gaitán himself. 'El pueblo' evolved as a categorical concept that was interpreted via Christian discourse as indicating the 'desheredados' – the utterly poor people or the dispossessed.[89] This idea of the people was turned into a myth by politicians and managed by the Church. The meaning of 'el pueblo', indeed, has three important political connections in this process. These are rhetoric, oratory and poetry – as it will be evident in the novel *Bulevar de los héroes*. These

86   *Le Robert Dictionnaire de la Langue Français*, 12th edn (Montréal: 1995).

87   This was one of the famous catchphrases of Jorge Eliécer Gaitán, who was also called 'el caudillo del pueblo' ('tribune of the people') by his followers. See Sharpless, *Gaitán of Colombia*, p. 60.

88   Abel, *Política*, p. 142.

89   Jaramillo has pointed to the importance of the concept of 'el pueblo' as well as the romantic interpretation of Christianity in Colombian political thought. See 'Tres etapas', p. 125.

connections are distinctive, but what they have in common is their political function and their ideological significance. Pivotal to those societal factors that kept changing the character of the audience are rhetoric and oratory. I have discussed above the instrumental role played by the press and the radio in this process. These ideological infrastructures made oratory and rhetoric more functional within the social context that I am discussing here.

Rhetoric is 'the art of speaking (and by extension, writing) effectively so as to persuade an audience'. It derives from the Greek *rethor*, meaning 'public speaker'.[90] Oratory is a branch of rhetoric and it is the conveyor of rhetorical speech. Oratory in fact became, during this period, entertainment for broad sectors of the population to whom speeches were addressed at the municipal theatre during the 'viernes culturales'.[91] Abel suggests in this respect, for instance, that at the 'teatro municipal' Gaitán pronounced an elaborate speech that was broadcast weekly to the nation. More importantly Abel stresses the effect it produced, which was guttural and hypnotic since the audience 'pagaba por entrar [...] y permanecía extasiada durante dos o tres horas'.[92] We find a similar picture of the way political ideas circulated among 'el pueblo' in *Siervo sin tierra* and *El día del odio* in which ideology comes through in simple language. Furthermore, ideological authority grew through the use of oratorical language and became a tradition and a respected ability. According to Abel, Gaitán y Gómez were 'buenos oradores', that quality though did not contributed to make any difference since in the contents the language they used was similar.[93] Oratory thereby gave prestige to those who possessed such skills; as such it was part of the 'letras' tradition as well as an intrinsic feature of political

---

90 Martin Gray, *A dictionary of literary terms* (York: York Press, 1999), p. 245.

91 Uribe Celis, *La mentalidad*, p. 65.

92 Abel, *Política*, p. 142. The 'teatro municipal' in Bogotá was re-named 'Teatro Jorge Eliécer Gaitán' on 8 March 1973. See at <http://www.teatrojorgeeliecer.gov.co/index.php?option=comcontent&view=article&id=127&Itemid=107> [Accessed 19 September 2009]

93 Abel, *Política*, p. 143.

training.[94] The bipartisan elite transformed this type of rhetoric into an art form. As Abel underlines 'un trozo de prosa inexacta pero bien escogida con olor a piedad y condimentada con referencias clásicas era mucho más alabado que cualquier otra clase de escritos'.[95] Thus 'letras' became the art of eloquence styled by a society of often elitist 'doctores' who stood deliberately apart from the 'mestizo' population stigmatised by the right-wing members.[96] Examples of this type of political orator were Laureano Gómez and Lucio Pabón Núñez, who were as notorious for their political deeds as they were notable for their oratorical skills. Gómez in his newspaper *El Siglo*, for example, wrote against Pablo Neruda during a visit the Chilean poet paid to Colombia, which elicited in turn Neruda's 'poemas punitivos'.[97]

Ideology, Poetry, Commitment and Novel

The poetic value of 'letras' is relevant to my analysis since ideology and power were intrinsically connected to poetry, often seen as the primordial genre in Colombia. As I have shown above, based on Eagleton's view, the

94 According to Abel, an oratorical duel could be a real disaster for a politician. See *Política*, p. 46.
95 Abel, *Política*, p. 48.
96 Laureano Gómez believed that a predominantly 'mestizo' country, for instance, was pointless 'since its population was not useful to political and economic unity of America, as it retained too many indigenous imperfections'. Against the liberal political conception radical stances considered that in American nations where the black population was high there was 'social disorder'. Haiti was mentioned as an example of a place where democracy was turbulent. Gómez suggested all-white populations in countries like Argentina, Chile and Uruguay brought political and economic stability. See Palacios, *Estado y clases sociales*, pp. 27–29.
97 On Neruda's 'poemas punitivos', see Adam Feinstein, *Pablo Neruda: A Passion for Life* (London: Bloomsbury, 2004), pp. 171–173. On the use of grammar and philology as a predominant conservative practice along with the interest in 'folclor' and interest in tradition, which persisted until the 1950s, see Deas, *Del poder*, p. 50.

Colombian political project was an idealistic invention which drew heavily on the European romantic, poetic world-view. Far from being a simple by-product of 'letras', poetry was not an epiphenomenal part of the culture; and indeed it was central to the power play at work in the novels of 1951–1987. In Gómez Corena's *El 9 de abril*, as already seen, a poet harangues 'el pueblo' on the radio, and in *Bulevar de los héroes*, as we will see, poetry is an important signifier of the ideological game underlying politics, to give only two examples. As I have emphasised above, it was because of its 'versificatory' qualities that poetry achieved prestige in Latin American society. Poetry, R.L. Williams maintains, has always been the most esteemed genre in Colombia and that it contributed to a legitimisation of 'letras' and 'letrados'. This is true to the extent that the momentum gathered by prose literature in the 1950s was prompted by the impetus of politics.[98] The generation of intellectuals, poets and politicians in which Gaitán grew up were active in a literary as much as a political sense in the 1940s and 1950s, and it was they who introduced the idea of commitment and political consciousness into discussions about literature.[99] Among the issues raised by these intellectuals was the loss of Panama which, together with the role played by foreign capital, persuaded these writers to demand protection for Colombian territory and its resources, and urged the restructuring of the state along with effective policies to meet the needs of a newly emerging industrial-urban society.[100] Intensely idealistic and strongly nationalist poets such as Luis Vidales and León de Greiff contributed to the formation of left-wing ideals. Luis Vidales, for his part, expressed himself with a voice closer to the sentiment of 'el pueblo' and was one of the founders and promoters of the Colombian communist party. Gutiérrez Girardot suggested that Vidales was a committed voice of the avant-garde in Colombia

---

98 Fernando Charry Lara, 'Los Nuevos', in *Manual de literatura colombiana*, vol. 2 (Bogotá: Procultura/Planeta, 1988), pp. 17–85 (p. 25).

99 Charry comments on the political-cum-literary debates among members of this generation among whom he counts Alberto Lleras Camargo, first president of the Frente Nacional, mentioned in Chapter One; and the poet León de Greiff. See 'Los Nuevos', p. 25.

100 Sharpless, *Gaitán*, p. 24.

who 'updated the country'.[101] The matter of the political commitment
of writers led to heated ideological debate at this time, particularly as a
result of the rise of the novel in the 1950s. Those debates flourished in the
work of writers, including Hernando Téllez, Eduardo Caballero Calderón
and Gabriel García Márquez. These writers focused almost obsessively on
novel writing, the writer's commitment and political pressures. Téllez, for
instance, drew attention not only to the rebellious position Caballero was
taking up vis-à-vis the oligarchy, but also to the growing anticipation for
the appearance of a great novelist.[102] Caballero Calderón commented on
the political fate that writers of the novel were facing because of the tough
times they were living through.[103] García Márquez, for his part, emphasised
the political pressures writers were facing and the compelling political commitment demanded by the intellectual environment of the time.[104] García
Márquez's discussion of the novel form can be seen as a continuation of the
'letrado' dialogue and its rule that 'letras' and power were inseparable. Of
all the authors studied in this book, Caballero Calderón was the epitome
of the 'letrado' figure as a result of being a member of the oligarchy, and
for that reason an exponent of its values. As Téllez wrote, Calderón was a
'escritor católico con hondas raíces feudales en su concepción del mundo y
de la sociedad [...] heredero legítimo de las oligarquías'.[105] The particular

101   See Rafael Gutiérrez Girardot, 'La literatura colombiana en el siglo XX', in *Manual
      de historia de Colombia*, vol. 3 (Bogotá: Procultura/Instituto Colombiano de Cultura,
      1984), pp. 447–536 (p. 494). 'Los Nuevos' were attracted by socialism and contributed
      to the tendency that gradually went leftwards. It was in parallel with this generation
      that the figure of Gaitán emerged, giving a new verve to liberalism, as I have shown
      in Chapter One.
102   Hernando Téllez, 'Literatura y testimonio', *El Tiempo, Lecturas Domicales*, 27 June
      1954, p. 1.
103   See Eduardo Caballero Calderón, 'El escritor ante una encrucijada', *El Tiempo, Lecturas
      Dominicales*, 1 November 1964, pp. 1, 5.
104   See García Márquez, 'Dos o tres cosas sobre "la novela de la violencia"', in *Eco*, 34/1,
      205, Bogotá (November 1978), 103–108 (first publ. in *La Calle*, 9 October 1959); see
      also Clemente Airó, 'Pro y contra en la novelística Colombiana', *El Tiempo, Lecturas
      Dominicales*, 24 February 1963, p. 1.
105   Hernando Téllez, 'Literatura y testimonio', *El Tiempo, Lecturas*, 1954, p. 1.

world-view conveyed by the author applied as much to party membership as to his adherence to 'letrado' culture. Up to the 1950s party membership was a crucial part of the cultural identity of a given generation. Santa argues that 'Colombians are born with a party card tied to their umbilical cord' and that this hereditary condition was passed through generations with a staunch commitment to the party to which the individual belonged.[106] This cultural specificity certainly applies in the case of Caballero Calderón, Plinio A. Mendoza and García Márquez; the latter's leftist position was influenced by his liberal grandfather who brought him 'más cerca de la rebeldía que del orden tradicional'.[107]

It was not only politics but also law which constituted the heritage of the 'letrado'. Law and 'letras' are, indeed, two things that have always gone hand in hand in Colombia.[108] Lawyers, traditionally in Colombia addressed as 'doctores' since they have obtained a title of 'doctor en leyes', were held to be the possessors of the intricate knowledge of language that connected society with power and also believed to be trained with the necessary skills required for socially elevated bureaucratic positions. It is not surprising, therefore, that both 'doctores' and bureaucrats have an exceptional place in the novels *Siervo sin tierra*, *La mala hora* and *Una y muchas guerras* already studied, as they represent the social role of power.[109] It is no coincidence that a writer such as Caballero Calderón was a law student before becoming a full-time writer, which did not, indeed, prevent him subsequently from taking up bureaucratic positions. Although

106 See Eduardo Santa, *Sociología política de Colombia* (Bogotá: Tercer Mundo, 1964), p. 31. More recently Plinio A. Mendoza asserted that 'en Colombia nacemos liberales o conservadores y yo soy de una familia liberal de abuelo y padre liberal aunque hoy ya no pertenezco a ningún partido ni siquiera a ese partido liberal que se me volvió socialista. Ingresó a la Internacional socialista', in *Contemporáneos*, televisión española, 28 March 2008, available at <www.youtube.com/watch?v=E_pY7pmqRy4> [Accessed 17 February 2009]

107 Some details on this aspect are discussed in Plinio A. Mendoza y Gabriel García Márquez, *El olor de la guayaba* (Barcelona: Mondadori, 1994), p. 123.

108 On Colombian legal rhetoric, lawyers and 'legalismo tinterillesco', see Uribe Celis, *La mentalidad*, pp. 152–153.

109 Gutiérrez Girardot, 'La literatura colombiana', p. 460.

García Márquez did not work in bureaucratic posts, as Caballero Calderón did, he was no exception to the 'letrado' rule. García Márquez, during his formative years, was linked to poets of the 'Piedra y Cielo' generation at his secondary school, and he enrolled later on as a law student before becoming a full-time writer, which suggests he followed the well-worn 'letrado' path.[110] García Márquez achieved a privileged position as a highly influential writer who has been fascinated by political power throughout his career.[111] Representative 'letrados' of twentieth century Colombia include Alfonso López Michelsen, liberal, and Belisario Betancur, conservative, both former presidents, and a novelist and poet respectively, both of whom were close friends of García Márquez. As Belisario Betancur confirmed it in his own words, in the writer's time: 'a García Márquez le gusta estar cerca del poder'.[112]

We have seen here a number of the factors which subtend the political scene analysed in Chapter One. The novels studied up to this point in this book are the product of a set of historical contingencies including bipartisanism, anticommunism, social exclusion and immobility, state absence, need for land reform, political resistance, transitional society, the growth of urban culture and, as such, many of the characters who people these novels are modelled either on the 'letrado' type – the poet, lawyer, penpusher or priest – or 'el pueblo' type – often illiterate, often powerless (she/he may be a peasant or an urban worker). In that sense the novels are arguably barometers of a complete set of historical tensions which were prevalent in the epoch they depict. These historical tensions together with the prominence of the 'letrado' are depicted in *Bulevar de los héroes*.

---

110   See Gabriel García Márquez, *Vivir para contarla*, pp. 246–248.
111   Interestingly in that respect is García Márquez's own answer: 'sí siento una gran fascinación por el poder […] es evidente en muchos de mis personajes', in *Olor*, p. 155.
112   See John Lee Anderson 'El poder de Gabo', in *Semana*, 909 (4–11 October 1999), 46–66 (p. 64).

Intellectuals, Revolution and Utopia: *Bulevar de los héroes*[113]

Bulevar de los héroes differs from the novels studied thus far in that it creates a more fantastic take on the articulation of politics and ideology in Colombian society. García Aguilar has written poetry, novels and also journalistic work like the previous authors and has made his way professionally by working in México, where the author lived for a long period before establishing his residence in Paris. García Aguilar's works also include *Tierra de leones* and *Tequila coxis* and, more recently *El viaje triunfal*, apart from *Bulevar de los héroes* that was selected as a finalist in the literary Plaza & Janés competition in Mexico. Details about García Aguilar's life are more plentiful than the criticism on his work, which is practically non-existent. García Aguilar himself writes in his 'blog literario desde París' he was born in Manizales (América Latina) (sic) and studied at the University of Vincennes (a reference that is found in *Bulevar de los héroes*), and he has always seen himself as a rebellious writer; as he said in an interview: 'En literatura hay que ser rebelde, toda fórmula o técnica fija debe ser trocada por lo aleatorio, disimétrico, raro, impredecible, inexplicable'.[114] Yet he is seen as a writer that subscribes to the recognisable traditions conveyed by writers of the Latin American Boom in which 'exoticism, politics and nostalgia are everywhere'.[115]

Living overseas seems to have contributed importantly to the form taken by *Bulevar de los héroes* as it appears to have provided the novel with a distanced view of the political process in Colombia. It brings together the issues of political power subtly blended with the vivid expression of

---

113   Eduardo García Aguilar, *Bulevar de los héroes* (México: Plaza & Janés, 1987). Further references to this novel are taken from this edition and only the page number is provided after quotations in the text.

114   See Eduardo García Aguilar's blog at <http://egarciaguilar.blogspot.com> [Accessed 23 April 2011]

115   See Ilán Stavans, 'Spanish Translations', in *World Literature Today*, 68, 2, University of Oklahoma (1994), 353–354. Stavans echoes Gregory Rabassa's prologue to *Boulevard of Heroes*, English version of García Aguilar's novel translated by Jay Miskowieck. Available at <http://www.jstor/stable/40150199> [Accessed 17 January 2010]

culture as represented and reflected by 'letrados' or 'doctores'. In fact it is that combination of ideology and power which is the main issue addressed by García Aguilar in *Bulevar de los héroes*. Commenting on the challenges he faced as a result of belonging to the so-called post-boom generation, that is, the generation that came after the Latin American Boom, García Aguilar suggested in an interview that his novel possesses the spirit of his generation which discovered the unfortunate trap set by ideologies. The ideological trap was exploited in Colombia, according to García Aguilar, by an ignoble class only interested in power for its own benefit. For that reason Colombians are better off overseas because 'Colombia es un país profundamente injusto dominado por una casta egoísta y obtusa que no está dispuesta a ceder un ápice de su poder a la mayoría pues la considera deleznable'.[116] This is also the reason why García Aguilar chose to live abroad since it allowed him the chance to see his homeland from a distance. Living abroad has contributed to his work to the extent that lived experience is filtered through an artistic eye-glass which allows for a distanced, measured world-view.

The actions and scenery found in *Bulevar de los héroes* are varied. Some of the ideas expressed in García Aguilar's novel are traceable back to the author's own views published in journalistic chronicles; the experiences and impressions described in his narrative are partly based on his everyday life in Colombia and partly on his life in France. One character represented in his novel is, for instance, the Colombian iconic figure, Camilo Torres, who impressed García Aguilar in his early years,

> la foto del padre Camilo Torres [...] en la primera plana de los periódicos me impresionó para siempre en ese lejano febrero de 1966, cuando niño aún, supe que lo habían matado a los 37 años de edad, el 15 de ese mes, en un combate.[117]

This sort of impression in García Aguilar's novel conveys ideological significance as a result of what it represents within the historical

---

116   See Felipe Agudelo Tenorio, interview with Eduardo García Aguilar, 'A nuestra generación le tocará pagar los platos rotos del Boom', in *El Espectador, Magazin Dominical*, 167, 8 June 1986, pp. 9–10.

117   See Eduardo García Aguilar's blog at <http://egarciaguilar.blogspot.com> [Accessed 23 April 2011]

contingencies that underline the narrative: 'Camilo Torres [...] niño bien de la alta clase bogotana, que excepcionalmente se había entregado a los pobres'.[118] *Bulevar de los héroes* portrays in a very unique manner an extremely rigid ruling class that manages to reproduce its power endlessly by means of inheritance from grandparents to parents and then to grandchildren. Some of the novel's characters mirror empirical Colombian figures of power such as Laureano Gómez or Berta de Ospina, who are portrayed in the fiction as involved in their power games while alternating their performance with narcissistic poets such as Guillermo Valencia or local thinkers such as Fernando González. Many of the characters in the novel are historical political and ideological actors of the past who, for the author, still reflect the present: 'las cosas han cambiado muy poco en el país, que vive inmerso en sus mismas obsesiones bajo el mando de los nietos de los líderes de entonces'.[119] Moreover, these characters are found alongside symbolic icons that inspired the ideals of previous generations such as Marx, Lenin and Che Guevara. There are frequent references to class difference and revolutionary change interspersed in the novel, which point to the new directions the fictionally recreated society was taking by the late 1980s. As R.L. Williams suggests in reference to novels published in the 1980s, 'the directions for the Colombian novel were more heterogeneous than they had ever been before'.[120] In the late 1980s the novel in Colombia went in new directions, and García Aguilar's novel reflects this.

Insurgency Towards the Bolivarian Ideal

The events of *Bulevar de los héroes* occur in many different places but the central one is the 'República de los Andes' and the novel is built around the story of a man whose ideal it is to bring about the revolution. The

---

118 Ibid.
119 Ibid.
120 See Raymond Leslie Williams, *The Colombian Novel 1844–1987* (Austin: University of Texas Press, 1991), p. 187.

protagonist, Petronio Rincón, is nicknamed 'el loco'; one day he decides
to become an insurgent and he makes his way to 'el monte'. Petronio is in
essence an idealist whose projected revolution in Los Andes looks to the
founding of a 'mundo feliz' based on the 'ideal Bolivariano' (7). The story
goes backwards and forwards in time, but moves progressively from the
past to the present in Petronio's life. Family-wise Petronio is a well-off man
whose privileges included not only material goods but also the education
and knowledge his friends could not afford; he reads J.A. Galán, and dreams
of re-creating Tupac Amaru's rebellion (53). By the same token during
Petronio's formative years life brought him to interact with writers and
artists, as his father – before he was tragically assassinated – had been a man
who turned from writing poetry to a life dedicated to power (144–145). In
his adolescence Petronio made a decision to join the revolutionary group
to begin 'el juego de la revolución' (37) though he trains to become a lawyer
before embarking on his revolutionary path. It is boredom and stagnation
(53) which make Petronio think he needs to move on (68–69) but, more
particularly, it is the murder of the priest, Antón Botero, that persuades
him to finally join the guerrilla (94). Petronio, like his great grandfather
who founded the city 'la Enea' in 'República de Los Andes' (112), founds
'El Edén, primer territorio libre de América' (84) in a small town in the
middle of the forest, in which he creates a government in an old mansion
populated by ghosts. Later on when he is arrested Petronio denounces the
'odiosa dictadura de la democracia constitucional' (139) and then is given
asylum in the French embassy and sent into exile (140). In Paris he meets
immigrants, finds a job, goes to Vincennes University and studies politics,
economics and ideologies (73). Petronio then meets Adela, a European, and
travels to some cities in France and Spain (80) but all the while nursing his
dream of returning to the tropics (81). Meanwhile we see other countries
embarked on the struggle for freedom through revolution; Third-World
countries fight to achieve democracy, peace and 'internacionalismo proletario' (153). Petronio suffers from a psychological crisis and he is led
away to a lunatic asylum where he hallucinates and sees 'Simón Bolívar, el
mesías de la gesta latinoamericana' (154–158). Re-connected to his ideal he
finally goes through tough times and he meets leaders of South American
regions working to organise people to create a 'gobierno independiente'

(175). Although he is committed with the cause of the revolution it proves impossible in the end to topple the 'república de los doctores'.

The Inherited Ideology of 'Letras' and the 'Letrado'

Bulevar de los héroes is clearly a work that offers a more universal vision of the articulation of political power when compared with the previous eight novels. It articulates the category of 'letras' and 'letrados' vividly and throws a critical light on the social role of the 'letrado'; it shows how for more than fifty years in Colombia the ideology of bipartisanism kept society stagnant, but it does so in a humorous way. In achieving that it also depicts in symbolic guise the ideological path that political subversion took during the 1980s.

We have seen in the previous novels how the presence of letrado is hidden beneath a number of disguises such as the 'tinterillo' (penpusher) in *Una y muchas guerras*, the frustrated, disenchanted and even non-committed intellectual in *Años de fuga*, the 'memoriales' or letter writer in *La mala hora*, and as the 'doctores' in *Siervo sin tierra*. In García Aguilar's novel the 'letrado' finds expression as the utopian dreamer who makes a mockery of his historic past, since behind the 'letrado' there lies the figure of the committed intellectual who lived for many decades in a society which stagnates while dwelling on the past and is overwhelmed by the boredom of living under a 'odiosa dictadura de la democracia constitucional' (139). The 'letrado' is one and the same, that is, the person who possesses the know-how essentially expressed through the knowledge of legal instruments, that is the knowledge of law, which also enables him to be eloquent and to excel in politics.

Ideology is expressed via the struggle between the 'letrado' and the protagonist, Petronio, who represents an organic intellectual in Gramsci's sense, who takes on his role as a liberator. Gramsci's organic intellectuals are explained as those 'who come into existence on the original terrain of an essential function in the economic production'.[121] This 'organic

---

121 See *Antonio Gramsci: Selections from Prison Notebooks*, ed. by Q. Hoare and G. Nowell Smith (London: Lawrence and Wishart, 1971), pp. 5–10. For Gramsci, 'organic'

intellectual' is reproduced by the upper class but his knowledge allows him to see the stagnation of power, which leads him to rebel against that old structure, i.e. that ideology of domination, becoming thereby a new force, a new voice in search for power and the organic participation of the people.[122]

These meanings and how they are expressed in the novel may be explored through Terry Eagleton's view with reference to ideology as a 'body of meanings and values encoding certain interests relevant to social power'.[123] In accordance with this thought ideologies lend coherence to groups or classes to mould them into 'unitary' structures, although they are not as '"pure" and unitary', partly because ideologies 'exist in relation to other ideologies'.[124] Thus, true to its meaning 'a successful ruling ideology must engage significantly with genuine wants, needs and desires'.[125] Therefore the dominant ideology 'has continually to negotiate with the ideology of its subordinates'.[126]

First it is important to analyse the significance of 'letras' and 'letrados' expressed in the novel via the cultural inheritance of the central character, Petronio. Petronio is an organic intellectual who brings with him the 'body of meanings and values encoding certain interests relevant to social power', though he becomes the nemesis of those meanings and values and, as such, is portrayed in the novel in a critical and at times humorous way.

Petronio is the heir of 'letrado' culture in every sense, for his father, a representative of the old traditional upper class, was a writer who moved smoothly into power while exchanging his art of writing poetry for the arrogance of power: 'el arte de mandar y medrar en las antesalas de la infamia'

---

intellectuals come into existence through a 'struggle to assimilate and conquer' the 'traditional' intellectual from the 'dominant social groups'.

122   Terry Eagleton, *Criticism and Ideology: A Study in Marxist Literary Theory* (London: Verso, 1986), pp. 102–103.

123   See Eagleton, *Ideology: An Introduction* (London: Verso, 1991), p. 45.

124   Ibid., p. 45.

125   Ibid., p. 45.

126   Ibid., p. 45.

(144–145). The suggestion is that power and politics are rather infamous, even abominable (145). Petronio is so close to power that he knows its secrets and hypocrisy and particularly the country's incompetent management (38). The 'letrado', indeed, is caricatured in the figure of Arnaldo Faria Utrillo, a chronicler and poet (126–128), typifying the unmistakable solemn style the ruling class paraded in front of the meek, general population. Faria Utrillo epitomises the 'ilustrado' held as the poet of 'la república', who is also the priest of the cult of words, the innovator of rhyme and the expert in 'Alejandrinos y Heptasílabos' in poetic verse. This world of solemnity, which characterises politics and pervades Colombian society, provides insight into the political 'type' who sits in power while oiling the machinery of bureaucracy with 'metáforas y sinalefas' (141). This aspect of politics in Colombia has been noted by historians in observations such as 'La política colombiana ha contenido desde un principio un vigoroso elemento ideológico y pedagógico'.[127] Such a combination of politics and literature became contentious in the 1970s when writers and artists were often hated, for being leftwingers, by the government (147); the novel shows the mixture of ideologies that coalesce in a social event. For example, at the poet Faria Utrillo's funeral, Maoists, Trotskyists and followers of the ideas of Che Guevara attend and exchange photos of the 'Sagrado Corazón' for those of Marx and Lenin; it is an event at which people read poems and sing songs like 'soy pirata y navego en los mares [...]' (147–149). While bringing to the fore representative ideological figures such as Marx and Lenin the novel also implies a disingenuous cultural décalage in which the sacred is mixed with the profane, that is, Marx appears as equivalent to the 'Sacred Heart' and vice versa. The effect is made all the more grotesque as a result of the popular song recited at the same time.[128] It is thus that 'letrado' ideology presents itself as the dominant ideology as portrayed in

---

127 For a discussion of the Colombian 'letrado' together with his particular trait of combining the art of *letras* with the exercise of politics see Malcom Deas, 'Miguel Antonio Caro y amigos: gramática y poder en Colombia', in *Del poder y la gramática* (Bogotá: Tercer Mundo, 1993), pp. 25–60 (p. 28).

128 The lyrics of *'Soy pirata y navego en los mares'* is a popular Colombian children's song.

Bulevar de los héroes, that of the dominant social class.[129] A stagnant society built by an upper class devoted to the cult of 'la letra' and built on the 'café' economy (38) provides an important symbolic point of reference in this novel, since it feeds into other cultural practices such as old religious rituals combined with political speeches as well as the persecution underlying bipartisan gang culture (37–39).

However, it is that old culture which for a long time kept Colombia in a state of status quo which turns Petronio into a rebel within his own class; he looks for a change in that society and for reforms to make it fairer. Petronio as a character brings that ideology to the point at which it critically reflects on itself; in effect, via Petronio, ideology is 'ideologised'. These reflections are the new 'thought' that de-legitimises the legitimacy of the unalterable old regime. If there was an ideology which was unitary in *Bulevar de los héroes* it was failing and not engaging significantly with the genuine wants, needs and desires of the people.[130]

If the genuine aspirations of 'el pueblo' were comprehended by anyone, it was Camilo Torres in his social project. As I have shown in Chapter One it was almost inevitable that Camilo should become an important inspiration for the Colombian novel. As mentioned above, García Aguilar declared he was impressed 'para siempre' as a young man when he learned Father Camilo Torres had been killed and Camilo Torres is alluded to in the novel via the priest Antón Botero who, like Camilo, died in the mountains soon after he joined the guerrilla (94). Botero subsequently becomes for Petronio a model of the political commitment to freedom; Petronio adds the symbolism implied by Bolívar and the Cuban revolution in his expressed intention to create a 'República de los Andes, primer paraíso de América' (95). The Bolivarian utopia is modelled on an aspiration held by the political Colombian armed opposition, as shall be seen later. But Petronio's political aspirations are also treated ironically in sections of the novel. Before going to the 'monte' the protagonist is shown as a character prone to conspiracy and the boycotting of group events.

---

129   Eagleton, *Ideology*, p. 45.
130   Eagleton, *Ideology*, p. 45.

With wry humour the novel gives a picture of Petronio during his university days as heir of the 'letrado' culture, attempting to organise a worker's union boycott of the 'Tertulia literaria Guillermo Valencia', as well as organisations such as 'La gota de leche' supported by the governor Berta Arnulfina Ochoa who acted as 'cacique inamovible de las zonas Andinas' (65) and whose members are the woman's sycophants (65–67). This is clearly disdainful reference to the literary groups and the conservative 'modernista' poet and also the conservative president Ospina's wife.[131] The lower rungs of society are extremely important for Petronio and his convictions lead him to create a 'servicio sexual proletario' which pressurises Berta Arnulfina Ochoa and contributes to her downfall. Petronio is a social observing character who thinks his 'conciudadanos' lead insouciant lives and that their arrogance prevents them from seeing beyond their limited horizons: 'Creían que La Enea era el centro del mundo y se hundían [...] con el cerebro encadenado al cretinismo' (53). That self-centred environment has been produced by the legal tradition, he thinks. It is for this reason Petronio is the prototype of Gramsci's organic intellectual, for he is intellectually a product of his own society; he is, after all, a lawyer: 'típico abogado de tierra fría, mediocre y abúlico, devorado por los códigos y el trabajo oscuro de las tristes provincias' (53), and thus a character who represents some facets of the lawyer figure in Colombian society, even if – paradoxically – he becomes their nemesis through the same process.

---

131 Mockery is clearly directed at Valencia, the 'modernista' poet and conservative politician regarded as a lofty representative figure of the 'letrado', and also wryly criticised by Gutiérrez Girardot. See Rafael Gutiérrez Girardot, 'La literatura colombiana en el siglo XX', in *Manual de historia de Colombia*, vol. 3 (Bogotá: Procultura/Instituto Colombiano de Cultura, 1984), pp. 447–536 (pp. 452–453). The name Berta Arnulfina is a transposition of the conservative president Mariano Ospina Pérez's wife, Berta de Ospina. Ospina Pérez was in power on 9 April 1948 and his wife is famously known for her strong and bossy character and conservative views which were expounded in her column 'El Tábano', in Laureano Gómez's newspaper, *El Siglo*.

Ideological Struggle

The internal splits in revolutionary movements are also depicted in the
story, particularly those that implied leadership issues in the guerrilla groups
(16–18). Petronio prefers to focus on the idealism of the revolutionary
since he dreams of founding 'El Edén, primer territorio libre de América'
(84), an echo of what in the 1960s Cuba stood for. As I have pointed
out above, during the 1960s Cuba was one of the main ideological influences in the revolutionary movements which grew in Colombia and its
motto was widely repeated among the youth: 'Cuba, territorio libre de
América' – Cuba's pivotal role was also depicted in *Años de fuga* as we have
seen. Petronio, inspired by the Cuban revolution, founds 'El Edén, primer
territorio libre de América', a small village in the middle of the forest (84)
which supports its people with free education, housing and food, and rejects
nationalisation and expropriation (85–86). The creation of a government
for the new independent republic gives rise, however, to the old ghosts of
conservatives, suggesting the new republic is still haunted by the past. The
old mansion had been a hide-out for a Nazi refugee fleeing the world's law
courts and has been abandoned after the people's superstitions linked it
with previous governments presided over by Gómez and Urdaneta in the
1950s (87), as discussed in Chapter One.

But the dream turns sour and the 'New Republic' is overtaken by
the ghosts of the past. Petronio criticises the regime and he is arrested.
He attacks the two-party system, and, in particular, he loudly denounces
the stagnation caused by the influence of the 'Corazón de Jesús' and the
'república de los doctores' and also the 'régimen legalista [...] aristocracia
racista y las humillaciones que aquel pueblo había tenido que soportar en
silencio' (139), as well as 'las traiciones sucesivas a quienes por ingenui-
dad o tontería desearon alguna vez acogerse a las amnistías propuestas
por azules o rojos' (139). Petronio also rejects the 'odiosa dictadura de la
democracia constitucional', whose rules and regulations are against the
'negros, mulatos y mestizos' of that society (139). Clearly alluding to what
Gómez represented and echoing the crusades against the left wing of that
era, Petronio's exile becomes inevitable when he learns about a group of

'ancianas devotas' who found an organisation in order to kill communists (140). The Nazi connections within the conservative party become clear when we hear about a German called Werner Gerhardt, who had been an ally of 'los godos' (105) when the entire country was starving (106). Petronio is eventually offered asylum at the French embassy. Exile means entry into a world of broader horizons in which he learns about politics and economics; there his comrades are aware of Petronio's revolutionary zeal and they invite him to listen to speakers from different parts of the world including ministers of defeated governments because he wants to deepen his knowledge of different ideologies (73). When attending university student marches and protests Petronio meets Adela Dampierre who tells him about her desire to participate as a 'guerrillera' in the revolution in the tropical forest. Adela's heroes range from Che Guevara to Latin American revolutionary singers, she reads the Che Guevara diaries and shows her affinity with Petronio through her interest in taking part in the Latin American struggles for freedom and change. She feels there is a link between the French revolution, its espousal of human rights and the development of the Cuban revolution (77–78). The connection between France and Latin America comes as a reminder of the ideological conceptualisation of the Cuban revolution made by French intellectual Régis Debray, who, together with Che Guevara was an influential figure in the continent during the 1960s.[132]

The revolution is depicted against the backdrop of an international conspiracy. Soon after, while travelling through France and Spain Petronio reads about Adela's assassination in the papers; she is depicted as a revolutionary. Her involvement included participation in acts of solidarity with writers and intellectuals and among her readings they had found 'las tesis del presidente Mao' and revolutionary poetry (98).

---

132   On the ideological influence played by Régis Debray over the Latin American intellectuals in these decades see Jorge G. Castañeda, *La utopía desarmada* (Bogotá: Tercer Mundo, 1994), pp. 84, 95.

In search for what lay behind Adela's tragedy Petronio finds out about a conspiracy in which fascists, communists and anarchists (82, 102) were involved, as well as a plot against the 'movimiento obrero': Adela's case is known as a 'proletarian secret' (104). A letter of hers reveals she was involved in leftist movements managed by Werner Gerhardt, a sinister individual whose contact had been a Nazi though he claimed to be a 'Marxist-Leninist' (130–131). After reading that Adela had been deceived and therefore had disappeared as her life was at risk, Petronio pursues Gerhardt to be told, once they come face to face, that he, Gerhardt, has a manic pleasure produced by 'la ambición de poder [...] el placer de dominar' and the need to kill in order to stay in power (134–135). These revelations drive Petronio to question his own life and his leadership in the 'República de los Andes'. In this way power, ideologies in the 'Third-World' countries and the struggle for democracy, peace, international proletarianism, and the aligning with the empire from 'más allá de los Urales' (in effect, the USSR) come into question (152–153).

Ideal, Disenchantment and Utopia

After experiencing a breakdown Petronio ends up in a lunatic asylum where he hallucinates and sees 'Simón Bolívar, mesías de la gesta latinoamericana' (154–158). In his vision Petronio is asked by Bolívar to carry on the struggle for 'la liberación del pueblo' and he thinks he might be 'el nuevo gran barbudo del paraíso socialista' (159). The clear allusion to the Cuban revolution in the reference to the 'barbudos' of the Sierra Maestra suggests that, for Petronio, the political ideal is one which fuses the ideology of the Cuban revolution with Bolívar's dream, and is redolent of Hugo Chávez's vision in modern-day Venezuela, becoming also an omen of it. This fusion may be referred to the Bolivarian Revolution promoted by the Venezuelan president Hugo Chávez, who won the presidency in the elections in 1999, reinforcing since then the relationship with the Cuban socialism, before his early death. Endorsing ideas of freedom, social inclusion, majority rule and direct democracy, the Bolivarian Revolution maintained a policy in favour of the deprived, defended and promoted social services such as health and education in an attempt to free the country from illiteracy, while keeping corruption under control.[133] These were the notions that oriented ideologically Petronio's idealism to found in essence a 'mundo feliz' based on the 'ideal Bolivariano' (7), as he began, with 'El Edén' as the 'primer territorio libre de América' (84).

Petronio's story then becomes more allegorical as he experiences delirium and utopia (163). There is an entrance to a tunnel towards an immense open field called the 'zona del olvido' and other trips to many different places in which Petronio learns that those who reach the oblivion zone never return and they are condemned to live in a dream-like state (147). This world described in the novel seems partly utopian and partly limbo-like. In the next step there are more encounters with idealist South American leaders who attempt to organise ignorant people. In a place called Noega, for instance, the leader and Petronio find that their ideals are in tune as they concur in their common admiration for the Jacobins (169). The subtle reference to 1789 is a clear allusion to the Jacobin society which espoused the notion of a democratic and truly free republic. After a period of working for this political ideal to create 'el primer gobierno independiente' (175), Petronio suddenly encounters Adela and start a new life together, close to the leader of Noega. Later on, going to a castle built by a desapeared tyrant who dedicated most of the public budget to make his power to become a religion, the question if life for them is reality or fiction elicits an Adela's hopeless response: 'No es lo uno ni lo otro, es algo peor [...] la zona del olvido', that is, oblivion, the prize to dreamers of impossible worlds and fallen into the trap of utopia (190). Utopia, as the state and place where everything is perfect, allows Petronio to see that never before were they so far from the people and Adela's answer is that the triumph for those who struggle to achieve redemption is directly proportional to that distance.

---

133 Detailed aspects about the Bolivarian Revolution are found in Raúl A. Sánchez Urribarri, 'Venezuela, turning further left?', in *Leftovers: Tales of the Latin American Left*, ed. by Jorge E. Castañeda and Marco A. Morales (London: Routledge, 2008), pp. 174–192 (pp. 187–188).

This suggests that being close to power inevitably means being far from the people (191).

Disillusioned with utopia, Petronio and Adela leave to later arrive to 'República Libertilandia'. There they meet new friends and also some old acquaintances, such as the writer who, at the beginning of the century had drafted the instrumental legislation to the 'República de los Andes' to render it the 'república de los doctores'; and in which Petronio had been such a nuisance. No doubt this passage, judging also by the general tone of the novel, is a critique of the Colombian political system that was still clinging into power when the novel itself was published, 1987.

It is possible that the reference in 1987 to the 'República Libertilandia' was a prescient allusion to the change which was about to occur to the Colombian constitution in 1991, four years later, and which would have major implications for bipartisanism. The unequivocal 'letrado' who meets Petronio favours a return to utopia and proposes bringing progress to the 'zona del olvido' and indeed Noega, where the venerable leader was a totalitarian boss. But Petronio and Adela are against 'ideologías ciegas' and in favour of 'libre industria, igualdad de oportunidades y en favor de los derechos del hombre' (198). They hold an election where a man called Apolinar Frías wins as a result of representing 'libertinaje positivista y moderno' (199). As a result of the election the city Nueva Pensilvania is founded with a 'Bulevar de los Héroes' (199) and Petronio regrets his past life which according to him was a 'edad estéril dedicada a las letras' (200–2001). The comment comes as a criticism to the long unproductive time the 'traditional' letrados revolved around themselves and their peers, the upper society, denying the mass a fair share of welfare in the process, suggesting that all that time was rather useless for being dedicated to letters.

Later on Petronio loses his left hand (222), a fact that has been interpreted to symbolise 'el fracaso de la guerrilla' by Pineda Botero.[134] Petronio losing his left hand might be rather seen as an omen of a new moment

---

134   See Alvaro Pineda Botero, *Del mito a la posmodernidad: la novela colombiana de finales del siglo XX* (Bogotá: Tercer Mundo, 1990), p. 128.

soon to begin: the pointless end of carrying on in that sort of struggle for power, but also the new era that the new Constitution would bring to the country. This prescience becomes clearer subsequently since the way to utopia has not ended, because it brings us to the 'god of revolutions', who tells Petronio he is the man destined to carry out the revolution that other men from the 'Andes' failed to complete (229). Petronio's answer is that he has lost his faith because the world is condemned to perpetual injustice. His answer is countered, though, by the observation that he isn't the one who decides because losing faith may be only a variant of faith and it is easy to convert incredulity into another religion (230). Petronio insists that 'la gran República de los Andes es una patria boba' and that its leaders are the biggest impostors on the planet.[135] Despite Petronio's reply he is given a sword, and this act is symbolic in that it is clearly a reference not only to Bolívar's sword – of which Petronio is now the spiritual guardian – but also to the subversive movement M-19, as mentioned in Chapter One, which became famous as a result of stealing Bolívar's sword. By accepting the sword Petronio becomes the heir not only of Bolívar's legacy but also the heir of the alternative politics of M-19 which was fighting against the sterile system of bipartisanism.[136] *Bulevar de los héroes* can, thus, be seen as a novel allegorising the growth of M-19; indeed Petronio's resemblance to Jaime Bateman (the leader

135   A satirical reference to a Colombian period that followed Independence after 1810 known as 'Patria Boba' for the confusion the liberators and leaders were in when they began to organise a republic, but nevertheless recurring to Anglo-American or French revolutionary rhetorical formulas. Compare in this respect Safford and Palacios, *Colombia: Fragmented Land, Divided Society* (Oxford: Oxford University Press, 2002), p. 89.

136   The reference reflects the factual event when the urban guerrilla movement M-19 stole Bolívar's sword when it was made public and returned it when integrated to the civil life as a political group after a process of amnesty followed by the reform of the national constitution. On the history of Bolívar's sword see <http://www.quintadebolivar.gov.co/coleccionEspada03.html> [Accessed 19 September 2009]

of M-19) is clear.[137] Petronio, like Bateman, disappears leaving behind an aura of legend and inspiration in the tropics, and the sword is then given to Cyrano, one of his sons (237). This portrays the legacy of the Bolivarian ideal advocated by Petronio which is symbolically conveyed to the successive generations. 'La espada de Bolívar había desaparecido del nicho en donde estaba expuesta desde hacía más de un siglo' (237) and the subversives, writers and poets were held responsible for the theft.[138] In the end, in the 'república de los doctores' the power was kept by the sons and grandsons of the presidents and dictators of yore.

It is with this blend of realism and mockery that *Bulevar de los héroes* expresses a unique take on the interplay between ideology and politics in Colombian society. We have seen the criticism of the 'república de los doctores' which Petronio opposes without success; as an organic 'letrado' he makes a different use of his knowledge so that he can encourage the people's participation in a fair society. The unequivocal moment of Petronio's defeat, though, is precisely the re-encounter with the old 'letrado' who offers to take progress back to the 'zona del olvido', which symbolises Petronio's utopia or the 'igualdad de oportunidades y en favor de los derechos del hombre' (198). Petronio rejects the solution of the old 'letrado' and, as argued above, his gesture embodies the hope for a new constitutional freedom in Colombia, one which is free from the old two-party system, which has held the country in shackles for so long, and which embodies the revolutionary fervour of

---

137   For a discussion of the political ideas and democracy advocated by M-19 see Jaime Bateman, *Oiga hermano* (n.p. M-19 Editor, 1986). See also Gabriel García Márquez, 'Bateman', in *Notas de prensa 1980–1984* (Bogotá: Norma, 1995), pp. 565–568.

138   The story of the sword ended when M-19 achieved amnesty and gave it back to the Bolívar house museum where it belonged. M-19 achieved legal political recognition after an amnesty process in the late 1980s and not only won representation for the writing of the 1991 Colombian constitution, but also elections for seats as members of parliament. At the time of writing this book one of the former M-19 leaders was elected mayor of Bogotá, in November 2011. See in this respect, Jaime Zuluaga Nieto, 'De guerrillas a movimientos políticos (Análisis de la experiencia Colombiana: el caso del M-19)', in *De las armas a la política*, ed. by Ricardo Peñaranda and Javier Guerrero (Bogotá: Tercer Mundo, IEPRI, 1999), pp. 1–74.

M-19. Embodying all that is hopeful for the future, Petronio – a mixture of the classical tradition suggested by his namesake, Petronio and the organic intellectual as understood by Gramsci – ultimately ends in defeat in his struggle with the forces of reaction that resiliently manage to reproduce power from one generation of relatives to another. Nevertheless, Petronio's legacy survives since the symbol of liberty and rebellion – the Bolivarian ideal represented in Bolívar's sword – with which he maintained his hopes for the construction of democracy, one in which people's needs are satisfied and the common good is intended, is left to his children as the emblematic ideal to which he dedicated his life.

Conclusions

The nine novels studied in this book present individualised ideological positions related to identifiable historical events deriving from political issues. As has been demonstrated throughout this study what becomes evident in the essential nuts and bolts of the story-telling are characters who operate according to ideologies favouring a system which benefits itself, i.e. bipartisanism in the majority of cases, as well as situations in which new historical forces come to the fore by opposing the repressive methods of a two-party governing structure resistant to change. In particular the historical contingencies that surrounded the struggle for power such as conspiracy, network organisation, landownership and power, resistance, exile and utopia are portrayed in different ways in these novels. The theme of conspiracy is touched upon in almost every one of them; such is the case with *El 9 de abril* and *El Cristo de espaldas*; the material limitations of poverty and the inability of a ruling class to address this problem looms large in *El día del odio*. The themes of landownership, deception throughout political networks and injustice were found to be predominant in *El Cristo de espaldas* and *Siervo sin tierra*. Class consciousness and the growth of a class struggle emerged as significant issues in *Viernes 9* and *La mala hora*. The 9 April 1948 is a key leitmotif in the first group of novels and returns in the 1980s novels via the authors' memory. Its recurrence though sheds light on matters such as the ambiguous status of the upper-class intellectual who oscillates between the left and traditional bipartisanism as in *Años de fuga* and the matter of partisan agency, as in *Una y muchas guerras*. The relationship between ideologies and utopia articulated in *Bulevar de los héroes* offers a new reading in the sense that it deals with the rivalry between the old tradition of the 'letrado' who favours the old two-party system and the new organic 'letrado', who is more open to notions such as social inclusion and a 'pueblo'-based utopia.

The theoretical approach provided by Terry Eagleton's views on social institutions, values and practices together with Jane Tompkins's notion of the novel as the 'product of historical contingencies' as well as other theoretical positions have allowed me to propose a new perspective on these novels which releases them from the narrow focus and isolation in which they were trapped for too long, that is, as simply 'novelas de la Violencia'. These nine novels focus on contemporary social, economic and power issues, as stimulated by the need for radical social change and reform. The period of thirty-six years within which these works were published demonstrates how the need for social reforms was formulated in different ways. The fact that these issues were combined in different jig-saw patterns in the novels also illustrates how important they were for writers in that they addressed the burning issues of the time as linked to social, economic and cultural matters. As a whole these works offer an insider's view of what the culture was thinking of itself when these works were written and published. The writers expressed the complexity of an old political system whose dysfunctional lines of command had reached the limits of their usefulness for society. The purpose of this book has been to contribute to the study of the role played by politics and ideology in nine representative novels of the period 1951–1987. I attempted to demonstrate the important questions the novels raise in relation to issues which are still current today. I believe that this study offers not only a fresh view but also a method with which to read the many more books of the same character written in Colombia during that span of time.

General Bibliography

Books

Abel, Christopher, *Política, iglesia y partidos en Colombia* (Bogotá: FAES/Universidad Nacional de Colombia, 1987).

Abercrombie, Nicholas, Hill, S. and Turner, B.S., *The Dominant Ideology Thesis* (London: George Allen & Unwin, 1980).

Alape, Arturo, *El Bogotazo: memorias del olvido* (Bogotá: Planeta, 1987).

——*La paz, la violencia: testigos de excepción* (Bogotá: Planeta, 1985).

Althuser, Louis, *Essays* (London: New Left, 1976).

Alvarez Gardeazábal, Gustavo, *El último gamonal* (Bogotá: Plaza & Janés, 1987).

——*Cóndores no entierran todos los días* (Bogotá: Plaza & Janés, 1979).

Andrade, María Mercedes, 'Ciudad y nación en las novelas del Bogotazo', in *Literatura y cultura: narrativa colombiana del siglo XX*, ed. by M. Jaramillo, B. Osorio and A. Robledo (Bogotá: Ministerio de Cultura, 2000), pp. 184–213.

Arango Ferrer, Javier, *Dos horas de literatura Colombiana* (Medellín: La Tertulia, 1963).

Arango, Manuel Antonio, *García Márquez y la novela de la violencia en Colombia* (México: Fondo de Cultura Económica, 1985).

——*Once novelistas latinoamericanos* (Bogotá: Carlos Valencia, 1985).

——*Tema y estructura en la novela de la revolución mexicana* (Bogotá: Tercer Mundo, 1984).

Arango Z., Carlos, *Farc veinte años. De Marquetalia a la Uribe* (Bogotá: Aurora, 1984).

Arenas Reyes, Jaime, *La guerrilla por dentro* (Bogotá: Tercer Mundo, 1975).

Aristizábal, Alonso, *Una y muchas guerras* (Bogotá: Planeta, 1985).

Balibar, Etienne and Macherey, Pierre, 'On Literature As An Ideological Form', in *Untying the Text: A Post-Structuralist Reader*, ed. by Robert Young (London: Routledge and Kegan, 1981), pp. 79–99.

Barbosa, Reinaldo, *Guadalupe y sus centauros: memorias de la insurrección llanera* (Bogotá: CEREC, 1992).

Bateman, Jaime, *Oiga hermano* (n.p. M-19 Editor, 1986).

Bedoya, Luis Iván and Escobar, Augusto, 'Religión y contexto social en *El Cristo de espaldas*', in *Ensayos sobre literatura colombiana y latinoamericana*, ed. by UNE, 137 (Bogotá: Biblioteca Banco Popular, 1989).

———*El Día Señalado, de Manuel Mejía Vallejo. Lectura crítica* (Medellín: Hombre Nuevo, 1981).

———*La mala hora, de Gabriel García Márquez. Lectura crítica* (Medellín: Hombre Nuevo, 1980).

———*La novela de la violencia en Colombia: Viento seco, de Daniel Caicedo. Lectura crítica* (Medellín: Hombre Nuevo, 1980).

Benedetti, Mario, 'Gabriel García Márquez o la vigilia dentro del sueño', in *9 Asedios a García Márquez* (Chile: Editorial Universitaria, 1969), pp. 11–21.

Behar, Olga, *Las guerras de la paz* (Bogotá: Planeta, 1985).

Bejarano, Jesús A., 'La economía', in *Manual de historia de Colombia*, vol. 3 (Bogotá: Procultura / Insituto Colombiano de Cultura, 1984), pp. 17–79.

Benjamin, Walter, 'The Author as Producer', in *Reflections: Essays, Aphorisms, Autobiographical writings* (New York: Schoken Books, 1978), pp. 220–238.

———'Critique of Violence' in *Reflections: Essays, Aphorisms, Autobiographical writings* (New York: Schoken Books, 1978), pp. 277–300.

Benson, John, 'El tema de la violencia en el periodismo de García Márquez: épocas y enfoques diferentes', in *Violencia y literatura en Colombia*, ed. by Jonathan Tittler (Madrid: Orígenes, 1989), pp. 63–80.

Berquist, Charles, *Coffee and Conflict in Colombia 1886–1910* (Durham: Duke University Press, 1981).

Betancourt Echeverry, Darío and García, Martha, *Matones y Cuadrilleros: origen y evolución de la violencia en el occidente colombiano 1946–1965* (Bogotá: Tercer Mundo, 1990).

Betancur, Belisario, *Poemas del caminante* (Bogotá: Villegas, 2005).

Boyers, Robert, *Atrocity and Amnesia: The Political Novel since 1945* (Oxford: Oxford University Press, 1985).

Botero, Mauricio, *El MRL* (Bogotá: Universidad Central, 1990).

Braun, Herbert, *The Assassination of Gaitán: Public Life and Urban Violence in Colombia* (Wisconsin: University of Wisconsin Press, 1985).

Bushnell, David, *The Making of Modern Colombia: A Nation in Spite of Itself* (Berkeley: University of California Press, 1993).

Caballero Calderón, Eduardo, *El Cristo de espaldas* (Medellín: Bedout, 1952).

———*Siervo sin tierra* (Medellín: Bedout, 1978).

Camacho Guizado, Eduardo, 'Estética del modernismo en Colombia', in *Manual de literatura colombiana*, vol. 1 (Bogotá: Procultura/Planeta, 1988), pp. 539–578.

Cardoso, Fernando Henrique and Faletto, Enzo, *Dependencia y desarrollo en América Latina* (México: Siglo XXI, 1987).

Carey, John, *The Intellectuals and the Masses* (London: Faber and Faber, 1992).

Carranza, María Mercedes, 'Silva y el modernismo', in *Poesía completa and De sobremesa*, by José Asunción Silva, edn centenario (Bogotá: Casa de Poesía Silva/Norma, 1996), pp. 35–43.

Castañeda, Jorge G., *La utopía desarmada: intrigas, dilemas y promesa de la izquierda en América Latina* (Bogotá: Tercer Mundo, 1994).

Castro Lee, Cecilia, *En torno a la violencia en Colombia: una propuesta interdisciplinaria* (Cali: Universidad del Valle: 2005).

Cataño, Gonzalo, *Educación y estructura social* (Bogotá: Plaza & Janés, 1989).

Child, Jorge, 'Correspondencia: la comedia de las contradicciones liberales', in *Mito 1955–1962. Selección de textos*, ed. by Juan Gustavo Cobo Borda (Bogotá: Insituto Colombiano de Cultura, 1975), pp. 301–315.

Cobo Borda, Juan Gustavo (compilador), *El arte de leer a García Márquez* (Barcelona: Belacqva, 2008).

——*Lecturas convergentes* (Bogotá: Taurus, 2006).

——*Lector impenitente* (México: Fondo de Cultura Económica, 2004).

—— *Letras de esta América* (Bogotá: Universidad Nacional de Colombia, 1986).

——'Poesía y Novela en Colombia en la década del 80: algunas tendencias', in *Colombia hoy*, ed. by Mario Arrubla (Bogotá: Tercer Mundo, 1978).

——'Lectura de Mito', in *Mito 1955–1962: Selección de textos* (Bogotá: Instituto Colombiano de Cultura, 1975), pp. 7–21.

—— (compilador), *Repertorio crítico sobre Gabriel García Márquez*, vol. 2 (Bogotá: Instituto Caro y Cuervo, 1975).

Colombia hoy: perspectivas hacia el siglo XXI, ed. by Jorge Orlando Melo, 15th edn(Bogotá: Tercer Mundo, 1995).

Colombia: violencia y democracia. Informe presentado al ministerio de gobierno. Comisión de estudios sobre la Violencia, ed. by Gonzalo Sánchez and others (Bogotá: Universidad Nacional de Colombia, 1987).

Charry Lara, Fernando, 'Guillermo Valencia', in *Manual de literatura colombiana*, vol. 1 (Bogotá: Procultura/Planeta, 1988), pp. 621–638.

——'Los Nuevos' in *Manual de literatura colombiana*, vol. 2 (Bogotá: Procultura/Planeta, 1988), pp. 17–85 (p. 25).

Christie, Keith, *Oligarcas, campesinos y política en Colombia* (Bogotá: Universidad Nacional, 1986).

'Concordato entre la Santa Sede y la República de Colombia', 31 December 1887, in *Conferencias Episcopales de Colombia*, vol. 1 (Bogotá: 1956).

Constitución Política Colombiana 1886 (Bogotá: Temis, 1975).

Curcio Altamar, Antonio, *Evolución de la novela en Colombia* (Bogotá: Instituto Caro y Cuervo, 1957; repr. Instituto Colombiano de Cultura, 1975).

Dabove, Juan Pablo, *Nightmares of the Lettered City: Banditry and Literature in Latin America 1816–1929* (Pittsburgh: University of Pittsburgh Press, 2007).

Dahl, Robert, *On Democracy* (New Haven: Yale University Press, 1998).

D'Allemand, Patricia, *José María Samper: nación y cultura en el siglo XIX colombiano* (Bern: Peter Lang, 2012).

Deas, Malcolm, *Intercambios violentos* (Bogotá: Taurus, 1999).

——*Del poder y la gramática* (Bogotá: Tercer Mundo, 1993).

——'Una tierra de leones: Colombia para principiantes', in *Del poder y la gramática y otros ensayos sobre historia, política y literatura colombianas* (Bogotá: Tercer Mundo, 1993), pp. 329–344.

De las armas a la política, ed. by Ricardo Peñaranda and Javier Guerrero (Bogotá: Tercer Mundo, IEPRI, 1999).

Debray, Regis, *Essais sur l'Amerique Latine* (Paris: Maspero, 1967).

Dix, Robert H., 'Political Oppositions Under the National Front' in *Politics of Compromise: Coalition Government in Colombia*, ed. by Albert Berry, Ronald Hellman and Mauricio Solaún (New Brunswick: Transaction Books, 1980).

——*Colombia: Political Dimensions of Change* (New Haven: Yale University, 1967).

Eagleton, Terry, *Literary Theory: An Introduction*, 2nd edn (Oxford: Blackwell, 1996; repr. 2004).

——*Ideology: An Introduction* (London: Verso, 1991).

——*Marxism and Literary Criticism* (London: Routledge, 1989).

——*Criticism and Ideology: A Study in Marxist Literary Theory* (London: Verso, 1978; repr. 1986).

——*Against the Grain* (London: Verso, 1986).

Ensayistas Colombianos del siglo XX, ed. by Jorge Eliécer Ruiz and Juan Gustavo Cobo Borda (Bogotá: Instituto Colombiano de Cultura, 1976).

Escobar, Eduardo, *Gonzalo Arango: correspondencia violada* (Bogotá: Instituto Colombiano de Cultura, Universidad de Antioquia, 1980).

Escobar Mesa, Augusto, *Ensayos y aproximaciones a la otra literatura colombiana* (Bogotá: Universidad Central, 1997).

Estrada Villa, Armando, *El poder político en la novelística de García Márquez* (Medellín: Universidad Pontificia Bolivariana, 2006).

Fajardo, Darío, 'La Violencia 1946–1964 su desarrollo y su impacto', in *Once ensayos sobre la violencia* (Bogotá: CEREC, 1985), pp. 259–295.

Fals Borda, Orlando, 'Lo sacro y lo violento, aspectos problemáticos del desarrollo en Colombia', en *Once ensayos sobre la violencia* (Bogotá: CEREC/Centro Gaitán, 1985), pp. 25–52.

——*Las revoluciones inconclusas en América Latina 1869–1968* (México: Siglo XXI, 1981).

——*Historia doble de la costa: Mompox y Loba*, vol. 1 (Bogotá: Carlos Valencia, 1980).

——*Subversion and Social Change in Colombia* (New York: Columbia University Press, 1969).

Feinstein, Adam, *Pablo Neruda: A Passion for Life* (London: Bloomsbury, 2004).

Fluharty, Vernon Lee, *Dance of the Millions: Military Rule and the Social Revolution in Colombia 1930–1956* (Pittsburgh: University of Pittsburgh Press, 1957).

Foley, Barbara, *Telling the Truth: The Theory and Practice of Documentary Fiction* (Ithaca: Cornell University Press, 1986).

Franco Isaza, Eduardo, *Las guerrillas del Llano* (Caracas: Editorial Universo, 1955).

Franco, Jean, *La cultura moderna en América Latina*, trans. Sergio Pitol (México: Grijalbo, 1983).

——*Critical Passions: Selected Essays* (Durham: Duke University Press, 1999).

Fuenmayor, Alfonso, *Crónicas sobre el Grupo de Barranquilla* (Bogotá: Instituto Colombiano de Cultura, 1978).

García Márquez habla de García Márquez en 33 grandes reportajes, ed. by Alfonso Rentería Mantilla (Bogotá: Rentería Editores, 1979).

Gabriel García Márquez, ed. by Peter Earle (Madrid: Taurus, 1981).

García Aguilar, Eduardo, *Bulevar de los héroes* (México: Plaza & Janés, 1987).

García Maffla, Jaime, 'Poesía romántica colombiana', *Manual de literatura colombiana*, vol. 1 (Bogotá: Procultura/Planeta, 1988), pp. 269–301.

García Márquez, Gabriel, *Vivir para contarla* (Barcelona: Mondadori, 2002).

——*El coronel no tiene quien le escriba* (Barcelona: Random House Mondadori, 2005) (first publ. 1961).

——*Los funerales de la mamá grande* (Barcelona: Random House Mondadori, 2003) (first publ. 1962).

——*La mala hora* (Barcelona: Bruguera, 1984) (first publ. 1962).

——'En busca del Silva perdido', in *Poesía completa and De sobremesa*, by José Asunción Silva, edn centenario (Bogotá: Casa de Poesía Silva/Norma, 1996), pp. 9–29.

——'Bateman', in *Notas de prensa 1980–1984* (Bogotá: Norma, 1995), pp. 565–568.

——*De viaje por los países socialistas: 90 días en la "cortina de hierro"* (Bogotá: Oveja Negra, 1982).

——'La literatura colombiana: un fraude a la nación', *Eco*, 33/5, 203, Bogotá (September 1962), 120–128.

——'Dos o tres cosas sobre "la novela de La Violencia"', *Eco*, 34/1, 205, Bogotá (November 1978), 103–108 (first publ. in *La Calle*, 9 October 1959).

Germani, Gino, *Authoritarianism, Fascism and National Populism* (New Brunswick: Transaction Books, 1978).

Gilhodés, Pierre, *Las luchas agrarias en Colombia* (Bogotá: La Carreta, 1974).

Girard, René, *Violence and the Sacred* (Baltimore: The John Hopkins University Press, 1977).

Goldmann, Lucien, *Towards a Sociology of the Novel* (London: Tavistock Publications, 1975).

——*Pour une Sociologie du Roman* (Paris: Gallimard, 1964).

Gómez Corena, Pedro, *El 9 de abril* (Bogotá: Iqueima, 1951).

Gómez Dávila, Ignacio, *Viernes 9* (México: Impresiones Modernas, 1953).

Gómez Martínez, Fernando, *Mordaza: diario secreto de un escritor público* (Medellín: Gráficos, n.d.).

González, Fernán, Bolívar, Ingrid and Vázquez, Teófilo, *Violencia política en Colombia: de la nación fragmentada a la construcción del estado* (Bogotá: CINEP, 2003).

Gramsci, Antonio, *Selections From the Prison Notebooks*, ed. by Q. Hoare and G. Nowell Smith (London: Lawrence and Wishart, 1971).

Gray, Martin, *A Dictionary of Literary Terms* (Essex: York Press, 1999).

Guberek, Simon, *Yo vi crecer un país*, 2 vols (Bogotá: Fundación Simón y Lola Guberek, 1987).

Guerrero, Javier, *Los años del olvido: Boyacá y los orígenes de la violencia* (Bogotá: Tercer Mundo, 1991).

Guillermoprieto, Alma, *Al pie de un volcán te escribo* (Bogotá: Norma, 1994).

Gutiérrez Girardot, Rafael, 'La literatura colombiana en el siglo XX', in *Manual de historia de Colombia*, vol. 3 (Bogotá: Procultura/Instituto Colombiano de Cultura, 1984), pp. 447–536.

Guzmán, Germán, *Camilo Torres*, trans. John D. Ring (New York: Sheed and Ward, 1969).

Guzmán Campos, Germán, Fals Borda, Orlando and Umaña Luna, Eduardo, *La violencia en Colombia: estudio de un proceso social*, 9th edn, 2 vols (Bogotá: Carlos Valencia, 1986).

Hampton, Christopher, *The Ideology of the Text* (Milton Keynes: Open University Press, 1990).

Hahn, Hannelore, *The Influence of Franz Kafka on Three Novels by Gabriel García Márquez* (New York: Peter Lang, 1993).

Hartlyn, Jonathan, *The Politics of Coalition Rule in Colombia* (Cambridge: Cambridge University Press, 2008) (first publ. 1988).

Harss, Luis, *Los nuestros* (Buenos Aires: Sudamericana, 1977).

Hart, Stephen, *Gabriel García Márquez* (London: Reaktion Books, 2010).

——'García Márquez's Short Stories', in *The Cambridge Companion to Gabriel García Márquez*, ed. by Philip Swanson (Cambridge: Cambridge University Press, 2010), pp. 129–143.

——*Gabriel García Márquez: Crónica de una muerte anunciada* (London: Grant & Cutler, 2005).

——'The House of the Spirits by Isabel Allende', in *The Cambridge Companion to the Latin American Novel*, edited by Efrain Kristal (Cambridge: Cambridge University Press, 2005), pp. 270–282.

——*Religión, política y ciencia en la obra de César Vallejo* (London: Támesis Books, 1987).

Helg, Aline, 'Education and Training in Colombia, 1940s-1960s', in *Welfare, Poverty and Development in Latin America*, ed. by Christopher Abel and Colin M. Lewis (London: MacMillan, 1993).

Henderson, James, *Modernization in Colombia: The Laureano Gómez Years 1889-1965* (Florida: University Press of Florida, 2001).

——*Cuando Colombia se desangró* (Bogotá: El Ancora, 1984).

Henríquez Ureña, Pedro, *Obra crítica* (México: Fondo de Cultura Económica, 1960).

Hernández, Germán, *La justicia en llamas* (Bogotá: Carlos Valencia, 1986).

Hobsbawm, Eric, *Bandits* (London: Weidenfeld & Nicolson, 1969).

——'La anatomía de "La violencia en Colombia"', in *Once ensayos sobre la violencia* (Bogotá: CEREC, Centro Gaitán, 1985), pp. 13–23.

——*Age of Extremes: The Short Century 1914-1991* (London: Abacus, 1995).

——*Interesting Times: A Twentieth Century Life* (London: Abacus, 2003).

Houen, Alex, *Terrorism and Modern Literature: From Joseph Conrad to Ciaran Carson* (Oxford: Oxford University Press, 2002).

Howe, Irving, *Politics and the Novel* (London: New Left Books, 1961).

Jakobson, Roman, 'Two Aspects of Language', in *Literary Theory: An Anthology*, ed. by Julie Rivkin and Michael Ryan (Oxford: Blackwell, 2004), pp. 76–80.

Jameson, Fredric, *The Political Unconscious: Narrative as a Socially Symbolic Act* (Ithaca: Cornell University Press, 1981).

Jaramillo Uribe, Jaime, 'El proceso de la educación, del virreinato a la época contemporánea' in *Manual de historia de Colombia*, vol. 3 (Bogotá: Procultura/Instituto Colombiano de Cultura, 1984), pp. 249–337.

——*La personalidad histórica de Colombia y otros ensayos* (Bogotá: Instituto Colombiano de Cultura, 1977).

——'Etapas de la filosofía en la historia intelectual de Colombia', in *Ensayistas colombianos del siglo XX* (Bogotá: Instituto Colombiano de Cultura, 1976), pp. 217–230.

——*Antología del pensamiento político colombiano*, vol. 2 (Bogotá: Bancode la República, 1970).

Jaramillo Vélez, Rubén, *Colombia: la modernidad postergada* (Bogotá; Temis, 1994).

Juten, Paul, *Notas críticas a la bibliografía de la literatura de La Violencia con algunas observaciones sobre una aproximación literaria*. Paper presented at II Simposio Nacional Sobre La Violencia en Colombia, Universidad Pedagógica y Tecnológica de Colombia, Chiquinquirá, 6 September 1986.

Kalmanovitz, Salomón, 'El desarrollo histórico del campo colombiano', in *Colombia Hoy* (Bogotá: Siglo XXI, 1995), pp. 257–307.

Karl Marx: Selected Writings, ed. by David McLellan (Oxford: Oxford University Press, 1978).

La Capra, Dominick, *History, Politics and the Novel* (Ithaca: Cornell University Press, 1987).

Lara, Patricia, *Siembra vientos y recogerás tempestades* (Bogotá: Oveja Negra, 1982).

Lara Parada, Ricardo and Castaño, Oscar, *El guerrillero y el político* (Bogotá: Oveja Negra, 1984).

Lara Romero, Gladys, *Imaginación social y novela de la Violencia en Colombia* (Bogotá: Gráficos, 2006).

La vorágine: textos críticos, ed. by Monserrat Ordóñez Vila (Bogotá: Alianza Editorial Colombiana, 1987).

Leftovers: Tales of the Latin American Left, ed. by Jorge E. Castañeda and Marco A. Morales (London: Routledge, 2008).

LeGrand, Catherine, *Frontier Expansion and Peasant Protest in Colombia 1850–1936* (Albuquerque: University of New Mexico, 1986).

Lleras, Alberto, *Mi gente. Memorias*, vol. 1 (Bogotá: Banco de la República, 1976).

Londoño-Vega, Patricia, *Religion, Culture and Society in Colombia: Medellín and Antioquia, 1850–1930* (Oxford: Clarendon Press, 2002).

Long-Term Trends in Latin American Economic Development, ed. by Miguel Urrutia (Washington: Inter American Development Bank and Johns Hopkins University Press, 1991).

López de Mesa, Luis, 'Nosotros y la esfinge', in *Ensayistas colombianos del siglo XX* (Bogotá: Instituto Colombiano de Cultura, 1976), pp. 37–50.

López Michelsen, Alfonso, 'Ensayo sobre la influencia semítica en María', in *Ensayistas colombianos del siglo XX* (Bogotá: Instituto Colombiano de Cultura, 1976), pp. 205–208.

——*Esbozos y atisbos* (Bogotá: Antares, 1980).

——*Los elegidos* (Bogotá: Antares, 1953).

López Tamés, Román, *La narrativa actual de Colombia y su contexto social* (Valladolid: Universidad de Valladolid, 1975).

Lukács, Georg, *Studies in European Realism* (London: Merlin Press, 1989).

——*The Historical Novel* (London: Merlin Press, 1962).

Macherey, Pierre, *A Theory of Literary Production* (London: Routledge, 2006).

——*The Object of Literature* (Cambridge: Cambridge University Press, 1995).

McMurray, George, *Gabriel García Márquez* (New York: Ungar, 1977).

Maddison, Angus, 'Economic and Social Conditions in Latin America, 1913–1950', in *Long-Term Trends in Latin American Economic Development*, ed. by Miguel

Urrutia (Washington: Inter American Development Bank and Johns Hopkins University Press, 1991), pp. 1–22.

Mannheim, Karl, *Ideology and Utopia*, collected works, vol. 1 (London: Routledge, 1997).

Manual de historia de Colombia, 3 vols (Bogotá: Procultura/Instituto Colombiano de Cultura, 1984).

Manual de literatura colombiana, 2 vols (Bogotá: Procultura/Planeta, 1988).

Marcos, Juan Manuel, 'Mujer y violencia social en *Cien años de soledad*', in *Violencia y literatura en Colombia*, ed. by Jonathan Tittler (Madrid: Orígenes), pp. 91–95.

Martin, Gerald, *Gabriel García Márquez: A Life* (London: Bloomsbury, 2008).

——*Journeys through the Labyrinth: Latin American Fiction in the Twentieth Century* (London: Verso, 1989).

Marulanda, Elsy, *Colonización y conflicto: las lecciones del Sumapaz* (Bogotá: Tercer Mundo, 1991).

Maturo, Graciela, *Claves simbólicas de Gabriel García Márquez* (Buenos Aires: García Cambeiro, 1972).

Mena, Lucila Inés, *La función de la historia en Cien Años de Soledad* (Barcelona: Plaza & Janés, 1979).

Medhurst, Kenneth N., *The Church and Labour in Colombia* (Manchester: Manchester University Press, 1984).

Medina, Medófilo, *La protesta urbana en Colombia en el siglo XX* (Bogotá: Aurora, 1984).

Mendoza, Plinio Apuleyo, *Aquellos tiempos con Gabo* (Barcelona: Plaza & Janés, 2000).

——*El olor de la guayaba* (Barcelona: Mondadori, 1994).

——*La llama y el hielo* (Bogotá: Planeta, 1984).

——*Años de fuga* (Bogotá: Plaza & Janés, 1979).

Menton, Seymour, *La novela colombiana: planetas y satélites*, 2nd edn (México: Fondo de Cultura Económica, 2007) (first publ. 1978).

Mito 1955–1962 Selección de Textos (Bogotá: Instituto Colombiano de Cultura, 1975).

Minta, Stephen, *Gabriel García Márquez: Writer of Colombia* (London: Jonathan Cape, 1987).

Molano, Alfredo, *Los años del tropel: relatos de la violencia* (Bogotá: CEREC/CINEP, 1985).

Montaña Cuéllar, Diego, *País formal, país real* (Buenos Aires: Platina, 1963).

Mora, Luis María, *La gruta simbólica y reminiscencias del ingenio y la bohemia en Bogotá* (Bogotá: Biblioteca Banco Popular, 1988).

Novela colombiana ante la crítica 1975–1990, ed. by Luz Mary Giraldo, (Cali: Univalle/Javeriana, 1994).

Nieto Rojas, José María, *La batalla contra el comunismo* (Bogotá: Empresa Nacional de Publicaciones, 1956).

Noguera Mendoza, Aníbal, 'José María Vargas Vila', in *Manual de literatura colombiana*, vol. 1 (Bogotá: Procultura, 1988), pp. 303–336.

Novelas y crónicas: J.A. Osorio Lizarazo, ed. by Santiago Mutis Durán (Bogotá: Instituto Colombiano de Cultura, 1978).

Ocampo López, Javier, *Colombia en sus ideas*, 3 vols (Bogotá: Universidad Central, 1999).

Once ensayos sobre la violencia (Bogotá: CEREC/Centro Gaitán, 1985).

Ong, Walter J., *Orality and Literacy: The Technologizing of the Word* (New York: Methuen, 1982).

Oquist, Paul, *Violence, Conflict and Politics in Colombia* (New York: 1980).

Ortega Ricaurte, J.V., Ferro, Antonio, *La gruta simbólica* (Bogotá: Biblioteca Banco Popular, 1981).

Ortiz, Carlos Miguel, *Estado y subversión en Colombia: la violencia en el Quindío años 50* (Bogotá: CEREC, 1985).

Osorio Lizarazo, José Antonio, *El día del odio* (Buenos Aires: López Negri, 1952).

Osorio Tapias, Abraham, *¿Por qué mataron a Gaitán?* (Bogotá: Iqueima, 1948).

Palacios, Marco, *Coffee in Colombia 1850–1970: An Economic, Social, and Political History* (Cambridge: Cambridge University Press, 2002).

——*Entre la legitimidad y la violencia: Colombia 1875–1994* (Bogotá: Norma, 1995).

——*Estado y clases sociales en Colombia* (Bogotá: Procultura, 1986).

Pardo, Jorge Eliécer, *El jardín de las Hartmann* (Bogotá: Plaza & Janés, 1978).

Parsons, James, *Antioqueña Colonization in Western Colombia* (Berkley: University of California Press, 1949).

Pasado y presente de la violencia en Colombia, ed. by Gonzalo Sánchez and Ricardo Peñaranda (Bogotá: CEREC, 1986).

Paz, Octavio, *El laberinto de la soledad* (México: Fondo de Cultura Económica, 1981).

——*Posdata* (México: Fondo de Cultura Económica, 1981).

Pécaut, Daniel, *Crónica de dos décadas de política Colombiana 1968–1988* (Bogotá: Siglo XXI, 1990).

——*Orden y violencia: Colombia 1930–1954*, 2 vols (Bogotá: Siglo XXI, 1987).

Penuel, Arnold M., *Intertextuality in García Márquez* (South Carolina: Spanish Literature Publication Company, 1994).

Peña Gutiérrez, Isaías, *La narrativa del Frente Nacional* (Bogotá: Universidad Central, 1982).

——*La generación del bloqueo y del estado de sitio* (Bogotá: Punto Rojo, 1973).

Peñarete Villamil, Fabio, *Así fue la gruta simbólica* (Bogotá: Tipografía Hispana, 1972).

Pineda Botero, Alvaro, *La esfera inconclusa: novela colombiana en el ámbito global* (Medellín: Universidad de Antioquia, 2006).

——*Del mito a la posmodernidad: la novela colombiana de finales del siglo XX* (Bogotá: Tercer Mundo, 1990).

Pizarro Leongómez, Eduardo, *Las Farc (1946–1966): de la autodefensa a la combinación de todas las formas de lucha* (Bogotá: Tercer Mundo, 1991).

——'La guerrilla revolucionaria en Colombia', in *Pasado y presente de la violencia en Colombia* (Bogotá: CEREC, 1986), pp. 391–411.

Portal, Marta, *El proceso narrativo de la revolución mexicana* (Madrid: Espasa, 1980).

Rama, Angel, *La ciudad letrada* (Hanover: Ediciones del Norte, 1984).

——'Diez problemas para el novelista latinoamericano', in *La novela en América Latina 1920–1980* (Bogotá: Instituto Colombiano de Cultura/Procultura, 1983), pp. 33–98.

——*La novela en América Latina: panoramas 1920–1980* (Bogotá: Procultura/Instituto Colombiano de Cultura, 1982).

——*Rubén Darío y el modernismo* (Caracas: Imprenta Universitaria, 1970).

——'Un novelista de la violencia Americana', in *9 asedios a García Márquez* (Santiago de Chile: Editorial Universitaria, 1969), pp. 107–125.

Ramos, Julio, *Divergent Modernities: Culture and Politics in Nineteenth Century Latin America* (London: Duke University Press, 2001).

Restrepo, Laura, 'Niveles de realidad en la literatura de la "violencia" colombiana', in *Once ensayos sobre la violencia* (Bogotá: CEREC/Centro Gaitán, 1985), pp. 117–169.

Richani, Nazih, *Systems of Violence: The Political Economy of War and Peace in Colombia* (Albany: State University of New York Press, 2002).

Roldán, Mary, *Blood and Fire, La Violencia in Antioquia, Colombia, 1946–1953* (London: Duke University Press, 2002).

——*Genesis and Evolution of La Violencia in Antioquia: Colombia 1900–1953* (Massachusetts: Harvard University, 1992).

——*Literary Theory: An Anthology*, ed, by Julie Rivkin and Michael Ryan (Oxford: Blackwell, 2004).

Romero, José Luis, *Las ciudades y las ideas* (México: Siglo XXI, 1984).

Ruiz, Jorge Eliécer, 'Situación del escritor en Colombia', in *Mito 1955–1962*, ed. by Juan Gustavo Cobo Borda (Bogotá: Instituto Colombiano de Cultura, 1975), pp. 63–77.

Rudé, George, *Ideology and Popular Protest* (Chapel Hill, NC: University of North Carolina, 1995).

Russell, John, *Reciprocities in the Non-fiction Novel* (London: University of Georgia Press, 2000).

Ryan, Michael, *Literary Theory: A Practical Introduction* (Oxford: Blackwell, 1999).

Said, Edward W., *Beginnings, Intentions and Method* (London: Granta Books, 1997).

Safford, Frank and Palacios, Marco, *Colombia: Fragmented Land, Divided Society* (Oxford: Oxford University Press, 2002).

Safford, Frank, *The Ideal of the Practical: Colombia's Struggle to Form a Technical Elite* (Austin: University of Texas Press, 1976).

Saldívar, Dasso, *Gabriel García Márquez: el viaje a la semilla. La biografía* (Madrid: Alfaguara, 1997).

Sánchez, Gonzalo and Meertens, Donny, 'Political Banditry and the Colombian Violencia', in *Bandidos*, ed. by Richard W. Slatta (London: Greenwood Press, 1987), pp. 151–170.

——*Bandoleros, gamonales y campesinos* (Bogotá: El Ancora, 1985).

Sánchez, Gonzalo, *Guerre et politique en Colombie* (Paris: L'Harmattan, 1998).

——'Los Estudios sobre La Violencia: balance y perspectivas', in *Pasado y presente de la violencia en Colombia* (Bogotá: CEREC, 1986).

——*Ensayos de historia social y política del siglo XX: Los bolcheviques del Líbano; Las ligas campesinas en Colombia; Las raíces históricas de la amnistía* (Bogotá: El Ancora, 1985).

Sánchez Urribarri, Raúl A., 'Venezuela, turning further left?', in *Leftovers: Tales of the Latin American Left*, ed. by Jorge E. Castañeda and Marco A. Morales (London: Routledge, 2008), pp. 174–192.

Santa, Eduardo, *Sociología política de Colombia* (Bogotá: Tercer Mundo, 1964).

Santamaría, Ricardo and Silva, Gabriel, *Proceso político en Colombia: del Frente Nacional a la apertura democrática* (Bogotá: CEREC, 1984).

Schmitt, Carl, *The Concept of the Political* (Chicago: The University of Chicago Press, 1996).

Sharpless, Richard, *Gaitán of Colombia: A Political Biography* (Pittsburgh: Pittsburgh University Press, 1978).

Sims, Robert Lewis, *The Evolution of Myth in Gabriel García Márquez: From La Hojarasca to Cien Años de Soledad* (Miami: Universal, 1981).

Silva, José Asunción, *Poesía completa and De sobremesa*, edn centenario (Bogotá: Casa de Poesía Silva, Norma, 1996).

Silva, Herzog, *Trayectoria ideológica de la revolución mexicana* (México: Fondo de Cultura Económica, 1984).

Silva, Renán, *República liberal, intelectuales y cultura popular* (Medellín: La Carreta, 2005).

Slatta, Richard W., *Bandidos* (London: Greenwood Press, 1987).

Tejada, Luis, *Libro de crónicas* (Bogotá: Triángulo, 1961).

Téllez, Hernando, '¿Pero hay tradición humanística?', in *Ensayistas colombianos del Siglo XX* (Bogotá: Instituto Colombiano de Cultura, 1976), pp. 167–170.

——'La novela en Latinoamérica', in *Ensayistas colombianos del siglo XX* (Bogotá: Instituto Colombiano de Cultura, 1976), pp. 173–178.

The Cambridge Companion to Gabriel García Márquez, ed. by Philip Swanson (Cambridge: Cambridge University Press, 2010).

The German Ideology, in *Karl Marx: Selected Writings*, ed. by David McLellan (Oxford: Oxford University Press, 1978).

Tirado Mejía, Alvaro, 'Colombia: siglo y medio de bipartidismo', in *Colombia hoy* (Bogotá: Siglo XXI, 1995), pp. 103–178.

——*Aspectos sociales de las guerras civiles en Colombia* (Bogotá: Instituto Colombiano de Cultura, 1976).

Tompkins, Jane, *Sensational Designs: The Cultural Work of American Fiction 1790–1960* (Oxford: Oxford University Press, 1985).

Torres, Camilo, *Cristianismo y revolución* (México: Era, 1970).

Tovar Zambrano, Bernardo, 'Modernización y desarrollo desigual de la intervención estatal: 1914–1946', in Gonzalo Sánchez y Ricardo Peñaranda (compiladores), *Pasado y presente de la violencia en Colombia* (Bogotá: CEREC, 1986), pp. 167–181.

Troncoso, Marino, 'De la novela *En La Violencia* a la novela *De La Violencia*: 1959–1960 (hacia un proyecto de investigación)', in *Violencia y literatura en Colombia*, ed. by Jonathan Tittler (Madrid: Orígenes, 1989), pp. 31–40.

Trujillo Montón, Patricia, 'Problemas de la historia de la novela colombiana del siglo XX', in *Leer la historia: caminos a la historia de la literatura colombiana*, ed. by Carmen Acosta, Diógenes Fajardo, Iván Padilla and Patricia Trujillo Montón (Bogotá: Universidad Nacional de Colombia, 2007), pp. 61–107.

Untying the text: A Post-Structuralist Reader on Literature as an Ideological Form, ed. by Robert Young (London: Routledge and Kegan, 1981).

Uribe Celis, Carlos, *La mentalidad del colombiano: cultura y sociedad en el siglo XX* (Bogotá: Alborada, 1992).

——*Los años veinte en Colombia: ideología y cultura* (Bogotá: Aurora, 1985).

Urrutia, Miguel, 'El desarrollo del movimiento sindical y la situación de la clase obrera', in *Manual de historia de Colombia*, vol. 3 (Bogotá: Procultura/Instituto Colombiano de Cultura, 1984), pp. 179–245.

Valencia Goelkel, Hernando, 'La mayoría de edad', in *Ensayistas colombianos* (Bogotá: Instituto Colombiano de Cultura, 1976).

Valencia Solanilla, César, 'La novela colombiana contemporánea en la modernidad', in *Manual de literatura colombiana*, vol. 2 (Bogotá: Procultura/Planeta, 1988), 463–510.

Valencia Villa, Hernando, *Cartas de batalla: una crítica del constitucionalismo colombiano* (Bogotá: Universidad Nacional de Colombia/CEREC, 1987).

Vargas, Germán, *Sobre literatura colombiana* (Bogotá: Fundación Literaria Simón y Lola Guberek, Colección Literaria, 1985).

Vargas Llosa, Mario, *García Márquez: historia de un deicidio* (Barcelona: Barral, 1971).

Vidales, Luis, *La insurrección desplomada* (Bogotá: Iqueima, 1948).

Violencia y literatura en Colombia, ed. by Jonathan Tittler (Madrid: Orígenes, 1989).

Violence in Colombia: The Contemporary Crisis in Historical Perspective, ed. by Charles Berquist, Ricardo Peñaranda and Gonzalo Sánchez (Wilmington, DE: Scholarly Resources, 2001).

Violent Origins: Ritual Killing and Cultural Formations, ed. by Robert Hamerton-Kelly (Stanford: Stanford University Press, 1987).

Waging War and Negotiating Peace 1990–2000, ed. by Charles Berquist, Ricardo Peñaranda and Gonzalo Sánchez (Wilmington, DE: Scholarly Resources, 2001).

Welfare, Poverty and Development in Latin America, ed. by Christopher Abel and Colin M. Lewis (London: MacMillan, 1993).

Whitebrook, Maureen, *Identity, Narrative and Politics* (New York: Routledge, 2001).

Williams, Raymond Leslie, *The Colombian Novel 1844–1987* (Austin: University of Texas Press, 1991).

——'Manuela: la primera novela de "La Violencia"', in *Violencia y literatura en Colombia*, ed. by Jonathan Tittler (Madrid: Orígenes, 1989), pp. 19–29.

——*Gabriel García Márquez* (Boston: Twayne Publishers, 1984).

——*Aproximaciones a Gustavo Alvarez Gardeazábal* (Bogotá: Plaza & Janés, 1977).

——*La novela colombiana contemporánea* (Bogotá: Plaza & Janés, 1976).

Williams, Raymond, *The Long Revolution* (London: Hogarth Press, 1992).

Zalamea, Jorge, *El sueño de las escalinatas* (Bogotá: El Ancora, 1984).

——*El gran burundún burundá* (Buenos Aires: Imprenta López, 1952).

Zamosc, Leon, *The Agrarian Question and the Peasant Movement in Colombia* (Cambridge: Cambridge University Press, 1986).

Zapata Olivella, Manuel, *La calle 10* (Bogotá: Iqueima, 1960).

Zuluaga Nieto, Jaime, 'De guerrillas a movimientos políticos (Análisis de la experiencia Colombiana: el caso del M-19)', in *De las armas a la política*, ed. by Ricardo Peñaranda and Javier Guerrero (Bogotá: Tercer Mundo, IEPRI, 1999), pp. 1–74.

Documents, Papers and Articles

Anderson, John Lee, 'El poder de Gabo', in *Semana*, 'Documento', 909 (4–11 October 1999), 46–54.

Agudelo Tenorio, Felipe, interview with Eduardo García Aguilar, 'A nuestra generación le tocará pagar los platos rotos del Boom', in *El Espectador, Magazín Dominical*, 167, 8 June 1986, 9–10.

Airó, Clemente, 'Pro y contra en la novelística colombiana', *El Tiempo, Lecturas Dominicales*, 24 February 1963, 1, 12.

Arango, Gonzalo, 'Cómo ser jurado en tres lecciones', *El Tiempo, Lecturas Dominicales*, 6 June 1965.

Caballero Calderón, Eduardo, 'El escritor colombiano en una encrucijada', *El Tiempo, Lecturas Dominicales*, 1 November 1964.

——'La novela y el mundo de la creación literaria', *El Tiempo, Lecturas Dominicales*, 21 April 1963.

——'Reflexiones y prospectos sobre la novela', *El Tiempo, Lecturas Dominicales*, 14 April 1963.

Castro Caycedo, Germán, interview with García Márquez, '"Gabo" cuenta la novela de su vida' (1), *El Espectador*, 16 March 1977, p. 5-A.

——interview with García Márquez, '"Gabo" cuenta la novela de su vida' (2), *El Espectador*, 17 March 1977, p. 5-A.

Collazos, Oscar and Manuel Mejía Vallejo (interview), 'Sólo tratando nuestra realidad saldremos del plano lugareño', *El Tiempo, Lecturas Dominicales*, 20 June 1965.

Dabove, Juan Pablo, 'Los pasquines como alegoría de la disolución de la ciudadanía en "La mala hora" de Gabriel García Márquez', in *Revista de Crítica Literaria Latinoamericana*, 26, 52 (2000), 269–287. Available at <http://www.jstor.org/stable/4531133> [Accessed 26 November 2008]

D'Allemand, Patricia, 'Silencios y reticencias de la crítica en Colombia', in *Bulletin of Spanish Studies*, 84, 4–5 (2007), 529–548. Available at <http://dx.doi.org/10.1080/14753820701452485> [Accessed 23 January 2009]

Díaz-Callejas, Apolinar, 'El estado de sitio ante la constituyente colombiana', in *Nueva Sociedad*, 112 (March-April 1991), 66–72. Available at <http://www.nuso.org> [Accessed 26 March 2009]

Flórez Góngora, Miguel Angel, 'El círculo de conspiraciones sobre el 9 de Abril de 1948', *El Espectador*, 9 April 2012. Available at <http://www.elespectador.com/noticias/politica/articulo-337056-el-circulo-de-conspiraciones-sobre-el-9-de-abril-de-1948> [Accessed 10 October 2012]

Gago, Víctor, interview with Plinio Apuleyo Mendoza, in *Contemporáneos*, Libertad Digital TV, 28 March 2008. Available at <http://www.youtube.com/watch?v=E_pY7pmqRy4> [Accessed 17 February 2009]

Garcés Lloreda, María Teresa, 'Paz, apertura política y representación', in *Análisis, conflicto social y violencia en Colombia. Documentos ocasionales*, 50, Bogotá: CINEP, 1988, pp. 13–18.

González, Fernán E., '¿Hacia un nuevo colapso parcial del Estado?', in *Análisis, conflicto social y violencia en Colombia. Documentos ocasionales*, 50, Bogotá: CINEP, 1988), pp. 5–12.

Laverde Amaya, Isidoro, 'Ojeada histórico crítica sobre los orígenes de la literatura colombiana', in *Boletín Cultural y Bibliográfico*, separata, 2 (Bogotá: Banco de la República/Biblioteca Luis Angel Arango, 1963).

Luchting, Wolfgang A., Untitled Review, in *World Literature Today*, 54, 3, University of Oklahoma (1980), p. 409. Available at <http://www.jstor.org/stable/40135088> [Accessed 9 November 2009]

Mena, Lucila Inés, 'Bibliografía anotada sobre el ciclo de la Violencia en la literatura colombiana', in *Latin American Research Review* (in *Research Reports and Notes*), 13, 3 (1978), 95–107. Available at <http://links.jstor.org/sici?sici=0023 8791%281978%2913%3A3%3C95%3ABASECD%3E2.0.CO%3B2-J> [Accessed 22 October 2007]

Message of Jean Paul II to the President of Bishops' Conference of Colombia, Archbishop Alberto Giraldo Jaramillo of Medellín, Vatican, 9 May 2002. Available at <http://www.vatican.va/holy_father/john_paul_ii/speeches/2002/june/documents/hf_jpii_spe_20020606_conf-episc-colombia_en.html> [Accessed 17 September 2011]

Osorio, Oscar, 'Siete estudios sobre la novela de la Violencia en Colombia, una evaluación crítica y una nueva perspectiva', in *Poligramas*, Revista Literaria, Universidad del Valle, 25, Cali, Valle del Cauca (June 2006), 85–108. Available at <http://poligramas.univalle.edu.co/25/osorio.pdf> [Accessed 29 March 2009]

Peña Gutiérrez, Isaías, 'De la niebla a los muros', *Boletín Cultural y Bibliográfico*, 21, 2, Biblioteca Luis Angel Arango, 1984. Available at <http://www.banrepcultural.org/blaavirtual/publicacionesbanrep/boletin/boleti3/bol2/niebla.htm> [Accessed 17 March 2010]

Posada Carbó, Eduardo, 'Fiction as History: The Bananeras and Gabriel García Márquez's One Hundred Years of Solitude', in *Journal of Latin American Studies*, vol. 30, 2 (May, 1998), pp. 395–414. Available at <http://links.jstor.org/sic i?sici=0022216X%281998050%2930%3A2%3C395%3AFAHTBA%3E2.0.CO %3B2-L> [Accessed 22 October 2007]

Quiroga Cifuentes, Alvaro, 'Evolución, objeto y universalidad en la literatura de la Violencia en Colombia', II Simposio nacional sobre la Violencia en Colombia. Universidad Pedagógica y Tecnológica de Colombia, 4, 5, 6, 7 September 1986. *Memorias de eventos científicos colombianos*, 1, 57, Bogotá: ICFES, 1987.

Quiroga Cifuentes, Alvaro, and Williams, Raymond Leslie (interview), 'Un Colombianista Norteamericano', *El Espectador, Magazín Dominical*, 198, 17 April 1985.

Ramsey, Russell W., 'Critical Bibliography on La Violencia in Colombia', in *Latin American Research Review* (in *Topical Review*), 8, 1 (1973), 3–44. Available at

<http://links.jstor.org/sici?sici=00238791%28197321%298%3A1%3C3%3AC
BOLVI%3E2.0.CO%3B2-5> [Accessed 22 October 2007]
Reviews and critical comments on *Novela y poder*, by Raymond Leslie Williams, *El
Espectador, Magazín Dominical*, 426, 23 June 1991, 6–13.

Russell, Ramsey, 'Critical Bibliography on la Violencia in Colombia', *Latin American
Research Review*, 8, 1 (1973), 3–44.

Sánchez, Gonzalo and Bakewell, Peter, 'La Violencia en Colombia: New Research,
New Questions', in *The Hispanic American Historical Review*, 65, 4 (November, 1985), 789–807. Available at <http://links.jstor.org/sici?sici=00182168%
28198511%2965%3A4%3C789%3ALVICNR%3E2.0.CO%3B2-L> [Accessed
19 July 2006]

Sánchez, Gonzalo, 'Intelectuales, poder y cultura nacional' in *Análisis Político*, 34
(1998), 99–119.

Santos Molano, Enrique, 'La novela y los novelistas' in *Revista Credencial*, 203, 2006.
Available at <http://www.banrepcultural.org/blaavirtual/revista/credencial/
noviembre2006/novela.htm> [Accessed 9 July 2012]

——'La novela en Colombia', *El Tiempo, Lecturas Dominicales*, 3 September 1961.

Silva Romero, Ricardo, 'De ayer a hoy: año Caballero Calderón 1910–2010',
document, 23 April 2010). Available at <http://www.bibliotecanacional.
gov.co/recursos_user/documentos_bnc/catalo-caballeroe.pdf> [Accessed 11
September 2011]

Stavans, Ilán, 'Spanish Translations', *World Literature Today*, 68, 2, University of
Oklahoma (1994), 353–354. Available at <http://www.jstor/stable/40150199>
[Accessed 17 January 2010]

Téllez, Hernando, Umaña Bernal, José and Rojas Herazo, Héctor, 'Tres escritores y
un tema ineludible: ¿por qué carecemos de una novelística?', *El Tiempo, Lecturas
Dominicales*, 2 December 1962.

Téllez, Hernando, 'Literatura y violencia', *El Tiempo, Lecturas Dominicales*, 15 November 1959, p. 1.

——'Literatura y testimonio', *El Tiempo, Lecturas Dominicales*, 27 June 1954, p. 1.

Tirado Mejía, Alvaro, 'El MRL y la cultura', in *Credencial Historia*, 3, March 1990, at
<http://www.banrepcultural.org/blaavirtual/revistas/credencial/marzo1990/
marzo2.htm> [Accessed 21 March 2009]

Wise, David, 'La función de la historia en *Cien Años de Soledad*', in *Hispania* (*Reviews;
Latin American Literature*), 66, 1 (March 1983), 141–42. Available at <http://
links.jstor.org/sici?sici=00182133%28198303%2966%3A1%3C141%3ALFDLH
E%3E2.0.CO%3B2-O> [Accessed 19 July 2008]

Theses

Alvarez Gardeazábal, Gustavo, *La novelística de la violencia en Colombia* (BA thesis, Cali: Universidad del Valle, 1970).
Suárez Rondón, Gerardo, *La novela sobre la violencia en Colombia* (Doctoral thesis, Bogotá: Pontificia Universidad Católica Javeriana, 1966).

Lectures

Eagleton, Terry, 'Socialism and Culture', Barry Amiel & Norman Melburn Trust, Annual Lecture at Brunei Gallery, London, SOAS, 5 June 2008.
Mendoza, Plinio Apuleyo, Lecture on Gabriel García Márquez's life, with Gerald Martin and Dasso Zaldívar, at London Metropolitan University, 8 December 2008.

Online Sources

<http://www.banrepcultural.org/blaavirtual/revista/credencial/noviembre2006/novela.htm> [Accessed 9 July 2012]
<http://www.bibliotecanacional.gov.co/recursosuser/documentosbnc/catalocaballeroe.pdf> [Accessed 23 April 2011]
<http://www.banrepcultural.org/blaavirtual/publicacionesbanrep/boletin/boleti3/bol2/niebla.htm> [Accessed 10 April 2010]
<http://www.banrepcultural.org/blaavirtual/revista/25/inicio> [Accessed 10 April 2010]
<http://www.banrepcultural.org/blaavirtual/revistas/credencial/marzo1990/marzo2.htm> [Accessed 21 March 2009]
<http://www.banrepcultural.org/blaavirtual/historia/notabilidades/notabilidades67.htm> [Accessed 18 November 2008]
<http://dx.doi.org/10.1080/14753820701452485> [Accessed 23 January 2009]

<http://www.elespectador.com/noticias/politica/articulo-337056-el-circulo-de-con-spiraciones-sobre-el-9-de-abril-de-1948> [Accessed 10 October 2012]

<http://www.eltiempo.com/archivo/documento/CMS-7847423> [Accessed 17 February 2011]

García Aguilar, Eduardo, <http://egarciaguilar.blogspot.com> [Accessed 23 April 2011]

<http://www.jstor.org/stable/40135088> [Accessed 9 November 2009]

<http://www.jstor.org/stable/4531133> [Accessed 26 November 2008]

<http://links.jstor.org/sici?sici=00238791%281978%2913%3A3%3C95%3ABASEC D%3E2.0.CO%3B2-J> [Accessed 22 October 2007]

<http://links.jstor.org/sici?sici=00238791%281973321%298%3A1%3C3%3ACBOLV I%3E2.0.CO%3B2-5> [Accessed 22 October 2007]

<http://www.nuso.org> [Accessed 25 March 2009]

<http://www.oed.com.libproxy.ucl.ac.uk/search?searchType=dictionary&q=pasqu inade&searchBtn=Search> [Accessed 26 November 2008]

<http://poligramas.univalle.edu.co/25/osorio.pdf> [Accessed 29 March 2009]

<http://www.quintadebolivar.gov.co/coleccionEspada03.html> [Accessed 19 September 2009]

<http://www.teatrojorgeeliecer.gov.co/index.php?option=comcontent&view=arti cle&id=127&Itemid=107> [Accessed 19 September 2009]

<http://www.vatican.va/holy_father/john_paul_ii/speeches/2002/june/documents/ hf_jpii_spe_20020606_conf-episc-colombia_en.html> [Accessed 17 September 2011]

<http://www.youtube.com/watch?v=E_pY7pmqRy4> [Accessed 17 February 2009]

Index

Hispanic Studies: Culture and Ideas

Edited by
Claudio Canaparo

This series aims to publish studies in the arts, humanities and social sciences, the main focus of which is the Hispanic World. The series invites proposals with interdisciplinary approaches to Hispanic culture in fields such as the history of concepts and ideas, the sociology of culture, the evolution of visual arts, the critique of literature, and the uses of historiography. It is not confined to a particular historical period.

Monographs as well as collected papers are welcome in English or Spanish.

Those interested in contributing to the series are invited to write with either the synopsis of a subject already in typescript or with a detailed project outline to either Professor Claudio Canaparo, Department of Iberian and Latin American Studies, School of Arts, Birkbeck College, 43 Gordon Square, London WC1H 0PD, UK, c.canaparo@sllc.bbk.ac.uk, or Peter Lang Ltd, oxford@peterlang.com.